# TRADE AND DEVELOPMENT POLICIES

# TRADE AND DEVELOPMENT POLICIES

Leading Issues for the 1980s

Alexander J. Yeats

St. Martin's Press   New York

ISBN   0 – 312 – 81203 – 5

**Library of Congress Cataloging in Publication Data**

Yeats, Alexander J.
  Trade and development policies.

  Bibliography: p.
  Includes index.
  1.  Underdeveloped areas—Commerce.   I.   Title.
HF1413.Y45          380.1′09172′4          80–16463
ISBN 0–312–81203–5

To my father
  . . . and now Alexis

# Contents

# List of Tables and Figures

TABLES

FIGURES

# Acknowledgements

This book, which constitutes the second of a two-part survey of developing country trade problems, was written during my stay as Visiting Scholar at the Institute for International Economic Studies at the University of Stockholm. As was the case with the first volume (*Trade Barriers Facing Developing Countries*, London: Macmillan, 1979), research support was provided by the Bank of Sweden's Tercentenary Foundation as part of a comprehensive project on the New World Economic Order.

In the course of my work, I have been able to draw on the advice of several individuals at the Institute and the United Nations Conference on Trade and Development. Marian Radetzki, Carl Hamilton, Arne Jon Isachsen, Sven Grassman and several other colleagues at the Institute made numerous helpful comments as did Gary Sampson, Jack Stone, Ho Dac Tuong and Alfred Maizels—all staff members of UNCTAD. Special thanks are also due Dr Lary Franko for suggestions on the transnational chapter and Dr Hal Lary for comments on the chapter dealing with the future composition of developing country trade. Finally, I would like to express my appreciation to various members of the computer centre at the University of Stockholm who assisted in the preparation and analysis of data.

I would also like to thank the editors of *World Development*, *The Journal of Development Economics*, *American Journal of Agricultural Economics*, and *Oxford Economic Papers* for permission to reproduce parts of previously published studies.

*Stockholm and Geneva*                                   *Alexander J. Yeats*
*1979*

# 1 Trade and Development Issues for the 1980s

Over the last several decades, economists have debated the relevance of two alternative strategies for developing countries to achieve industrialisation and growth. One camp, whose spokesmen included a number of prominent Latin American economists, stressed the potential advantages of growth through 'import substitution' policies. This strategy suggests high tariff and nontariff barriers be erected around domestic industries to replace foreign supply. Under a protective umbrella of artificial trade restraints, it was theorised that local firms would have the opportunity to achieve economies of scale associated with larger production volumes, or to lower unit costs through specialisation or factors associated with the learning curve. However, a number of practical disadvantages often resulted from attempts to apply import substitution policies with the result that this strategy has experienced declining professional favour.[1]

While import substitution has fallen in esteem, 'outward-oriented' strategies for industrialisation and growth have been increasingly advocated. Under an outward-oriented strategy, LDCs are advised to reduce artificial trade restraints and open the domestic economy to the stimulating effects of foreign competition. Also, domestic producers are encouraged to take full advantage of export opportunities in foreign markets and thereby experience gains that would not be achieved if output were geared solely to domestic demand. Keesing (1967) lists four potentially favourable influences of such a strategy: increasing returns connected with economies of scale and market size, learning effects and the improvement of human capital, beneficial effects from competition and close communication with other countries including the familiarisation with advanced techniques from abroad, and potentially favourable demonstration effects.

Without doubt, the enthusiasm for the outward-looking approach was kindled by the success of countries such as Korea, Hong Kong, Taiwan and Brazil which adopted such policies, as well as accomplishments in the area of trade liberalisation over the previous two decades.[2] In 1968, the Kennedy Round negotiations produced agreement on a broad series of tariff cuts which significantly reduced import duties on a wide range of products exported by developed and developing countries. Generalised System of Preference (GSP) schemes were also launched by developed market economy countries (DMECs) in the early 1970s under which some LDC exports are admitted to industrial markets duty free, or at rates below MFN tariffs. While little progress was made on important issues such as agricultural protectionism or the reduction of nontariff barriers, the outlook through the early 1970s was still for freer market access and trade liberalisation.

For several reasons, there is now considerably less optimism concerning removal of trade barriers and the success of export-oriented growth policies. The growth of industrial countries, which had been sustained at relatively high rates during the previous two decades, fell off sharply in 1974 and has failed to return to previous levels. The international monetary system, based on fixed parities and the convertibility of currencies into gold, has collapsed, with the result that unstable exchange rates and disequilibrating movements of capital are a common occurrence. High rates of inflation persist in many developed nations in spite of continuing conditions of slack economic activity, while unemployment remains high by historical standards. Many industrial countries have not adjusted to the higher energy costs resulting from continuing Organisation of Petroleum Exporting Countries' price increases. In response to these adverse economic developments strong sentiments for increased protectionism have surfaced with new trade restraints applied in a variety of key sectors such as steel, shipbuilding, textiles and electronics. The nature and products covered by these restrictions are such as to have serious detrimental effects on the potential export earnings and industrialisation prospects of developing countries.

These and related developments accent the need to re-evaluate basic trade and development strategies for the 1980s. For example, in a related study Arthur Lewis (1978) compiled historical series which show that the period following the culmination of hostilities in Korea up to the early years of the 1970s marked a truly remarkable interval for international trade and economic relations. Over 1953–73, Lewis showed that world trade expanded at an annual rate of 8 per cent, while trade in manufactures grew by 11 per cent. In comparison, the normal rate of growth in trade prior to this interval was much lower; 3·5 to 4 per cent during 1813–1900, and about 1 per cent per year over 1910–40.

Thus, the expansion in post-war trade was unmatched by similar rates of growth in previous eras.

These developments, rising protectionism, continuing sluggishness in developed market economies, and the realisation that the trade expansion of the 1960s and early 1970s may have been a historical anomaly, have important implications for future development policies. Specifically, if rapid expansion and liberalisation of world trade are not carried over into the 1980s it will be necessary to re-examine the advantages of import substitution as opposed to outward-oriented growth strategies. Also, growing protectionism in DMECs places a premium on new outlets for LDC manufactures. As such, trade and other forms of cooperation among developing countries themselves, or between LDCs and socialist nations, should have a much higher priority than during the 1960s and 1970s. Existing international institutions such as the General Agreement on Tariffs and Trade, the International Monetary Fund, or the United Nations Conference on Trade and Development are also likely to require considerable modification in response to conditions in the 1980s.

## SELECTION OF ISSUES: THE LDC VIEWPOINT

Two important documents effectively summarise the developing country viewpoint concerning the major trade and development issues for the 1980s: a special report by the Secretary-General of UNCTAD (May 1976) discusses a broad range of development problems that will require solutions in the next decade; in addition, an UNCTAD (July 1978) symposium of prominent economists and government officials was convened specifically for the purpose of identifying the major issues that would face LDCs during the 1980s. As background, the panel suggested that the main current problems are: the continuing sluggishness of economic activity after the 1974–6 recession, the associated slowdown in world trade, the persistence of historically high rates of unemployment and inflation, the maldistribution of current account payments balances, and the instability of exchange rates. All of these factors were thought likely to pose continuing problems for the 1980s. Structural factors such as the collapse of the international monetary system established at Bretton Woods, the breakdown of the GATT trading rules (manifested in the increasing share of world trade accounted for by intra-firm transactions and new forms of protectionism which bypass GATT rules), the emergence of chronic shortages of key resources such as energy and food, and the decline of some developed country industries were also predicted to be of continuing importance during the next decade. Given these basic problems, the UNCTAD panel considered their policy implications and solutions. While there was a lack of consensus on some issues, the following points emerged from these deliberations:

—From the LDCs' viewpoint, the present world situation required a fundamental *restructuring* of international economic relations and not merely traditional measures to stimulate recovery in the industrial countries. Several specific proposals were advanced, including: a redeployment of industries from developed to developing countries; a more equitable control over science and technology; institutional changes such as reform of the international monetary and financial system; establishment of international commodity agreements; measures for regulating the activities of transnational corporations; and the promotion of collective self-reliance among developing countries.

—A majority of the participants felt that access to developed country markets would be a vital issue for the 1980s since the benefits include opportunities to exploit economies of scale in production, and comparative advantages in the manufacture of certain products, notably processed primary commodities. It was argued that, in imposing 'voluntary' export restrictions on developing countries, and in applying import restrictions under the GATT 'safeguard' clause, developed countries were discriminating against LDCs. It was also noted that developing countries which were just beginning to export manufactures would suffer most from these measures in the 1980s.[3]

—Considerable attention was devoted to the question of 'collective self-reliance' which many felt would be a major issue for the 1980s. Three aspects of this strategy were discussed: measures aimed at achieving political solidarity, improving the developing countries' negotiating position with industrialised nations, and an expansion of economic transactions among LDCs. However, a divergent view envisaged collective self-reliance as a process by which the LDCs would 'delink' (detach) themselves from developed countries to escape conditions of enforced integration into the world economy under conditions of 'unequal exchange'.

Thus, according to the UNCTAD panel, as well as the report of the Secretary-General of UNCTAD, collective self-reliance, unequal exchange, market access, and the search for new outlets, will be among the most pressing problems confronting developing countries in the 1980s.

In considering the potential impact of LDC industrialisation, Alfred Maizels (1979) foresees major changes for existing institutions and the world economy during the next decade. Specifically, Maizels suggests that the industrialisation of the underdeveloped countries to anywhere near the levels attained by the present DMECs will involve vast changes in resource use, patterns of production, consumption and trade, and in socio-economic structures. Changes in relative prices and in the terms-of-trade between nations will also be involved.

Maizels concludes that the existing international economic system, built on a vertical exchange of commodities for manufactures, may have serious problems in adjusting to a two-way flow of manufactures between developed and developing countries. Such an adjustment would not seem a likely result of the normal working of market forces, rather positive and complementary policies by both developed and developing countries would be involved. A key element for the LDCs centres on the promotion of structural change in their own economies to facilitate the expansion of intra-trade. The developing countries also need to pursue appropriate domestic policies such as the mobilisation of their resources to meet the elementary needs of their populations, and to exploit potential complementarities of their economies by closer economic cooperation. Establishment of such a 'self-reliant' strategy would also strengthen the countervailing power of the LDCs against transnationals, and help to ensure that these corporations' activities promote economic development.

In assessing the potential obstacles to these institutional and economic changes, Maizels is highly concerned with activities of transnationals. Specifically, he suggests that:

while there is insufficient information available to make any precise assessment of their role in manufacturing and exports of developing countries, these corporations now seem to have a major influence on the pace and pattern of industrialisation in the majority of developing countries. It is also held that these corporations have established effective control over a large and growing portion of LDC export trade. This trend has been accentuated by the growing network of trade barriers imposed by developed countries on the traditional manufactured exports of developing countries.

*Interdependence or structural change*
A key question to be resolved concerns the nature of the trade and development policies for the 1980s. One school of thought is the

'interdependence' approach which holds that by improving and co-ordinating the functioning of the international economy, within the context of existing economic and political institutions, maximum achievable benefits will accrue to both developed and developing countries. However, this approach has been effectively challenged on the ground that the historical record shows such action holds little promise for LDCs. For example, during the 1960s and early 1970s the international economy was operating at what now seem to be high levels of efficiency, yet the position of most developing countries was static or deteriorated. If the LDCs could not achieve basic development objectives in the favourable economic climate that prevailed in this period, this suggests that major changes are needed in international economic, social, and political institutions since the longer-term international economic outlook suggests that it will be difficult to return to conditions prevailing in 1960–73.

Perhaps the major policy paper presented to the fifth session of the United Nations Conference on Trade and Development (UNCTAD (May 1979)) argued forcefully and convincingly for the need for basic institutional changes in international economic relations. The report began by noting that the existing international economic system has not provided adequate support for developing countries over the last two decades. Even before the onset of what was the worst post-war recession in 1974, it was apparent that the International Development Strategy for the Second United Nations Development Decade was likely to be a failure. Over 1970–3, economic expansion was largely concentrated in medium and high income developing countries. The poorer nations, with over half of the third world's population, achieved an annual growth rate of about 2 per cent, which was about equal to their population growth. As a result, these countries failed to achieve practically every target of importance in the UN International Development Strategy. That such failures occurred in a period of impressive growth in most DMECs was a source of concern and loss of confidence that growth could be transmitted from developed to developing countries, at least within the confines of existing economic institutions.[4]

After 1973 the debate concerning the nature of appropriate development policies intensified since LDC economic conditions deteriorated from what were already unsatisfactory levels. Over 1974–5, growth in the more advanced LDCs fell sharply, while per capita output in the poorer countries was static or declined. UNCTAD (May 1979) notes these developments 'brought increasing recognition of the need for radical changes in the institutional framework of international economic relations, and it was in this climate that the General Assembly adopted in 1974 the Declaration and Programme of Action on the Establishment of a New International Economic Order'. Since this document has key implications for the types of institutional economic reforms needed, it is reproduced in an appendix to this book.

Given the proposition that third world economic development cannot be accelerated without restructuring the existing international order, it appears that the preoccupation of the DMECs with their own continuing domestic economic problems have diverted attention from the need for such reforms. In fact, the emphasis placed on domestic economic recovery has some negative implications for implementation of basic institutional changes.

The current accent on domestic economic recovery carries with it the implicit assumption that the key to international problems lies in the economic recovery of the industrialised nations, and the consequent expansion of the international economy and trade. This line of reasoning essentially argues for a return to the international processes at work before 1974, i.e., for a continuing of the existing system restored to its pre-recession levels with some marginal adjustments. In this schema, the third world's development is dependent on the transmission of growth from the developed countries via the expansion of the latters' markets, and the resulting increase in demand for raw materials and other LDC products. Emphasis on economic recovery in the DMECs also suggests that the current crisis is essentially cyclical and that economic recovery in developed countries can be achieved independently of basic structural reforms in international institutions. However, the main problem with this (interdependence) line of reasoning is that LDCs were not able to achieve development targets in the pre-1974 period so it is difficult to see what they might gain by any return of industrial countries to these former levels of economic activity.

Another difficulty with the 'interdependence' approach is that it fails to recognise the tie between the current economic difficulties of the DMECs and the imbalances between developed and developing countries. In other words, it ignores the potential contribution of a substantial strengthening of the LDC economies, with a corresponding increase in their purchasing power, to the current economic problems of developed countries. Increasing LDC purchasing power would be a particularly effective way of raising demand for developed countries' capital goods industries which have been operating at very low levels of capacity utilisation.

*Industrialisation and basic needs*

While the historical record shows that institutional reforms are needed to facilitate third world development, other important lessons can be learned from past experiences. Specifically, over 1960–73 a small number of LDCs experienced expansion in real GDP and trade, but there is considerable evidence that the resulting benefits did not disseminate widely through their economies. Experience with specific trade and industrialisation projects in a number of LDCs also shows that large segments of the population may not experience any resulting gains. In cases, it has been suggested that these activities are conducted in 'enclaves' with no influence on vast segments of the population. Since the trade and industrialisation projects may only benefit a minority of the population they can lead to greater income inequalities and a heightening of social tensions. To some extent these industrialisation projects have also influenced mass migrations to urban centres as members of the rural population compete for the relatively few newly created jobs. Too often, this migration forces individuals to live in urban slum conditions which would be viewed as intolerable by even the poorest strata of society in Western societies.

A few simple statistical comparisons quickly illustrate the abject poverty of most third world inhabitants, and the need to ensure that trade and development projects are such as to convey maximum benefits to the masses. For example, the differential in incomes between the richest and poorest nations is very large. Of the 4 thousand million people in the world today, about half live on a subsistence income of 50 cents or less per day. Thus, the abject poverty in many developing countries places people at the minimum level of subsistence with the result that famine, disease, and malnutrition are constant occurrences.

Gross differences also exist in other measures of economic well-being. At present, life expectancy in some of the advanced developed countries ranges to well over 70 years, yet a number of LDCs have not been able to attain a figure of half this level. Educational opportunities also vary widely between developed and developing nations. In Europe or North America, literacy rates are well over 90 per cent, but in many developing countries of Asia or Africa more than 90 per cent of the population can neither read nor write. Gross differences exist in employment opportunities between the developed and developing world. While unemployment rates for most industrial nations have historically ranged between 4 and 6 per cent, recent UN statistics show that over 20 per cent of the population in Algeria, Bolivia, Jamaica, Surinam and a number of other developing countries are without gainful employment. Surveys by the

United Nations also show that the majority of the population in many third world countries are without housing, sanitation, health, transport, or education facilities that meet minimum acceptable standards. Just as institutional reforms are needed to facilitate growth transmission in the international economy, basic changes are required in the mechanism through which the benefits of growth are transmitted internally in the developing countries themselves. To facilitate this effort, recent thinking on development policy often stresses that internal resources in the LDCs be mobilised to satisfy the basic human needs of the population. The emphasis here is considerably different from trade policies such as import substitution or the outward-oriented approach. While trade and industrialisation are still viewed as important elements in the overall strategy, it is recognised that these activities may not make a maximum contribution to the elevation of living standards. It is toward this effort, and a reduction in the gap between developed and developing countries, that the basic needs strategy is directed.

In some cases, the policy conclusions of basic needs and the trade-development strategies may be different. For example, the outward-oriented approach argues that LDC efforts be directed toward development of industries in which the country has a comparative advantage and export markets appear profitable. Hopefully, such action will produce a steady supply of foreign exchange to finance future development projects, and the country will also experience important learning effects and other benefits from trade. However, basic needs argue that the primary problem in LDCs is the eradication of poverty. Unless the export venture makes a direct immediate contribution to improvement of living standards, its required investments and claim on productive resources deserves a lower priority than alternatives which will have these desired effects.[5]

While this book does not attempt a comprehensive evaluation of the relative merits of trade related policies as opposed to basic needs strategies, it acknowledges that the latter's humanitarian objectives deserve a high priority for the 1980s. It is also recognised that achievement of these objectives is dependent upon reforms in the developing countries themselves. In cases, the scope of these reforms require changes in the established institutional arrangements and will involve land tenure, the distribution of income, political power, and policies toward industry and agriculture. However, unlike other aspects of the New World Economic Order these changes will have to be initiated on the part of the developing countries. While much attention has been directed to the demands that LDCs have made on industrial nations, these basic internal reforms may constitute the key to the success or failure of the new order. If the LDCs demonstrate that they do not have the political will or convictions to initiate these required broad changes in their own domestic economies, it will certainly influence the industrial countries' treatment of LDC demands for changes in international economic relations.

## SCOPE OF THE PRESENT STUDY

As the preceding discussion indicates, this book attempts to assess the major *trade-related* development issues for the 1980s. However, one point should be stressed at the outset. To avoid casting too wide a net, the discussion largely focuses on major problems which directly link trade to development policies. Thus, while such issues as world food problems, debt relief, or international monetary reform will no doubt be major issues for the next decade, they are touched on only obliquely in their relation to trade policy. A more important omission may be a lack of direct discussion of energy problems which will undoubtedly influence production and trade policies of both developed and developing countries. Perhaps the most direct influence of higher energy costs will be felt on LDC freight rates. Indeed, a study by Finger and Yeats (1976) suggests that higher energy costs associated with OPEC pricing policy may have wiped out the gains associated with Kennedy Round tariff cuts. Even more important, the continuing OPEC price increases have resulted in a severe drain on scarce LDC financial reserves. Instead of being directed toward productive domestic investments, which would increase future trade flows, an increasingly larger percentage of these reserves are being appropriated by OPEC pricing practices.

Concerning specific issues, the rise of the new protectionism in LDC export markets will undoubtedly be a key concern for the developing countries in the 1980s. Due to the complexity and importance of this issue, it has been treated separately in the first of this two-part survey (see Yeats (1979)). However, the present volume does touch on ways developing countries could respond to this occurrence in their external markets. All too often, it is assumed that the new protectionism is a purely exogenous phenomenon from the policy viewpoint of developing countries. This is not entirely correct since it will be argued (particularly in Chapter 3) that LDCs have options to counter these unfavourable developments.

Chapter 2 sets the tone for much of the discussion in this book by examining the ways existing international institutions constrain the gains that developing countries could realise from trade. In particular, attention is directed to the problem and results of unequal exchange in developing country import and export markets. Empirical illustrations, drawn from actual trade patterns, illustrate the magnitude of the losses developing countries experience due to their lack of countervailing power. Various policy alternatives are also considered through which LDCs might be able to correct some imbalances. Chapter 3 evaluates what may well be the most promising avenue for LDCs to approach the problem of institutional reform: collective self-reliance and the expansion of intra-trade. Specific suggestions are offered as to how developing country contacts might be broadened including a new proposal for establishing preferences for intra-trade.

Chapters 4 and 5 deal respectively with the problem LDCs have in the commodity sector, and the potential influence of transnational corporations on developing countries' trade. Concerning commodities, Chapter 4 reviews the elements of, and need for, an integrated programme such as that advanced by UNCTAD. However, the accent in this chapter differs somewhat from that of the integrated programme. While the latter stresses the need for achieving commodity price stabilisation through operations of a common fund, it appears that many of the desired objectives could also be realised by measures aimed at transferring the processing function for primary commodities back to the developing countries. Increased LDC processing could also make a contribution to reducing unemployment and increasing export earnings, as well as having a number of other potentially beneficial economic effects.

In analysing LDC economic problems, the potential role that the socialist countries can play in the industrialisation effort has been largely neglected. However, the rise of the new protectionism in the West places a premium on the search for additional markets for LDC exports. Chapter 6 shows that the socialist countries have considerable potential as such outlets, and have historically been operating below standards set by the DMECs. However, this chapter shows that the foreign exchange constraint is an important barrier to any potential expansion of 'East–South' trade. One solution rests on developed market economy countries lowering trade barriers against socialist products, particularly in agriculture, with the increase in foreign exchange earnings being used to expand trade with developing countries. Alternative courses of action, such as barter or buy-back arrangements, are also evaluated.

Chapter 7 examines existing empirical evidence concerning future

LDC exports to developed countries. This discussion appears to be of prime importance since it attempts to show which industries will come under increased pressure from LDCs in the 1980s. It appears that the rise of the new protectionism may have been caused, in part, by the rapidity with which LDCs moved into new export areas such as steel, shipbuilding, nonferrous metals, shoes, light capital equipment, and other sectors in the 1970s. Evidence as to the probable new directions or areas of LDC export expansion is examined so, with advanced notice, pressures for a similar spread of protectionism may be reduced.

Before turning to the subject matter of this book, a point should be made concerning the topics selected as the leading trade and development issues for the 1980s. In many respects, these issues are not new since transnationals, commodities, and unequal exchange have been recognised as major LDC problems in the past. Also, the problem of contemporary protectionism (discussed in the companion volume) has its roots in the 1960s and 1970s when developing countries began to emerge as important exporters of manufactured goods. Thus, many of the major trade and development issues for the 1980s will not be new ones, but are problems which have continued for some time. It is hoped that the discussion and analysis in this two-part survey will be helpful in understanding the basic issues associated with these problems.

# 2 Unequal Exchange and the Gains from Trade

The classical model of trade according to comparative advantage is based on several assumptions which must be relaxed when applying the theorem in practice. Aside from the problem of having to generalise from a two-country two-commodity framework, comparative advantage rests on the presumption of identical production functions, full employment, and factors of production being internationally immobile. A further requirement is that perfect competition exists within and between countries. This latter stipulation appears especially inappropriate in describing relations between most developed and developing nations.

A variety of factors relating to finance, transportation, culture and the historical pattern of economic development may tie LDCs to a metropolitan state.[1] In cases, liner conferences have established routes between given developing nations and one, or a relatively few, industrial countries so the potential for broadened trade contacts is limited. Language, financial ties, as well as established marketing and distribution systems are frequently such that developing countries have little external flexibility in trade relations. Finally, the export structures of many LDCs, centring on the production of primary goods and raw materials, have developed historically to serve the needs of a metropolitan state. This specialised pattern of commerce works to further limit the trading possibilities for developing countries.[2] Industrial nations, in contrast, normally have considerably broader contacts, and more diversified trade structures, so their dependence on any one developing country is limited.

In short, the normal situation is one in which a developing country disposes of its exports in a market characterised by varying degrees of monopoly power, while imports of manufactures and capital equipment are subject to control by one or a few metropolitan states. In this environment the power to influence commercial relations clearly lies with the developed nations. The marketing and distribution systems for many developing country products are also controlled by elements based in industrial nations. This adds to the potential for abuse of monopoly power which would work against the LDCs. Much of the debate concerning the new international order centres on ways to redress the vast imbalances in economic power between developed and developing countries. Clearly this discussion will carry over and assume even greater importance in the 1980s.

A key question centres on the extent to which developed nations employ their market power to influence commercial relations with developing countries. This chapter surveys the institutional factors which work against the LDCs in import and export markets, and also provides a quantitative evaluation of the ways in which this monopoly control may be exercised. Various policy actions developing countries might initiate to offset this influence are examined where evidence of the abuse of this power is uncovered.

## UNEQUAL EXCHANGE IN LDC IMPORT MARKETS

Price theory has traditionally held that the degree of competition in a market is related to the number and size distribution of competing units. The smaller the number of competitors, and the more unequal their size, the lower is the probability that there will be aggressive competition. The importance of maintaining or stimulating competition is that lower prices and profits, and a more efficient allocation of resources, generally prevail in markets where active competition exists.

Numerous studies have attempted to assess the influence of market structure on performance in industrial markets. With some measure of prices or profits as an indicator of performance, and the concentration ratio serving as a proxy for the relative power of competing units, a statistically significant positive relation has been found between prices, profits and the level of concentration.[3] Further work has also analysed the influence of other barriers to competition on performance. With few exceptions, these studies have shown that factors which foster monopoly control of markets lead to higher prices and profits than those prevailing in more competitive situations.[4]

While considerable attention has been devoted to the study of selling prices in domestic markets of industrial countries, these analyses have now been extended by UNCTAD (1968), Hewett (1974), Yeats (June 1978) and others to the systematic investigation of prices in international trade. The conclusions parallel those which would be predicted by theory. When monopoly elements exist in international markets, prices and profits rise above levels which would prevail in a more competitive environment. This has important implications since the problem of whether industrial nations abuse market power and extract excessive profits, whether alternative sources of supply offer lower prices, or whether trade and tariff policies result in higher import prices, can be crucial for developing countries. Since many LDCs are typically faced with the problem of making optimal use of limited financial reserves, it is important that they pay the lowest possible prices for imports of industrial equipment and related inputs required for economic growth. However, if market imperfections exist, or if competition is less vigorous than it might be under some alternative structural form, there is the possibility that some developing nations may be paying in excess for imports or receive less than fair prices for exports.

### Institutional factors in import markets

A variety of institutional factors combine to work against developing countries in their efforts to achieve the best possible terms for imports. Helleiner (1978) concisely summarises the problem in noting that 'it is known that restrictive trade practices – national and international cartels, the abuse of positions of dominant market power in individual markets, etc. – are common at the international level where antitrust laws are weak or nonexistent or unenforceable. Public investigations are few, the relevant practices are subject to constant change, and agreements are usually clandestine, but available information about private restrictions indicates persuasively that their number has been large enough to constitute a significant problem for the world trading community.' Edwards (1972) notes that among the restrictive practices which are most frequently found internationally, and for which there is publicly available evidence, are inter-firm agreements for the allocation of territorial markets; pooling and allocation of patents, trademarks, and copyrights; fixing of prices and price relationships including discriminatory pricing; allocation of total amounts of export business; and establishment of reciprocal, exclusive, or preferential dealing. At the national level, inter-firm agreements on exports extend not only to the allocation of foreign markets, but even to individual foreign customers, allocation of specific goods to be exported, fixing of prices and levels of bidding on foreign contracts, and the selection in advance of the firm that will submit the lowest bid.

For various reasons, these institutional factors and practices seem likely to have an adverse differential effect on developing countries. In the DMECs, the existence of antitrust laws relating to import trade, more aggressive market competition, and the degree of intra-industry trade tend to moderate losses associated with such practices. However, most of the moderating forces do not seem generally applicable for developing countries. Helleiner specifically suggests that:

> these countries are likely to pay higher prices than are paid by industrialised countries for products controlled by cartel arrangements because their relatively small size reduces the incentive for cartel members to risk frictions by cheating while they also offer limited incentives for firms not participating in these arrangements to establish competitive distribution networks. When foreign firms reach agreements as to the allocation of export markets in the developing countries, the agreements are much less likely to come unstuck through market pressures than are similar agreements concerning larger markets in the industrialised countries.

The likelihood that competitive practices will be stimulated by enforcement of anti-restrictive practices legislation is considerably lower in the LDCs since many of these countries have not even enacted such measures. These considerations lead Tumlir and Robinson (1975) to conclude that 'cartel arrangements and the abuse of dominant positions are probably more widespread and damaging in imports to developing than to developed countries'.

*Iron and steel prices: a case study*
For a test of these propositions concerning monopoly power, data on French exports were compiled from various issues of the United Nations *World Trade Annual*. This source provided detailed information on the quantity and value of shipments (f.o.b.) on a joint product-by-country basis. The decision to examine French export prices was based on the fact that this country had well defined colonial ties with a number of different developing countries. However, there is no reason to believe that empirical results would differ significantly if trade relations between another industrial nation and its former colonial associates had been chosen for analysis.[5] Furthermore, by confining the statistical analysis to the 1964–73 period, it was possible to observe the behaviour of relative prices over an interval when special French reverse preferences were being extended to other members of the European Economic Community.[6] As such, the opportunity exists to examine the effect of increased competitive pressures on French firms due to the loss of

special preferences in these markets. The results are therefore relevant to other LDCs which have some capacity to increase competition in their own import markets.

Employing a selection of iron and steel products, over 3400 unit values were computed for exports to former French colonial associates and other developed and developing countries. As indicated in Table 2.1, this selection covered almost $5 billion in trade, or approximately 37 per cent of France's iron and steel shipments during 1964–73. Iron and steel unit values were studied since these products are generally homogeneous, with the result that statistical problems caused by quality variations would be minor.[7] Another factor was that most of the associated countries had little or no domestic production to effectively compete with foreign sources of supply. In this situation, import prices had the potential to be determined largely by foreign firms.

TABLE 2.1  Comparison of Sample Statistics with Total French Iron and Steel Exports over the Period 1964–73

| Period | French iron and steel exports Sampled for unit value comparisons | | Total value of French exports ($000) | Per cent of exports in sample |
| | No. of unit values computed | Value of shipments ($000) | | |
| --- | --- | --- | --- | --- |
| 1964–65 | 699 | 779281 | 1854617 | 42·0 |
| 1966–67 | 684 | 714683 | 1874646 | 38·1 |
| 1968–69 | 617 | 812641 | 2135326 | 38·1 |
| 1970–71 | 695 | 1135507 | 3087850 | 36·8 |
| 1972–73 | 730 | 1443396 | 4273801 | 33·8 |
| Total | 3425 | 4885508 | 13226240 | 36·9 |

*Source*: All data on French iron and steel shipments were taken from United Nations, *World Trade Annual*, Vol. 3 (New York: Walker and Company, various issues).

Table 2.2 compares prices for the associated nations with those paid by other developing and developed countries. Shown here are unit values, quantities, and value of shipments for France's major export products. While the underlying statistics have been computed on an annual basis, the results are presented for successive two-year periods in the interests of brevity, and to reduce the influence of any unrepresentative shipments. To assist in the comparisons, the ratio of non-associated to associated country unit values was computed for each item. As such, a figure of less than unity indicates that the associated French unit value exceeds that of the matched country group. Finally,

TABLE 2.2 Analysis of Iron and Steel Unit Values for French Shipments to Associated and Non-associated countries[a]

| SITC | Product-importing country group | 1964–1965 shipments | | | | 1966–1967 shipments | | | | 1968–1969 shipments | | | |
|---|---|---|---|---|---|---|---|---|---|---|---|---|---|
| | | Quantity (tons) | Value ($000) | Unit value | Ratio | Quantity (tons) | Value ($000) | Unit value | Ratio | Quantity (tons) | Value ($000) | Unit value | Ratio |
| 673.21 | Iron simple steel bars | | | | | | | | | | | | |
| | French associates | 153179 | 16296 | 106·39 | — | 159512 | 16142 | 101·20 | — | 149339 | 15872 | 106·28 | — |
| | Developed countries | 868453 | 82813 | 95·36 | 0·896 | 824549 | 77299 | 93·74 | 0·926 | 966790 | 91479 | 94·62 | 0·890 |
| | Developing countries | 246979 | 21538 | 87·20 | 0·819 | 224614 | 18690 | 83·20 | 0·822 | 140372 | 12616 | 89·87 | 0·845 |
| 673.41 | Iron simple steel big sections | | | | | | | | | | | | |
| | French associates | 63834 | 7376 | 115·55 | — | 67698 | 8073 | 118·78 | — | 67653 | 8034 | 118·75 | — |
| | Developed countries | 625025 | 62346 | 99·74 | 0·863 | 773720 | 73622 | 95·15 | 0·801 | 875238 | 83760 | 95·70 | 0·806 |
| | Developing countries | 47735 | 4369 | 91·52 | 0·792 | 65144 | 6141 | 94·26 | 0·793 | 72345 | 7496 | 103·61 | 0·872 |
| 673.51 | Iron simple steel small sections | | | | | | | | | | | | |
| | French associates | 114160 | 14248 | 124·81 | — | 85108 | 9980 | 117·26 | — | 72740 | 8537 | 117·36 | — |
| | Developed countries | 380524 | 40801 | 107·22 | 0·859 | 330677 | 32132 | 97·17 | 0·829 | 424448 | 38575 | 90·88 | 0·774 |
| | Developing countries | 25298 | 2463 | 97·35 | 0·780 | 17109 | 1867 | 109·12 | 0·931 | 20828 | 2132 | 102·36 | 0·873 |
| 674.31 | Iron simple steel thin uncoated | | | | | | | | | | | | |
| | French associates | 46912 | 7242 | 154·37 | — | 48015 | 7011 | 146·02 | — | 56879 | 8654 | 152·15 | — |
| | Developed countries | 2217468 | 293566 | 132·39 | 0·857 | 1918382 | 246907 | 128·70 | 0·881 | 2055304 | 263669 | 128·29 | 0·843 |
| | Developing countries | 207927 | 25252 | 121·45 | 0·787 | 240992 | 27785 | 115·32 | 0·790 | 169431 | 21897 | 129·24 | 0·849 |
| 674.81 | Iron simple thin coated | | | | | | | | | | | | |
| | French associates | 76661 | 17258 | 225·12 | — | 52274 | 12286 | 235·03 | — | 41963 | 9174 | 218·62 | — |
| | Developed countries | 245903 | 43364 | 176·35 | 0·783 | 204066 | 35245 | 172·71 | 0·735 | 327153 | 54281 | 165·91 | 0·759 |
| | Developing countries | 47339 | 7695 | 162·55 | 0·722 | 36965 | 5616 | 151·93 | 0·646 | 17668 | 2790 | 157·91 | 0·722 |
| 677.01 | Iron simple steel wire | | | | | | | | | | | | |
| | French associates | 41765 | 7326 | 175·41 | — | 36159 | 6416 | 177·44 | — | 30440 | 5544 | 182·13 | — |
| | Developed countries | 85292 | 13396 | 157·06 | 0·895 | 94787 | 15291 | 161·32 | 0·909 | 114761 | 19251 | 167·75 | 0·921 |
| | Developing countries | 54284 | 7133 | 131·40 | 0·749 | 29891 | 3971 | 132·85 | 0·748 | 23072 | 3302 | 143·12 | 0·785 |
| 678.50 | Iron and steel tube fittings | | | | | | | | | | | | |
| | French associates | 5915 | 4688 | 792·56 | — | 5938 | 4647 | 782·59 | — | 6633 | 5870 | 884·97 | — |
| | Developed countries | 25510 | 15539 | 609·13 | 0·769 | 32066 | 21487 | 670·09 | 0·857 | 33489 | 25053 | 748·10 | 0·845 |
| | Developing countries | 6624 | 4204 | 634·66 | 0·801 | 8034 | 5364 | 667·66 | 0·853 | 8532 | 6494 | 761·13 | 0·860 |

| 670.00 Other iron and steel products | Quantity (tons) | Value ($000) | Unit Value | Ratio | Quantity (tons) | Value ($000) | Unit Value | Ratio | Quantity (tons) | Value ($000) | Unit Value | Ratio |
|---|---|---|---|---|---|---|---|---|---|---|---|---|
| French associates | 12112 | 18321 | 151·26 | — | 11447 | 17999 | 157·24 | — | 16224 | 27928 | 172·14 | — |
| Developed countries | 37628 | 45802 | 124·03 | 0·820 | 36662 | 44220 | 135·38 | 0·861 | 45147 | 60723 | 141·15 | 0·820 |
| Developing countries | 14675 | 16245 | 118·79 | 0·782 | 15001 | 16492 | 129·57 | 0·824 | 21343 | 29510 | 138·57 | 0·805 |
| Total of above shipments | | | | | | | | | | | | |
| French associates | 514538 | 92755 | | | 466151 | 82554 | | | 441871 | 89613 | | |
| Developed countries | 4485803 | 597627 | | | 4214909 | 546203 | | | 4842330 | 636791 | | |
| Developing countries | 650861 | 88899 | | | 637750 | 85926 | | | 473591 | 86237 | | |
| Total | 5651202 | 779281 | | | 5318810 | 714683 | | | 5757792 | 812641 | | |
| Premium paid by associated French (per cent) | | +15·5 | | | | +14·6 | | | | +16·7 | | |

| SITC | Product-importing country group | 1970–1971 shipments | | | | 1972–1973 shipments | | | |
|---|---|---|---|---|---|---|---|---|---|
| | | Quantity (tons) | Value ($000) | Unit Value | Ratio | Quantity (tons) | Value ($000) | Unit Values | Ratio |
| 673.21 | Iron simple steel bars | | | | | | | | |
| | French associates | 167552 | 23898 | 142·63 | — | 147150 | 29359 | 199·51 | — |
| | Developed countries | 991142 | 132221 | 133·40 | 0·935 | 605761 | 105797 | 174·65 | 0·875 |
| | Developing countries | 175580 | 22044 | 125·54 | 0·880 | 120776 | 22135 | 183·27 | 0·918 |
| 673.41 | Iron simple steel big sections | | | | | | | | |
| | French associates | 82364 | 13229 | 160·61 | — | 91229 | 18026 | 197·59 | — |
| | Developed countries | 935027 | 125990 | 134·74 | 0·839 | 896349 | 148585 | 165·77 | 0·839 |
| | Developing countries | 65336 | 8610 | 131·78 | 0·820 | 79287 | 13278 | 167·46 | 0·848 |
| 673.51 | Iron simple steel small sections | | | | | | | | |
| | French associates | 55651 | 8347 | 149·99 | — | 71433 | 13387 | 187·41 | — |
| | Developed countries | 362613 | 49058 | 135·29 | 0·902 | 310609 | 51948 | 167·36 | 0·893 |
| | Developing countries | 10290 | 1368 | 132·94 | 0·886 | 32698 | 5874 | 179·64 | 0·959 |
| 674.31 | Iron simple steel thin uncoated | | | | | | | | |
| | French associates | 66786 | 11763 | 176·13 | — | 100957 | 21634 | 214·29 | — |
| | Developed countries | 2349548 | 366291 | 155·90 | 0·885 | 2602650 | 500275 | 192·22 | 0·897 |
| | Developing countries | 147601 | 23937 | 162·17 | 0·920 | 114469 | 20609 | 180·04 | 0·840 |
| 674.81 | Iron simple thin coated | | | | | | | | |
| | French associates | 38287 | 8019 | 209·44 | — | 63267 | 18735 | 296·13 | — |
| | Developed countries | 434013 | 83416 | 192·19 | 0·918 | 511516 | 123201 | 240·85 | 0·813 |
| | Developing countries | 22285 | 3855 | 179·99 | 0·826 | 40770 | 9301 | 228·13 | 0·770 |

TABLE 2.2 (*Contd.*)

| SITC | Product-importing country group | 1970–1971 shipments | | | | 1972–1973 shipments | | | |
|---|---|---|---|---|---|---|---|---|---|
| | | Quantity (*tons*) | Value (*$000*) | Unit value | Ratio | Quantity (*tons*) | Value (*$000*) | Unit value | Ratio |
| 677.01 | Iron simple steel wire | | | | | | | | |
| | French associates | 34321 | 9957 | 290·11 | — | 27611 | 8528 | 308·86 | — |
| | Developed countries | 103266 | 25707 | 248·94 | 0·859 | 152161 | 45793 | 300·95 | 0·974 |
| | Developing countries | 12808 | 2335 | 182·30 | 0·628 | 7174 | 1946 | 271·25 | 0·878 |
| 678.50 | Iron and steel tube fittings | | | | | | | | |
| | French associates | 11493 | 12904 | 1122·77 | — | 10294 | 13271 | 1289·20 | — |
| | Developed countries | 39952 | 37145 | 929·74 | 0·828 | 47192 | 51034 | 1081·41 | 0·839 |
| | Developing countries | 10874 | 11604 | 1067·13 | 0·950 | 9968 | 13362 | 1340·49 | 1·040 |
| 670.00 | Other iron and steel products[b] | | | | | | | | |
| | French associates | 15119 | 29525 | 195·28 | — | 21212 | 44575 | 210·14 | — |
| | Developed countries | 47200 | 83610 | 177·14 | 0·907 | 59160 | 119456 | 201·92 | 0·960 |
| | Developing countries | 23005 | 40674 | 176·81 | 0·905 | 21906 | 43287 | 197·60 | 0·940 |
| | Total of above shipments | | | | | | | | |
| | French associates | 471573 | 117642 | | | 533153 | 167515 | | |
| | Developed countries | 5262761 | 903438 | | | 5185398 | 1146089 | | |
| | Developing countries | 467779 | 114427 | | | 427048 | 129792 | | |
| | Total | 6202113 | 1135507 | | | 6145599 | 1443396 | | |
| | Premium paid by associated French (per cent) | | +11·0 | | | | +11·3 | | |

[a] The associated country group includes both members of the Central African Union; Chad, Central African Republic, Gabon, Congo as well as the West African Union; Dahomey, Ivory Coast, Mali, Mauritania, Niger, Senegal and Upper Volta. Also included were Tunisia, Morocco, Guinea, Madagascar, Togo, Reunion, Mauritius, Algeria and Mozambique.

[b] Since this group includes four different five-digit SITC items the *overall* unit values have been computed using associated country trade weights.

*Source:* Alexander J. Yeats, 'Monopoly Power, Barriers to Competition, and the Pattern of Price Differentials in International Trade', *Journal of Development Economics* (June 1978), pp. 171–2.

the table also shows the premium paid by the associated countries in each of the five periods.

The data in Table 2.2 strongly suggest that the associated countries pay in excess for iron and steel imports. Overall, the adverse price differentials facing these nations range from a high of 16·7 per cent during 1968–9, to 11 per cent in 1970–1. The unit values for individual products show that these adverse prices were maintained across all types of iron and steel shipments. In only one instance, that for iron and steel tube fittings during 1972–3, does a non-associated group (developing countries) record a unit value exceeding that of the French associates.

While it is difficult to draw firm conclusions, the recent experience suggests that the adverse price margins have been reduced in the 1970s. The overall premium paid by these nations averaged close to 15 per cent during 1964–9, but this margin fell to about 11 per cent over 1970–3. A factor here may have been the extension of preferential tariff margins to other EEC members, and the resulting increase in competitive pressures on French manufacturers. Loss of special tariff preferences has decidedly eroded France's market share in some associated countries, and may have initiated a pricing policy aimed at arresting these declines.[8] However, even with the extension of reverse preferences, Table 2.2 suggests the associates still pay an adverse price differential of over 10 per cent for their iron and steel imports.[9]

While the preceding comparisons show that the associated country's unit values have been consistently, and considerably, above those for the non-associated groups, the analysis provides no indication as to the reasons for these differences. For example, if shipments to the non-associated countries are consistently larger, the price differentials may be due to economies of scale. Alternatively, the spread between associated and non-associated unit values may be due to structural factors such as concentration of suppliers, or the dominant position France has maintained in many of the associated country's markets.

Since differences in the import unit values may be caused by various factors, correlation analysis was used to account for the observed variations. To evaluate the influence of geographic concentration, variables were tested which showed the percentage of iron and steel (SITC 67) originating in the largest, and three largest, OECD countries. While these measures parallel the concentration ratios used in structure-performance studies of domestic markets, there is a special problem in that similar ratios can mask different distributions of competing foreign firms. In support of the country ratios, however, firms headquartered in the same exporting nation may have a tendency to participate in cartel arrangements, or collusive oligopoly decisions concerning foreign prices. Also, iron and steel production is generally among the most concentrated of industries so the potential number of exporting firms is limited.

Two variables were selected to test the relation between the size of the market and the pattern of relative prices: the relative quantity (tons) of each country's iron and steel imports from France was computed to determine if larger shipments were associated with lower prices. Also, the absolute magnitude of each nation's total imports from all sources was tested. Analysis of results from these variables may indicate whether there are economies of scale associated with larger shipments, or whether French pricing policies are different for large export markets where countervailing power may be influential.

Other variables employed include the number of alternative (country) suppliers of iron and steel to determine if a larger variety of contacts, and potentially greater sources of information on competitive prices, are related to unit value differences. Dummy variables were also used to designate transactions between France and another developed country, while a second dummy registered shipments from France to a former colonial associate.

*Correlation results*

Using this detailed information, French export price relatives were correlated with various market structure and related variables which might be expected to influence prices. The results are summarised in Table 2.3. To assist in evaluating this information, results which are significant at the 99 per cent confidence level are marked with an asterisk.

As shown in the first column of the table, five explanatory variables have a significant influence on French export prices. As is the case with the industrial organisation studies, variables relating to market structure influence relative prices. For example, a highly significant positive relation ($r = 0.38$) exists between relative prices and the percentage of imports controlled by the largest supplying countries. Thus, those nations which are heavily dependent on relatively few suppliers pay for this domination of domestic markets through higher import prices. In this respect, the significant positive association between market concentration and prices, observed in studies of domestic markets, also holds for prices in international trade.

Another result which accents the importance of market characteristics is the significant inverse association ($r = -0.45$) between relative

TABLE 2.3 Correlation Analysis Between Iron and Steel Relative Import Prices in 1968–9 and Selected Explanatory Variables

| | Relative price | Market structure variables | | Market size[a] | | Dummy variable | |
|---|---|---|---|---|---|---|---|
| | | Number of trade contacts | Share of three largest suppliers | Relative quantity | Total imports | Associated countries | Developed countries |
| Number of contacts | −0·448* | 1·000 | | | | | |
| Share of three largest | 0·384* | −0·762* | 1·000 | | | | |
| Relative quantity | −0·134 | 0·355* | −0·150 | 1·000 | | | |
| Total imports | −0·157 | 0·474* | −0·219* | 0·842* | 1·000 | | |
| Associated country group | 0·604* | −0·778* | 0·680* | −0·216* | −0·337* | 1·000 | |
| Developed country group | −0·200* | 0·593* | −0·441* | 0·454* | 0·598* | −0·515* | 1·000 |
| GNP per capita | −0·287* | 0·560* | −0·385* | 0·575* | 0·716* | −0·517* | 0·799* |

* Statistically significant at the 99 per cent confidence level.
[a] Total imports reflect the total value of iron and steel (SITC 67) imports from all sources while the relative quantity (tons) refers to shipments of each five-digit SITC product from France.

Source: Alexander J. Yeats, 'Monopoly Power, Barriers to Competition, and the Pattern of Price Differentials in International Trade', *Journal of Development Economics* (June 1978), p. 175.

prices and the number of trading partner (country) contacts. Thus, those importing countries maintaining trade relations with a larger number of exporters, and theoretically benefiting from greater competition and information on comparative prices, pay less for their imports. Unfortunately, from the view of development policy, there is evidence that the smaller, poorer countries may not normally be able to attract a larger number of trading contacts since this variable is positively correlated with GNP per capita, market size, relative quantities purchased, and the developed country dummy. Thus, developing nations, *acting in isolation*, may not be able to maintain the trade contacts or other market conditions leading to lower import prices.

Somewhat surprisingly, the data fail to reveal a strong association between relative prices and either of the market size variables. While import prices are negatively correlated with both the relative quantities purchased and total imports, these associations fail to achieve statistical significance at the 99 per cent level. Thus, market size may have a relatively minor *direct* influence on prices as compared to the structure variables and related competitive factors. However, the overall effect of size is probably considerable since Table 2.3 shows this variable strongly influences market structure which, in turn, is directly associated with relative prices.

Aside from these relations, the correlation between relative prices and the association dummy ($r = 0.60$) is one of the strongest in the table. This suggests that the special relations between France and the associated countries insulate suppliers from active competition and allow prices to rise above those dictated by market structure and related influences. As such, it would seemingly benefit the associated countries to encourage alternative trade contacts, or adopt policy measures aimed at reducing the market power of French manufacturers.

While the correlation between relative prices and the explanatory variables are the focus of this analysis, some of the intercorrelations between the independent variables are also of interest. For example, a number of specific factors seem to be working against a more favourable price position for the associated countries. Specifically, Table 2.3 shows that these nations have fewer trade contacts ($r = -0.77$), are generally smaller markets ($r = -0.34$), and also have significantly higher concentration ratios ($r = 0.68$). These factors undoubtedly contribute to higher import prices. Conversely, the developed countries have less concentrated markets, and a larger number of trade contacts. Thus, certain institutional characteristics of each country group seem to have an important influence on price relatives.

*Comparisons for selected African countries*

Another useful procedure for evaluating the level of import prices paid by the associated countries is to compare France's export unit values for shipments to similar African nations with and without French ties. If both the associated and non-associated countries are matched so as to have approximately equal geographic size, population, development, and other related characteristics, it may be hypothesised that the types and quality of items generally imported should be similar. As such, *persistent* variations in prices should be due to the feature in which the countries differ; the concentration of economic power France has in the associated markets, and the comparative lack of competition facing French products.

Several factors work against attempts to make the required price comparisons. The primary problem was that many African countries are still highly dependent on a limited number of industrial nations for their manufactured imports.[10] Thus, while it was possible to form a number of combinations of associated and non-associated countries with similar characteristics, there were relatively few in which France was an active trader in both markets. However, ten country combinations were found in which France had extensive trade relations. These combinations are shown in Table 2.4 along with the aggregate ratio of associate to non-associate unit values.

These results provide additional evidence that the associates pay in excess for French products. For example, of the 28 matched combinations these nations record higher overall unit values in all but one instance (Senegal–Ghana). The table also shows that the adverse price differentials may range to over 40 percentage points for the Ivory Coast and Upper Volta. Overall, the price margins of 18 per cent in 1962, and 13 per cent in 1969, are in line with the steel price differentials shown in Table 2.2. This suggests that a figure in the range of 10 to 20 per cent provides a reasonable approximation to the adverse price margins paid by the French associates as a group.

## DEVELOPING COUNTRY IMPORT POLICY

From the viewpoint of development policy, the results in Table 2.3, as well as those for supplementary studies, have important implications. Specifically, relative prices have been found to vary inversely with the number of trade contacts and market size. This suggests that there may be economies of scale associated with larger shipments, or that

TABLE 2.4 Ratio of French Unit Value Export Prices Charged Associated and Non-associated Countries for Common Four-Digit SITC Products

| *Associated/Non-associated* | *Unit value ratio*[a] | | |
|---|---|---|---|
| *country comparison* | *1962* | *1965* | *1969* |
| Madagascar–Uganda | na | 115 | 112 |
| Madagascar–Tanzania | na | 113 | 115 |
| Cameroon–Nigeria | 115 | 112 | 109 |
| Cameroon–Ghana | 127 | 120 | 113 |
| Ivory Coast–Nigeria | 105 | 102 | 105 |
| Ivory Coast–Ghana | 143 | 122 | 115 |
| Upper Volta–Nigeria | 109 | 106 | 112 |
| Upper Volta–Ghana | 127 | 130 | 141 |
| Senegal–Ghana | 98 | 102 | 103 |
| Senegal–Nigeria | 120 | 121 | 110 |
| Average | 118 | 114 | 113 |

[a] Each ratio shown is based on unit value comparisons for at least 100 different four-digit SITC items.

*Source*: Alexander J. Yeats, 'Monopoly Power, Barriers to Competition, and the Pattern of Price Differentials in International Trade', *Journal of Development Economics* (June 1978), p. 178.

countervailing power is a factor. However, the indirect effects of size on prices may be equally important since a strong inverse correlation exists between this variable and market concentration.[11] Thus, market size apparently produces structural features which influence both the level of competition and prices. However, it appears that developing countries can, at least partially, offset these unfavourable size and structural effects by cooperative trade arrangements.

*The potential for import cooperation*

Although substantial opportunities exist, import cooperation has only recently come under study as a means for improving the trade position of developing countries. The need for import cooperation results from imbalances in market power between developed and developing countries, and the fragmentation and small size of demand in the latter. The bulk of imports of about 130 developing countries is heavily concentrated in fewer than ten industrial nations with the result that the LDCs acting independently have little or no influence on conditions under which they purchase imports.

There are various reasons for believing that import cooperation might result in more equitable prices and improved gains from trade. The countervailing power resulting from collective bargaining by LDCs in trade relations with industrial countries' corporations should improve their capacity to secure better terms for imports. Even when practised at the national level, centralised trading seems to have led to more favourable prices. For example, UNCTAD (January 1975) notes that 'countries which practise state trading or other forms of centralised import regulation tend to have import price trends at least 30 per cent, and sometimes a great deal more, below the average for developing countries as a whole'.

Bulk orders could produce economies of scale in marketing, distribution, and service systems for many products. Dealing in larger quantities, on behalf of several importers, could make it easier to locate low-cost sources of supply. Frequently, it is not feasible for individual small-scale importers to conduct the research required for determination of the best price offered by alternative suppliers. Pooling expenses for this function, and sharing information, could produce substantial benefits for the cooperating importers.[12] Filing joint purchase orders might also enhance the importance of these transactions so the larger cooperative unit could actually be sought out by foreign firms.

Import cooperation could also lead to freight savings since economies of scale and other benefits can often be realised if homogeneous import cargoes like coal, grain, and wood were bulked for marine transport, or mixed liner cargoes were consolidated. Aggregation of small cargo shipments could offer savings if the size increase makes charter or contract methods feasible (which requires shipments sufficient to fill a vessel), as opposed to the parcel service offered by liners. However, even when aggregation of orders does not produce full loads, liner conferences normally grant reductions for larger consignments. Collectivisation of imports may produce savings through rationalisation of shipping services. A relatively frequent service, delivering small cargoes, is costly and inconvenient if liners must spend considerable berth time for the discharge of these consignments. A rationalised service, with fewer calls, may reduce both the average cost of shipments and the number of ports at which the liner must stop.

UNCTAD has shown that containerisation, or unit load transport systems, often can produce economies if cargo volumes are adequate. Of the various unit load systems—containers, pallets, roll-on/roll-off vehicles or LASH barges—containers are the most widely used.

However, small ports often cannot be efficiently served by containerised systems, while some LDCs might have difficulty, acting alone, in generating the sizeable initial investment needed for the implementation of these unitised transport modes. However, if cargoes are aggregated on a regional basis, accompanied by the appropriate intra-regional transport systems, unitisation procedures might be employed for the benefit of the cooperating nations.

Import cooperation may also produce benefits in international trade relations. For example, developed market economy countries which have formed regional groupings such as the EEC or EFTA have found that a joint approach to trade negotiations has advantages such as the enhanced market position and bargaining power of the group. The centrally planned economies are also given joint representation in international forums through the auspices of the Council for Mutual Economic Assistance. Cooperation on trade matters may allow the LDCs to negotiate from a combined position in such sessions.

In international trade negotiations such as the Tokyo Round, bargaining from a common position, with the larger combined market serving as an attraction, might enable LDCs to extract trade concessions which would otherwise not be achieved. Cooperative import arrangements could also make it possible for the developing countries to maximise their bargaining position among different trading partners. Finally, import cooperation may also provide a stimulus to other forms of potentially profitable integration. For example, the pooling of imports could demonstrate the feasibility of integrated production and trade policies. These could provide an important offset to the small size of demand in some LDCs which often works as a constraint against the development of basic industries like iron and steel, pulp and paper, motor vehicles and transport equipment, and a variety of capital goods subject to substantial economies of scale.

## UNEQUAL EXCHANGE IN EXPORT MARKETS

As was the case with imports, high concentration is commonplace in many developing country export markets which may be dominated by a small number of giant firms. For example, the largest cocoa-buying and processing firm in the world accounts for between 30 and 40 per cent of all transactions. In bauxite, six firms control between 50 and 60 per cent of world primary aluminium capacity, while similar concentration ratios occur for nickle, phosphates, copper, and other mineral industries.

Furthermore, important entry barriers such as large required investments, technological dominance, scale economies, and the ability of vertically integrated firms to pursue pricing policies aimed at eliminating rivals, tend to perpetuate the highly concentrated structures of these markets. Aside from the imbalances that result from the market power of these international firms there are other factors, such as the weak financial position of LDCs, which work against these countries in their export markets. Several investigations by the UNCTAD Secretariat demonstrate that foreign enterprises absorb a high percentage of the value of developing country exports and that LDCs may only receive 10 to 20 per cent of the consumer price for tea, 10 to 15 per cent for cocoa powder, 20 per cent for bananas, and 30 per cent for citrus fruit even though these items experience little or no processing between the exporter and the final consumer. It was also demonstrated that the margins absorbed by middlemen in the DMECs who handle the marketing and distribution function may be several times the value retained by developing country exporters.[13]

A recent study by Avramovic (1978) provides useful empirical information concerning the degree to which various institutional factors work against developing countries in their export markets. This analysis compared developed and developing country unit values as a percentage of world market prices for a selection of basic commodities over 1971–5. Recognising that the unit values may be subject to quality or product-mix differences, Avramovic attempted to account for these factors to the maximum account possible. However, the results, summarised in Table 2.5, show conclusively that the LDCs generally receive prices for their exports which were 15 to 20 per cent below those of the DMECs. While the lack of market power was cited as an explanatory factor, the inability of the developing countries to time sales over the cycle was also stressed. In other words, the foreign exchange requirements of some developing countries were so pressing that they were forced to sell in adverse market conditions while the developed nations were able to time sales to achieve higher prices.

*The policy implications*
This chapter assessed both institutional factors and empirical evidence of the biases that work against developing countries in their import and export markets. However, additional evidence could have been cited as to the existence of institutional biases against LDCs in other commercial sectors. For example, Helleiner (1978) makes a convincing case that technology, capital, and labour markets are such as to seriously

TABLE 2.5 Comparison of Export Unit Values as a Percentage of World Market Prices over 1971–5

| Product | All developing | African countries | Developed countries |
|---|---|---|---|
| Beef | 67·3 | 47·0 | 85·2 |
| Groundnuts | 92·0 | 84·3 | 107·5 |
| Groundnut oil | 85·6 | 81·3 | 101·4 |
| Rice | 81·6 | 114·2 | 103·3 |
| Wheat | 97·0 | na | 95·1[a] |
| Maize | 79·3 | 74·6 | 94·8 |
| Soybeans | 92·8 | na | 88·8 |
| Soybean cake | 87·3 | na | 96·0 |
| Soybean oil | 102·5 | na | 103·6 |
| Coconut oil | 85·3 | na | 104·7 |
| Palm oil | 83·8 | 83·6 | 126·2 |
| Tea | 87·2 | 74·0 | na |
| Cocoa | 78·1 | 78·4 | na |
| Sisal | 67·0 | 63·9 | na |
| Jute | 72·4[b] | na | na |
| Copra | 81·6 | 81·5 | na |
| Palm nuts | 84·7 | 88·5 | na |
| Palm kernel oil | 86·0 | 88·1 | na |
| *Average*: | | | |
| Median | 85·3 | 81·5 | 101·0 |
| Mean | 84·4 | 81·1 | 100·6 |
| Weighted[c] | 84·3 | 78·5 | 94·0 |

[a] Biased downward because of special US sales to the USSR in 1972–3. In other years wheat was sold by developed countries at or above the average world market price.
[b] Average of 80·5 for Bangladesh only.
[c] By value of exports in 1975.

*Source*: Adapted from Dragaslov Avramovic, 'Common Fund, Why and What Kind', *Journal of World Trade Law* (October 1978), p. 405.

disadvantage the developing countries. Yeats (November 1977) shows that similar problems exist in shipping since liner conference freight rates may work against industrialisation. Efforts and policy proposals to redress these imbalances lie at the centre of the objectives of the new international economic order.

In assessing these proposals, two different points should be noted. Firstly, the developing countries are asking for action to correct deficiencies in international economic institutions which have an adverse differential bias against them. In this respect, they are attempting to remove imperfections in existing markets so that they will be placed on an *equal footing* with the industrial countries. Secondly, the actions requested by the LDCs are related to measures adopted by the DMECs for their own internal markets. For example, in the United States a host of regulatory agencies have evolved such as the Federal Trade Commission, Justice Department, or Federal Deposit Insurance Corporation to insure that consumers are not exploited or abused by corporations that possess high degrees of market power. Does not the fact that the developed countries find it necessary to protect their own nationals from abuses of such power constitute a compelling case for extending similar regulatory functions to the international arena where these corporations also operate? At present, no such bodies or functions exist. It should also be noted that the developed countries have found it necessary to stabilise and subsidise the incomes and prices of their own primary product producers, particularly in the agricultural sector. Are not the existence of such stabilisation and subsidisation programmes as the Common Agricultural Policy evidence that similar price and income guarantees should also be extended to producers in developing countries? Indeed, basic questions such as these lie at the heart of many of the proposals for a new economic order.

# 3 Economic Cooperation among Developing Countries

A major element in the overall development strategy pursued by the United Nations Conference on Trade and Development is that LDCs should adopt policies aimed at promoting *collective self-reliance.* According to UNCTAD (May 1976), collective self-reliance embraces two essential elements: establishing common positions to increase the LDCs' bargaining power *vis-à-vis* the industrialised countries, and promotion of trade, investment, technological, and other forms of economic cooperation. If the LDCs succeeded in pursuing such policies, it should loosen economic ties to industrial nations. This could lead to considerably more freedom to follow independent policies directly geared to national development objectives, or rectify institutional imbalances of the sort discussed in the preceding chapter.

A cornerstone of the collective self-reliance strategy hinges on the creation of preferences for developing country intra-trade. Among the possible benefits from such preferences are: weakening the influence developed countries have on LDC trade policies, provision of further incentives (markets) to shift from primary product exports to semi-finished goods or manufactures, establishing a basis for other forms of mutually beneficial cooperative efforts, and creation of larger markets which could lead to more efficient allocation of resources or economies of scale in production and distribution. It has also been argued that trade preferences among developing countries might directly stimulate joint ventures in areas such as finance, insurance, transportation, marketing and distribution which could have important implications for trade relations with industrial nations.[1] Thus, while all forms of economic cooperation deserve a high priority, measures to stimulate intra-trade should be a major issue for the 1980s.

In spite of the potential benefits associated with such measures, previous trade expansion efforts have met with few concrete successes. A major problem is that many past attempts to establish preferences were on a regional basis. Since LDCs in the same region are often at similar levels of economic development, producing the same types of primary or semifinished goods, the opportunities for mutually beneficial trade were limited.[2] While efforts at creating inter-regional preferences have greater promise, these have not been particularly successful. The major accomplishment is the 1973 *Protocol for Trade Relations Among Developing Countries* under which approximately 500 items are exchanged at preferential tariffs by 16 developing countries. However, the effects have been minimal, as UNCTAD estimated the *Protocol* covered about 1 per cent of the contracting members' trade in 1974.

Given its importance in the overall development strategy, this chapter surveys the major aspects of developing country intra-trade. Drawing from economic theory, the potential benefits associated with economic cooperation and trade among developing countries are outlined. Institutional barriers to intra-trade are examined, and a statistical survey of the nature of this exchange is conducted. After an assessment of two alternative procedures for establishing preferences, the chapter closes with an evaluation of policy measures that would facilitate the expansion of trade among developing countries.

## BENEFITS OF ECONOMIC INTEGRATION

Given the importance placed by UNCTAD on LDC economic integration, a key question centres on the nature of the gains likely to result. Economists have normally classified such benefits in terms of static and dynamic effects. The former refer to the welfare gains or losses from a reallocation of trade, consumption and production. Individually, they include the terms-of-trade effect (i.e., the improved purchasing power of exports) resulting from the greater bargaining power of the partner countries; the production effect on inter-country substitution of trade; and the consumption effect associated with changes in relative prices.[3]

While these static effects have been discussed in theoretical works by Viner (1950) and Mead (1955), economists now feel that the 'dynamic' effects are likely to be of far greater importance. These dynamic effects refer to ways in which integration influences the growth rate of the participating countries through its impact on the volume and location of investment, achievement of economies of scale associated with larger markets, increases in economic efficiency and trade due to changes in competitive pressures and increased familiarity with trade policies of participating countries. Newly created external economies in finance, insurance, or transport may also provide a stimulus to production and trade. However, a potentially negative effect can result from the deterioration in the relative or absolute economic position of a member country due to a failure to achieve an equitable share of benefits from the integration scheme. These 'polarisation' effects are often caused by new enterprise gravitating to areas where an industrial base already exists. The problem may also be due to integration agreements under which poorer areas must purchase high-cost manufactures from more advanced partner countries—thus, in effect, subsidising their industries.

*Relative importance of static effects*

While traditional theory is better suited for analysis of the static effects of economic integration, it is conceded that these usually are relatively minor. Jabar (1971) cites empirical estimates of the static gains from developed countries' integration efforts which, as a percentage of GNP, reach a maximum of 1 per cent for Britain joining EFTA. For various reasons, the static effects of LDC economic integration are thought to be even less important. The range of goods produced in the developing countries is smaller so the possibilities for successful trade creation and diversion are more limited. Also, given the small size and relatively low GNP in most developing countries, economic integration may not do much to increase their terms-of-trade or bargaining power *vis-à-vis* the industrial countries or transnationals unless the unions are different in scope from existing schemes.

Several reasons suggest that LDCs would experience maximum benefits from a global integration effort. Specifically, Kreinin (1975) has identified key factors which influence the static effects of any integration plan. Firstly, the larger the union the smaller the scope for trade diversion. As a result, the better the chance the union will have a favourable effect. Secondly, the more similar production patterns are within the integration countries, and the larger the differences in their production costs, the greater the scope for trade creation. One proxy for production cost differences is the pre-integration tariff rates. Studies have shown that variations in such rates for specific industries are an indication of differences in production costs (see Table 3.2 for such a comparison). Tariff levels are also important. The higher the pre-union rates the better the chances for large trade creation. Finally, the lower the union's common external tariff, the less the discrimination against other nations and the smaller the scope for trade diversion.[4]

*Benefits in a dynamic framework*

Given that the potential static effects are relatively small, the attraction in LDC economic integration lies in the achievement of dynamic effects. Jabar (1971) recognises this point in noting that 'the emphasis should be on dynamic rather than static effects in evaluating the desirability of integration among LDCs. The present economic structure is not acceptable and each LDC is trying individually to introduce changes. These changes are not marginal but structural. Their net effect will not be felt over a short period of time. Accordingly, any evaluation of economic integration schemes should concentrate on the potential or dynamic effects'. Given this evaluation questions are raised as to the nature of these dynamic effects and how they are achieved through economic integration.

Most analyses of development problems recognise the potential importance of limited market size in many developing countries. For example, the 1970 population of 50 developing countries was under 5 million, while these nations had a GNP of under $2 billion. Even these statistics may not reflect the limited effective size of some markets given the constraints associated with a lack of transport, finance, marketing or other related functions. If economic integration results in larger markets and the achievement of scale economies, it can be an important catalyst for increased production, investment and employment. Such economies seem especially important in manufacturing processes like steel, machinery and chemicals.[5] Since these items are often inputs into other production processes, the scale economies may have important linkage effects.

Economists have also suggested that expanded trade and cooperation among LDCs may have important 'psychological' benefits associated with reduced dependence. In other words, successful cooperative ventures may make the LDCs less reluctant to undertake independent projects directly geared to industrialisation objectives. This line of reasoning also holds that economic cooperation could increase LDC bargaining power in import markets. As noted in Chapter 2, there is a pressing need for the developing countries to achieve some degree of countervailing power to rectify many of the imbalances that exist in these markets.

On some important issues the developing countries are fragmented and fail to negotiate from mutually beneficial positions. This may be due to a lack of effective lines of communication through which common interests can be identified. Keesing (1967) in particular stresses the importance of these communication links. Expanded commercial contacts would undoubtedly facilitate improved communication which could be a factor in identifying opportunities for cooperation.

Morton and Tulloch (1977) suggest intra-trade may ease development bottlenecks. Transport, telecommunications, finance, insurance and marketing functions have often evolved to service North–South trade and may not effectively contribute to development efforts. If intra-trade increased in importance, complementary institutions could evolve which would be more responsive to these needs. For example, new banking and financial links for inter-country payments seems likely to be a pre-condition for economic integration. Such financial institutions are likely to be more responsive to economic needs of developing countries. Integration may also assist the LDCs in overcoming the need to import industrial country technology, even though these may be inappropriate for local conditions (Chapter 5 has a further discussion of this problem).

In summary, these dynamic effects from integration are likely to have far more important consequences than the static gains normally discussed in economic theory. The main result of these effects should be to stimulate *institutional changes* in the LDCs. Since the primary concern of the Declaration and Programme of Action for a New International Economic Order (see Appendix) is for such changes, measures to stimulate developing country trade and integration are tied directly to the objectives of this important document.


## INSTITUTIONAL BARRIERS TO INTRA-TRADE

Given the potential benefits resulting from expanded trade and economic relations among LDCs, efforts must be directed toward removal of constraints to this exchange. To a large degree, institutional factors such as transport systems, finance and insurance, or monetary arrangements are important negative influences. However, the level and structure of protection in the LDCs themselves often has a serious detrimental impact on intra-trade.

### Transport costs and intra-trade
Developing countries' trade relations may be hampered by a variety of factors, but a major barrier is often the transportation problem. For example, liner routes often link LDCs to one, or a relatively few industrial nations. Since direct sailings may not exist, developing countries intra-trade can involve long delays and costly transhipment

through commercial centres. Even in adjoining developing countries, transport systems may be designed to facilitate movement of primary goods to ports, rather than to promote trade with neighbours. The lack of ships may also be an important factor, as LDCs owned about 7 per cent of the world fleet (in terms of gross registered tons) in 1975.

Other factors place a disproportionate transport cost burden on developing country intra-trade relative to shipments from industrial nations. Consignment size may be important since the larger shipments associated with developed country exports offer freight savings. For example, the IBRD estimated that Japan lowered transport costs per metric ton of iron ore more than 30 per cent over 1960–70 in spite of a 50 per cent increase in the distance of these shipments. A primary reason for the saving was the development of bulk carriers and compatible loading and unloading equipment. Most transport economists also agree that economies of scale can be realised for products like grains, ores, coal, bauxite, timber, rubber and jute. Larger size of shipments normally associated with developed country trade also allows freight savings of a different nature. As an example, UNCTAD estimates that dry cargo carriage in a 10,000 dwt vessel on a round-trip voyage of 2,500 miles costs $1·30 a ton, whereas the cost could be over 50 per cent lower in a 50,000 dwt ship.

An important problem arises where less than full shipments are involved. Since existing liner routes often do not service intra-LDC trade, small lots may require costly transhipment through a commercial centre. These indirect routes, plus the extra loading and unloading charges, may place a prohibitive transport burden on some potential intra-trade. A related factor causing adverse LDC freight rate differentials is that loading, unloading, and other facilities may not be geared to intra-trade. Normally, transport infra-structures have evolved to facilitate North–South trade and may not be readily adaptable to other patterns of exchange.[6]

Aside from these considerations, studies by Heaver (1973), UNCTAD (1969), Koch (1968), and Yeats (November 1977) show that liner conference freight rates may depart considerably from charges justified on a pure cost basis, and often reflect the relative bargaining position of individual shippers. Due to the volume of merchandise transported, financial resources available, and the fact that most liners are headquartered in industrial countries, there is no question where the superior bargaining power lies. While UNCTAD has urged the creation of collective groups to protect the interests of LDC exporters, the results have not as yet had any notable impact on freight rates.

TABLE 3.1 Average *ad valorem* Transport Costs for Eight Latin American Countries' Aggregate Trade with Other Developing Nations

| Importing country | Exporting country | | | | | | | |
|---|---|---|---|---|---|---|---|---|
| | Argentina | Brazil | Colombia | Chile | Mexico | Peru | Uruguay | Venezuela |
| Argentina | — | 19·6 | 93·9 | 12·9 | 10·3 | 7·1 | 7·1 | 55·0 |
| Brazil | 19·1 | — | — | 13·4 | 27·1 | — | 26·8 | 216·9 |
| Colombia | 31·6 | 8·8 | — | 9·3 | 14·4 | 11·7 | 4·7 | 38·4 |
| Costa Rica | — | — | 142·5 | 9·9 | 20·1 | — | — | 191·8 |
| Chile | 8·4 | 17·0 | 7·2 | — | 16·3 | 8·6 | 15·7 | 216·4 |
| Ecuador | 15·4 | 52·2 | 9·8 | 14·6 | 13·2 | — | — | 45·0 |
| Mexico | 8·8 | 47·4 | 25·0 | 37·5 | — | 21·7 | — | — |
| Peru | 11·9 | 53·7 | 10·9 | 24·5 | 9·1 | — | — | — |
| Uruguay | 38·5 | 43·1 | — | 13·2 | 10·5 | — | — | — |
| Venezuela | 22·0 | 21·0 | 12·9 | 3·5 | 6·5 | 95·0 | — | — |
| El Salvador | — | — | 62·9 | 5·9 | 24·7 | — | — | — |
| Guatemala | 21·9 | 84·1 | 5·6 | 13·5 | 12·0 | — | — | 176·7 |
| Honduras | — | 54·0 | 5·7 | — | 8·0 | — | — | — |
| Nicaragua | — | 83·5 | 15·0 | — | 26·5 | — | 45·0 | — |
| Panama | 14·0 | — | 5·8 | 15·9 | 39·4 | 11·5 | 8·2 | 92·8 |
| Dominican Rep. | 19·6 | — | 22·9 | — | — | — | — | — |
| Trinidad and Tobago | 16·7 | 40·0 | — | 27·3 | — | — | — | 23·0 |

*Source:* Adapted from Wilfred Prewo, 'The Structure of Transport Costs on Latin American Exports', *Weltwirtschaftliches Archiv* (Band 114, Heft. 2), p. 324.

Although it is acknowledged that these and other institutional factors in shipping work against intra-trade, there is little systematic empirical evidence concerning the exact magnitude of this bias. However, a pioneering study by Wilfred Prewo (1978) drew on a United Nations survey to estimate the aggregate bilateral transportation costs for Latin American intra-trade. The results are summarised in Table 3.1.

Before examining these data, several points should be noted. Firstly, the freight factors are for aggregate trade flows and have been derived using actual trade weights. This invariably leads to a *downward* bias in such estimates. Trade in items bearing very high transport charges is naturally depressed due to the incidence of these charges, while items with lower shipping costs are not greatly restricted. As such, high transport cost products enter the calculation of the overall average with low weights. The aggregate freight ratios in Table 3.1 would undoubtedly be higher if they were based on an unweighted transport cost average. A second point is that the figures refer to freight costs for intraregional trade. Since many of these countries' ports may be serviced by interlinking liner routes, costly transhipment may not be involved. Also, the distances between many ports may be smaller than in inter-regional trade. Transhipment and longer hauls could lead to higher transport rates than shown in Table 3.1.

In spite of these qualifications, *ad valorem* transport costs for some intra-trade are very high. Colombian exports to Argentina have freight factors of over 90 per cent, while freight rates of over 143 per cent are experienced on the former's shipments to Costa Rica. Venezuela's trade with other LDCs (primarily oil) often incurs transport factors of 100 to 200 per cent or more, while rates of 40 to 100 per cent occur throughout the matrix. In comparison, Finger and Yeats (1976) show that the average transport factor for US imports was about 9 per cent, a fraction of the freight costs experienced on many of these intra-trade flows.

*Protection in developing countries*
A further problem hampering LDC trade expansion is that systematic records are not available on tariff and non-tariff barriers applied by these nations. Due to its mandate for liberalising industrial country trade, GATT has established comprehensive records on trade barriers employed by these nations. These facilities have been an invaluable input into the multilateral trade negotiations since they provide a means for direct comparison of tariffs and other barriers on negotiating parties.

The pressing need for comprehensive information on trade barriers is accented by specific country studies which show that levels of protection

TABLE 3.2 Estimates of Nominal and Effective Protection in Sri Lanka, Iran and Pakistan; Select Industrial Groups

| Product group | Sri Lanka (Ceylon) Nominal protection | Effective rate High estimate | Effective rate Low estimate | Per cent difference | Iran Nominal protection | Effective rate High estimate | Effective rate Low estimate | Per cent difference | Pakistan Nominal protection | Effective rate High estimate | Effective rate Low estimate | Per cent difference |
|---|---|---|---|---|---|---|---|---|---|---|---|---|
| Food products | 20 | 232.5 | 61.0 | 281.1 | 20 | 73.4 | 52.4 | 40.1 | 130 | 3.1 | -3.5 | — |
| Beverages | 70 | 141.7 | 105.5 | 34.3 | 160 | 196.9 | 179.5 | 9.7 | 120 | 246.0 | 185.8 | 32.4 |
| Tobacco products | 10 | -16.2 | -59.5 | 72.8 | 250 | 286.3 | 283.5 | 1.0 | 210 | 364.7 | 324.6 | 12.4 |
| Textiles | 50 | 61.7 | 59.0 | 4.6 | 60 | 111.2 | 90.2 | 23.3 | 100 | 245.1 | 203.7 | 20.3 |
| Apparel | 60 | 160.1 | 126.9 | 26.2 | 90 | 258.3 | 182.4 | 41.6 | 220 | -180.0 | -441.8 | 59.3 |
| Leather and products | 120 | 478.7 | 331.0 | 44.6 | 60 | 564.2 | -750.0 | — | 50 | 361.6 | 104.6 | 245.7 |
| Wood products | 240 | 192.1 | 107.9 | 78.0 | 70 | 209.6 | 138.8 | 51.0 | 70 | 188.2 | 150.0 | 25.5 |
| Furniture | na | na | na | na | na | na | na | na | 100 | 270.5 | 200.0 | 35.2 |
| Paper and products | 50 | 93.9 | 77.1 | 21.8 | 20 | 79.2 | 50.3 | 57.4 | 80 | 977.6 | 231.1 | 323.0 |
| Printing and publishing | 100 | 294.3 | 178.6 | 64.8 | 20 | 38.9 | 26.3 | 47.9 | 30 | 38.0 | 35.9 | 5.8 |
| Industrial chemicals | 240 | 203.3 | 110.0 | 84.8 | 100 | 198.6 | 136.7 | 45.3 | 70 | 314.5 | 161.4 | 94.9 |
| Other chemical products | 50 | 55.8 | 54.8 | 1.8 | na | na | na | na | na | na | na | na |
| Synthetic resins | na | na | na | na | 40 | 77.3 | 50.0 | 54.6 | 70 | 335.0 | 125.2 | 167.6 |
| Misc. petroleum products | -40 | -39.7 | -42.7 | 7.0 | 50 | 166.1 | 124.5 | 33.4 | 30 | -4.9 | -23.6 | 79.3 |
| Rubber products | 40 | 121.9 | 107.1 | 13.8 | na | na | na | na | 140 | -326.7 | -921.7 | 64.6 |
| Plastic products | 80 | 133.7 | 110.9 | 20.6 | 30 | 45.5 | 39.7 | 14.6 | 220 | 751.3 | 625.0 | 20.2 |
| Pottery and glass | 30 | 320.3 | 73.3 | 336.9 | na | na | na | na | 160 | 303.8 | 258.2 | 17.7 |
| Nonmetallic mineral products | 30 | 768.2 | 87.1 | 782.0 | na | na | na | na | na | na | na | na |
| Iron and steel products | 40 | 39.4 | 35.2 | 11.9 | 40 | 35.9 | 31.7 | 13.2 | 60 | 530.0 | -46.2 | — |
| Nonferrous metals | na | na | na | na | na | na | na | na | 130 | 266.7 | 186.9 | 42.6 |
| Metal products | 180 | 191.9 | 190.6 | 0.6 | 40 | 82.8 | 57.7 | 43.5 | 90 | -329.2 | 180.9 | — |
| Machinery, non-electrical | 50 | 59.5 | 54.8 | 8.6 | 50 | 183.3 | 72.9 | 154.4 | 90 | 441.0 | 375.8 | 17.3 |
| Electrical machinery | 30 | 36.5 | 33.9 | 7.7 | 50 | 68.5 | 63.9 | 7.2 | 60 | 93.6 | 85.2 | 9.8 |
| Transportation equipment | 60 | 187.4 | 112.5 | 66.6 | 110 | 72.8 | 58.6 | 24.2 | 250 | -186.5 | -225.7 | 17.4 |
| Shipbuilding and repair | na | na | na | na | na | na | na | na | 70 | 360.6 | 136.6 | 164.0 |
| Profession equipment | 130 | 126.5 | 123.7 | 2.3 | 70 | 166.2 | 120.9 | 37.5 | 70 | 122.7 | 81.2 | 51.1 |
| Average | 75 | 174.7 | 92.7 | | 70 | 153.4 | 53.2 | | 110 | 216.9 | 82.9 | |

*Source:* Alexander J. Yeats, 'A Sensitivity Analysis of the Effective Protection Estimate', *Journal of Development Economics* (December 1976), p. 372.

in LDCs are often very high. Table 3.2 presents one such set of nominal and effective protection estimates derived for selected industries in Sri Lanka, Iran, and Pakistan. Nominal protection of over 50 per cent is a regular occurrence, while rates of over 200 per cent are observed for industrial chemicals, transportation equipment, tobacco, plastics and wood products. Studies by Balassa and the UN Economic Commission for Asia and the Far East (1972) also found that nominal protection rates in this range are common in developing countries.

The effective protection estimates reveal a further problem associated with effects to measure LDC protection. Coefficients of production costs for many manufacturing processes may be very sensitive to changes in import prices or variations in capacity utilisation. This, plus the fact that value added in LDC manufacturing is often lower than in industrial nations, can make estimates of effective protection highly unstable. Table 3.2 shows the normal yearly range in effective protection associated with changes in input costs or shifts in value added. The wide variance in these figures indicates that effective rates must be employed with considerable caution in empirical analyses of LDC protection policies. As a minimum, some measure of variability is needed to ensure that any point estimate is representative of longer-term levels.

In summary, several points emerge from analyses of developing country protection. Firstly, tariff levels are often very high and may range to several hundred per cent. This, coupled with the existence of nontariff barriers such as quotas, licensing systems, prohibitions, and foreign exchange controls suggest that LDCs' own protection may be a major constraint to intra-trade. A second factor is that the level and structure of protection may disadvantage industries in which the LDCs are internationally or domestically competitive, and therefore act as a drag on economic activity. For these reasons, rationalisation of protection in the developing countries themselves deserves a very high priority.

*Other obstacles to trade and integration*
Efforts to encourage intra-trade often involve attempts to establish customs unions among LDCs, just as the EEC links many of the countries of Europe. A major obstacle to such efforts are differences among the developing countries themselves. Differences in size or level of development can produce problems concerning the distribution of costs and benefits. Indeed, if the unions are formed to take advantage of larger markets, shift production to optimum localities, or develop transport or financial infrastructure, some geographic or industrial

sectors will be adversely affected. While it should be possible to compensate the disadvantaged sectors if the union produces positive benefits, inability to agree on the distribution of benefits may constrain the operation of integration schemes.

As compensation, Healey (1977) suggests some combination of the following measures will have to be implemented if the union is to remain functional:

—Balance of payments support through financial institutions of the union or external institutions.
—Credits for new investment on preferential terms for the most disadvantaged countries.
—Fiscal policy support measures. Import duties in LDCs often form a large part of total government revenue. If tariffs are reduced within the union, alternative fiscal measures must be implemented.
—Commercial policy measures have to be designed primarily for the needs of the least developed in the group.

Aside from the problems of the most disadvantaged countries, Healey also elaborates on other potential problem areas:

—There may be an inability to harmonise economic and social policies. For example, conflicts may exist between those advocating that market forces should provide a guide to allocation of economic activity as opposed to central planning.
—The competency of national bureaucracies in LDCs may not be equal to the task of administering the complex rules of an integration scheme.
—Political or long-standing historical tensions often severely constrain the operations of the integration schemes.

This chapter offers no *general* solutions to these problems, but acknowledges their existence can severely constrain LDC integration efforts. Solutions to these and other problems will have to be resolved. However, these will normally be determined by the nature of the individual countries involved in the specific integration effort and will vary on a case-by-case basis.

## CHARACTERISTICS OF INTRA-TRADE

Given the potential benefits and existing constraints associated with expanded integration and trade, it appears useful to examine some basic statistics on intra-trade. Such an evaluation could answer questions concerning the importance of this exchange in world trade and for individual developing countries. It also appears important to identify the key products in intra-trade since the composition of this exchange may differ from that between developing and developed nations.

### The level and structure of intra-trade

Table 3.3 examines the characteristics of LDC intra-trade. Shown here are 1970–5 trade values (excluding petroleum), both in total and for broad classes of goods. Each component's share is given to help evaluate its relative importance. As Table 3.3 indicates, food and beverages constituted 48 per cent of total exports in 1975, while manufactures'

TABLE 3.3 The Value and Composition of Developing Country Non-petroleum Intra-trade, 1970 to 1975

| Product group | Value of intra-trade ($ million) | | | | | |
|---|---|---|---|---|---|---|
| | *1970* | *1971* | *1972* | *1973* | *1974* | *1975* |
| Total | 7434 | 8107 | 9661 | 14298 | 20995 | 22226 |
| of which: | | | | | | |
| Foods and beverages | 3972 | 4236 | 4842 | 7077 | 10056 | 10740 |
| Chemicals | 472 | 511 | 679 | 990 | 1607 | 1634 |
| Manufactures | 2990 | 3360 | 4140 | 6231 | 9332 | 9852 |
| of which: | | | | | | |
| Nonferrous metals | 229 | 240 | 320 | 507 | 682 | 576 |
| Machinery and | | | | | | |
| transport | 646 | 811 | 1107 | 1663 | 2786 | 3235 |
| Textiles | 766 | 842 | 922 | 1426 | 1878 | 1917 |
| Other manufactures | 1349 | 1467 | 1791 | 2635 | 3988 | 4124 |
| | | | (Per cent) | | | |
| Total | 100 | 100 | 100 | 100 | 100 | 100 |
| of which: | | | | | | |
| Foods and beverages | 54 | 52 | 50 | 49 | 48 | 48 |
| Chemicals | 6 | 6 | 7 | 7 | 8 | 8 |
| Manufactures | 40 | 41 | 43 | 44 | 44 | 44 |
| of which: | | | | | | |
| Nonferrous metals | 3 | 3 | 3 | 4 | 3 | 3 |
| Machinery and | | | | | | |
| transport | 9 | 10 | 11 | 12 | 13 | 15 |
| Textiles | 10 | 10 | 10 | 10 | 9 | 7 |
| Other manufactures | 18 | 18 | 19 | 18 | 19 | 19 |

*Source*: Adapted from George Novak, *Trade Among Developing Countries* (Washington: World Bank, 18 August 1977).

share was 4 points lower. However, the two groups experienced different trends over the five-year period with food declining by 6 points while manufactures increased by 4 points. Chemicals' share rose by 2 percentage points primarily due to shipments of petroleum-based products.

Somewhat surprisingly, Table 3.3 shows that textiles accounted for only 7 per cent of intra-trade in 1975 and has been on a declining trend. Machinery and transport equipment are the most dynamic sector with exports increasing from $646 million in 1970 to about $3.2 billion five years later. However, the 1975 share for these items was still 4 percentage points below that for 'other manufactures' (19 per cent), a group composed of a number of labour-intensive manufactures in which the LDCs have production advantages.

Table 3.4 examines the origin and destination of non-fuel intra-trade. Shown here are 1955–75 values of exports originating in each of four LDC regions (America, Africa, West Asia, and South and South East Asia), and the destination of these shipments. As indicated, over 50 per cent of this trade ($11·6 billion) originated in South East Asia in 1975 with developing America accounting for $6·5 billion. In contrast, Africa and West Asia played a relatively minor role with only about $2 billion in 1975 trade.

Table 3.4 reveals another feature of LDC intra-trade: its largely regional character. In 1975, 76 per cent of developing America's intra-trade was intra-regional, although this represented a decline of over 10 percentage points from 1955. West Asia also had 70 per cent of its intra-trade destined within the region, while 65 per cent of South Asian trade is intra-regional. However, the table suggests that some of the most attractive trade opportunities may be inter-regional as this share has shown a steady increase except for West Asian countries.

Table 3.5 examines the importance of intra-trade to several developing countries. Shown here are the total values of manufactures exported by 20 selected LDCs in 1975 with the percentage accounted for by intra-trade. To assist in interpreting these figures, tabulations are also given for SITC 6 (basic manufactures), 7 (machinery and transport), and 8 (other manufactures).

While previous analyses show that intra-trade is relatively minor compared to world exports (about 6 per cent of total trade in 1976), Table 3.5 shows this exchange is of considerable importance to individual LDCs. For example, intra-trade accounted for 74 per cent of Argentina's total exports of manufactures in 1975, or 87 per cent of machinery and transportation equipment (SITC 7) shipments. In

TABLE 3.4 Regional Analysis of Developing Countries' Non-fuel Intra-trade, 1955 to 1975

| Exporter–Year | Total exports ($ million) | Destination of exports (per cent) | | | | |
|---|---|---|---|---|---|---|
| | | Developing America | Africa | West Asia | South and S.E. Asia | Total |
| **Developing America** | | | | | | |
| 1955 | 729 | 87·8 | 4·5 | 3·0 | 4·7 | 100 |
| 1960 | 631 | 84·0 | 5·9 | 3·8 | 6·3 | 100 |
| 1965 | 1228 | 83·9 | 6·5 | 4·2 | 5·4 | 100 |
| 1970 | 1959 | 85·7 | 5·0 | 1·9 | 7·4 | 100 |
| 1975 | 6464 | 75·8 | 10·8 | 9·1 | 4·3 | 100 |
| **Africa** | | | | | | |
| 1955 | 532 | 3·4 | 57·3 | 11·3 | 28·0 | 100 |
| 1960 | 670 | 6·0 | 50·7 | 14·9 | 28·4 | 100 |
| 1965 | 823 | 3·4 | 62·8 | 14·6 | 19·2 | 100 |
| 1970 | 935 | 3·7 | 59·3 | 11·4 | 25·6 | 100 |
| 1975 | 1889 | 7·9 | 55·3 | 19·6 | 17·2 | 100 |
| **West Asia** | | | | | | |
| 1955 | 158 | 1·9 | 15·8 | 69·6 | 12·7 | 100 |
| 1960 | 200 | 2·5 | 22·5 | 62·5 | 12·5 | 100 |
| 1965 | 315 | 4·8 | 14·3 | 68·2 | 12·7 | 100 |
| 1970 | 465 | 1·1 | 16·1 | 76·3 | 6·5 | 100 |
| 1975 | 2140 | 3·7 | 14·0 | 70·1 | 17·2 | 100 |
| **South and S.E. Asia** | | | | | | |
| 1955 | 2212 | 9·7 | 8·6 | 6·7 | 75·0 | 100 |
| 1960 | 2329 | 7·1 | 8·3 | 6·9 | 77·7 | 100 |
| 1965 | 2693 | 6·4 | 11·4 | 8·5 | 73·7 | 100 |
| 1970 | 3752 | 4·5 | 12·6 | 9·7 | 73·2 | 100 |
| 1975 | 11564 | 3·8 | 11·4 | 19·3 | 65·5 | 100 |
| **Total** | | | | | | |
| 1955 | 3631 | 24·2 | 15·2 | 9·3 | 51·3 | 100 |
| 1960 | 3830 | 19·2 | 16·2 | 10·7 | 53·9 | 100 |
| 1965 | 5059 | 24·6 | 18·8 | 12·2 | 44·4 | 100 |
| 1970 | 7111 | 26·6 | 16·9 | 12·1 | 44·4 | 100 |
| 1975 | 22057 | 25·3 | 15·2 | 21·3 | 38·2 | 100 |

*Source*: Adapted from UNCTAD, *Trade Among Developing Countries by Main SITC groups and by Regions* (TD/B/C.7/21) (Geneva: United Nations, 20 September 1978).

Colombia and Kuwait intra-trade represents over 90 per cent of total manufactures shipments, while in one half of these LDCs the proportion stands at 45 per cent. Thus, the message that emerges from Table 3.5 is

TABLE 3.5 The Composition and Relative Importance of Intra-trade in Manufactures for Selected Developing Countries in 1975
(values in $000)

| Exporter | Basic manufactures (SITC 6) | | Machinery and transport (SITC 7) | | Misc. manufactures (SITC 8) | | Total manufactures | Per cent intra-trade |
|---|---|---|---|---|---|---|---|---|
| | Value of exports | Per cent intra-trade | Value of exports | Per cent intra-trade | Value of exports | Per cent intra-trade | | |
| Argentina | 141409 | 44·7 | 399366 | 86·8 | 64293 | 55·3 | 605068 | 73·6 |
| Brazil | 748634 | 37·4 | 892204 | 65·6 | 391545 | 26·2 | 2032383 | 47·6 |
| Colombia | 143953 | 43·1 | 32202 | 86·7 | 73973 | 40·6 | 250128 | 47·9 |
| Costa Rica | 40693 | 95·9 | 14640 | 89·1 | 21817 | 95·4 | 77150 | 94·5 |
| Egypt | 265015 | 13·2 | 14720 | 70·8 | 136846 | 10·7 | 416581 | 14·4 |
| Hong Kong | 621482 | 28·8 | 672106 | 18·0 | 3138935 | 12·9 | 4432523 | 15·9 |
| India | 1398589 | 28·0 | 317489 | 76·7 | 320982 | 19·4 | 2037060 | 34·2 |
| Indonesia[a] | 92007 | 6·6 | 32059 | 69·3 | 20935 | 27·2 | 145001 | 23·4 |
| Iran[b] | 199109 | 25·7 | 32822 | 85·1 | 18613 | 24·8 | 250544 | 33·5 |
| Ivory Coast | 60194 | 70·0 | 44228 | 67·7 | 9450 | 55·6 | 113872 | 67·9 |
| Korea | 1479119 | 35·1 | 700746 | 24·6 | 1879689 | 4·1 | 4059554 | 18·9 |
| Kuwait | 95787 | 97·7 | 184630 | 96·3 | 33098 | 97·7 | 313515 | 96·8 |
| Malaysia | 676877 | 16·9 | 238775 | 43·4 | 220583 | 27·0 | 1136235 | 24·4 |
| Mexico[b] | 706978 | 15·2 | 285381 | 33·1 | 151757 | 28·9 | 1144116 | 21·5 |
| Morocco | 88834 | 41·0 | 6668 | 42·1 | 65980 | 7·0 | 161482 | 27·1 |
| Pakistan | 450797 | 49·4 | 6579 | 75·9 | 91135 | 27·4 | 548511 | 46·1 |
| Philippines | 233477 | 21·1 | 11772 | 50·2 | 106003 | 10·1 | 351252 | 18·8 |
| Singapore | 457943 | 72·4 | 1200002 | 45·3 | 371065 | 33·3 | 2029010 | 49·2 |
| Thailand | 310218 | 27·5 | 28532 | 84·7 | 250160 | 71·5 | 588910 | 49·0 |
| Venezuela | 43395 | 53·0 | 8403 | 42·4 | 6526 | 74·8 | 58324 | 53·8 |
| Total as above: | 8260510 | 33·1 | 5147324 | 50·0 | 7373385 | 16·9 | 20751219 | 31·5 |

[a] Excluding nonferrous metals, 53 per cent of Indonesia's exports of manufactures go to other developing countries.
[b] 1974 trade values.

that LDC intra-trade can assume, and has assumed, proportions of considerable importance to individual countries.[7]

*The potential volume of intra-trade*
Given the importance that intra-trade has reached for some developing countries, questions naturally arise as to the potential magnitude of this exchange. While it is difficult to form precise estimates, some rough approximations can be derived from analysis of existing trade flows. The methodology employed in making these projections is illustrated in Figure 3.1.

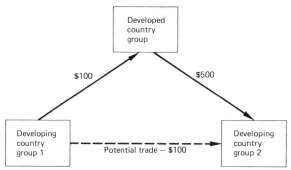

FIGURE 3.1 Numeric Illustration of the Procedure for Estimating the Potential Value of LDC Intra-trade

The figure assumes that the world is composed of a developed industrial country block and two groups of developing countries. Trade occurs with LDC group 1 exporting $100 million of product $j$ to the developed country block, while the latter exports $500 million of $j$ to LDC group 2. Given this situation, a measure of potential intra-trade is defined by,

$$P_{ij} = \frac{\text{LDC imports of } j \text{ from developed countries}}{\text{LDC exports of } j \text{ to developed countries}} \quad (0 \leqslant P_{ij} \leqslant 1)$$

$$(3\text{--}1)$$

where $P_{ij}$ shows the percentage of imports from developed countries which could be supplied by other LDCs. Thus, a value close to zero indicates a limited potential for LDC export expansion, while a value of unity shows that 100 per cent of imports could be obtained from other developing countries. A supplementary index,

$$P_{ej} = \frac{\text{LDC exports of } j \text{ to developed countries}}{\text{LDC imports of } j \text{ from developed countries}} \quad (0 \leqslant P_{ej} \leqslant 1)$$

$$(3\text{--}2)$$

TABLE 3.6   Analysis of Potential LDC Intra-trade in Labour-intensive Manufactures

| SITC | Description | 1975 imports ($000) OECD from LDCs | 1975 imports ($000) LDCs from OECD | Per cent LDC exports diverted | Per cent OECD exports replaced | Potential LDC intra-trade |
|---|---|---|---|---|---|---|
| 651.00 | Textile yarn and thread | 408621 | 1047455 | 1·00 | 0·39 | 408621 |
| 652.00 | Woven cotton fabrics | 578821 | 418763 | 0·72 | 1·00 | 418763 |
| 653.00 | Woven textile fabrics | 540641 | 1953509 | 1·00 | 0·28 | 540841 |
| 654.00 | Tulle and lace | 24165 | 162774 | 1·00 | 0·15 | 24165 |
| 655.00 | Special textile fabrics | 141162 | 447597 | 1·00 | 0·32 | 141182 |
| 656.00 | Made-up textiles | 252471 | 239571 | 0·95 | 1·00 | 239571 |
| 657.00 | Floor coverings | 511198 | 126198 | 0·25 | 1·00 | 125198 |
| 841.00 | Clothing except fur | 5466156 | 855484 | 0·16 | 1·00 | 856484 |
| 612.00 | Leather manufactures | 51179 | 58738 | 1·00 | 0·87 | 51179 |
| 831.00 | Travel goods | 321807 | 67238 | 1·00 | 1·00 | 67238 |
| 851.00 | Footwear | 879269 | 179120 | 0·21 | 1·00 | 179120 |
| 842.00 | Fur clothing | 83674 | 8389 | 0·20 | 1·00 | 8389 |
| 820.00 | Articles of rubber | 101282 | 1065377 | 0·10 | 0·10 | 101282 |
| 893.00 | Plastic articles | 309881 | 385874 | 1·00 | 0·80 | 309661 |
| 665.00 | Glassware | 51007 | 260936 | 1·00 | 0·20 | 51007 |
| 666.00 | Pottery | 42298 | 82083 | 1·00 | 0·52 | 42298 |
| 821.00 | Furniture | 213583 | 397468 | 1·00 | 0·54 | 213583 |
| 892.00 | Printed matter | 91657 | 547910 | 1·00 | 0·17 | 91657 |
| 732.90 | Motorcycles and parts | 7990 | 462652 | 1·00 | 0·02 | 7990 |
| 733.10 | Bicycles and parts | 42243 | 109291 | 1·00 | 0·39 | 42243 |
| 891.00 | Musical instruments | 220688 | 487449 | 1·00 | 0·45 | 220688 |
| 894.00 | Sporting goods | 590837 | 250031 | 0·42 | 1·00 | 250031 |
| 667.00 | Precious stones | 957785 | 776157 | 0·81 | 1·00 | 776157 |
| 897.10 | Gold jewellery | 88801 | 238318 | 1·00 | 0·37 | 88801 |

| Code | Product | | | | | |
|---|---|---|---|---|---|---|
| 551.00 | Essential oils | 91827 | 1·00 | 165977 | 0·55 | 91827 |
| 842.00 | Paper articles | 55167 | 1·00 | 446902 | 0·12 | 55167 |
| 896.00 | Office and stationery supplies | 8052 | 1·00 | 153091 | 0·05 | 8052 |
| 899.00 | Manufactures, n.e.s. | 349589 | 0·93 | 323377 | 1·00 | 323377 |
| 861.20 | Spectacles and frames | 21301 | 1·00 | 68588 | 0·32 | 21601 |
| 861.30 | Optical goods | 11772 | 1·00 | 15422 | 0·76 | 11772 |
| 861.40 | Photographic cameras | 89241 | 1·00 | 144471 | 0·62 | 89241 |
| 861.60 | Photographic equipment | 17789 | 1·00 | 246411 | 0·07 | 17789 |
| 851.70 | Medical instruments | 21062 | 1·00 | 320545 | 0·07 | 21062 |
| 864.10 | Watches and cases | 186404 | 1·00 | 693469 | 0·27 | 188404 |
| 864.20 | Clocks | 56044 | 1·00 | 201696 | 0·28 | 56044 |
| 678.50 | Tube fittings | 20006 | 1·00 | 468480 | 0·04 | 20006 |
| 693.00 | Wire products | 32392 | 1·00 | 423811 | 0·08 | 32392 |
| 694.00 | Nails and screws | 39594 | 1·00 | 215102 | 0·18 | 39594 |
| 695.00 | Hand tools | 67582 | 1·00 | 697165 | 0·10 | 67582 |
| 696.00 | Cutlery | 62605 | 1·00 | 111403 | 0·58 | 62605 |
| 697.00 | Household equipment | 12467 | 1·00 | 226827 | 0·55 | 124267 |
| 698.10 | Locksmith's wares | 27048 | 1·00 | 239282 | 0·11 | 27048 |
| 717.30 | Sewing machines | 31338 | 1·00 | 266728 | 0·12 | 31338 |
| 722.00 | Electric power machines | 303315 | 1·00 | 3404377 | 0·09 | 303315 |
| 729.40 | Automotive electrical equipment | 31475 | 1·00 | 318798 | 0·10 | 31475 |
| 729.90 | Electrical machinery, n.e.s. | 213189 | 1·00 | 1487445 | 0·15 | 213189 |
| 724.00 | Telecommunications apparatus | 1305415 | 1·00 | 3586373 | 0·36 | 1305414 |
| 725.05 | Domestic appliances, n.e.s. | 21653 | 1·00 | 111928 | 0·19 | 21653 |
| 725.05 | Space heaters | 87588 | 1·00 | 147412 | 0·59 | 87588 |
| 729.10 | Batteries and accumulators | 23591 | 1·00 | 241728 | 0·10 | 23591 |
| 729.20 | Electric lamps | 65662 | 1·00 | 128089 | 0·51 | 65662 |
| 729.30 | Thermionic valves | 975947 | 1·00 | 1151529 | 0·85 | 975947 |
| 812.40 | Lighting fixtures | 68116 | 1·00 | 234597 | 0·29 | 68115 |
| 891.10 | Sound recorders | 153499 | 1·00 | 328183 | 0·47 | 153499 |

TABLE 3.6 (*Contd.*)

| SITC | Description | 1975 Imports ($000) | | Per cent LDC exports diverted | Per cent OECD exports replaced | Potential LDC intra-trade |
| --- | --- | --- | --- | --- | --- | --- |
| | | OECD from LDCs | LDCs from OECD | | | |
| 712.00 | Agricultural machinery | 17859 | 2137239 | 1·00 | 0·01 | 17859 |
| 714.20 | Calculating machines | 272804 | 252611 | 0·93 | 1·00 | 252811 |
| 714.30 | Statistical machines | 87534 | 484490 | 1·00 | 0·18 | 87534 |
| 714.90 | Office machines | 160388 | 560643 | 1·00 | 0·29 | 160388 |
| 715.10 | Metal working machines | 23225 | 2245451 | 1·00 | 0·01 | 23225 |
| 715.20 | Other metal working machines | 2475 | 679365 | 1·00 | 0·00 | 2475 |
| 717.10 | Textile machinery | 10933 | 2665898 | 1·00 | 0·00 | 10933 |
| 718.10 | Paper mill machinery | 3230 | 450297 | 1·00 | 0·01 | 3230 |
| 718.30 | Food processing machines | 3446 | 533353 | 1·00 | 0·01 | 3446 |
| 719.20 | Pumps | 49517 | 2820989 | 1·00 | 0·02 | 49517 |
| 719.50 | Power tools, n.e.s. | 15716 | 982351 | 1·00 | 0·02 | 15718 |
| 719.60 | Other nonelectric machines | 14820 | 949190 | 1·00 | 0·02 | 14820 |
| 719.80 | Machinery, n.e.s. | 23684 | 2762186 | 1·00 | 0·01 | 23684 |
| 719.91 | Moulding boxes | 2564 | 148817 | 1·00 | 0·02 | 2564 |
| 719.92 | Taps and valves | 1924 | 1263379 | 1·00 | 0·00 | 1924 |
| 731.00 | Railway vehicles | 6261 | 851932 | 1·00 | 0·01 | 6261 |
| 732.80 | Motor vehicle bodies | 179677 | 3543032 | 1·00 | 0·05 | 179677 |
| 32.00 | Canned fish | 268362 | 177314 | 0·66 | 1·00 | 177314 |
| 31.40 | Meat and fish meal | 134391 | 20328 | 0·15 | 1·00 | 20328 |
| 411.10 | Oils of fish | 54888 | 268158 | 1·00 | 0·20 | 54888 |
| 52.00 | Dried fruit | 46081 | 24083 | 0·52 | 1·00 | 24083 |
| 53.00 | Preserved fruit | 482946 | 74978 | 0·16 | 1·00 | 74978 |
| 55.00 | Prepared vegetables | 329355 | 141198 | 0·43 | 1·00 | 141198 |
| 62.00 | Sugar and honey | 23537 | 59133 | 1·00 | 0·40 | 23537 |

| | | | | | |
|---|---|---:|---:|---:|---:|
| 99.00 | Food preparations | 65539 | 303891 | 1·00 | 0·22 | 65539 |
| 122.10 | Cigars and cheroots | 196 | 8993 | 1·00 | 0·02 | 196 |
| 611.00 | Leather | 368957 | 189178 | 0·51 | 1·00 | 189178 |
| 613.00 | Tanned for skins | 27982 | 26669 | 0·95 | 1·00 | 26669 |
| 621.00 | Rubber materials | 7968 | 177061 | 1·00 | 0·05 | 7968 |
| 248.00 | Shaped wood | 652073 | 229799 | 0·35 | 1·00 | 229799 |
| 631.00 | Plywood and veneers | 563587 | 100987 | 0·18 | 1·00 | 100987 |
| 632.00 | Wood manufactures | 204883 | 166984 | 0·82 | 1·00 | 166984 |
| 633.00 | Cork manufactures | 3793 | 16103 | 1·00 | 0·24 | 3793 |

Total projected increase    119554643

shows the proportion of total LDC imports from developed countries which could be displaced by the new intra-trade. In Figure 3.1, the group 1 countries could dispose of all existing exports in other LDCs ($P_{ij} = 1$), and are capable of displacing one-fifth ($P_{ej} = 0.20$) of the developed country exports.

The assumption behind these indices should be carefully noted since it is obvious that LDCs would *not* want to divert existing hard currency-earning exports from developed countries. The index (3–1) takes, as a base, a given export capacity for goods shipped to industrial markets and assumes that similar production volumes (through unutilised capacity or new investment) could be generated to satisfy requirements of other LDCs. These assumptions are probably reasonable for certain manufactures where long-run supply is elastic, but may be much less realistic for agricultural or natural resource-based goods. However, equation (3–1) may, in cases, understate potential intra-trade since existing LDC export capacity has often evolved to satisfy demand in industrial markets. New production ventures, geared specifically to LDC requirements, could involve different trade patterns and levels than that resulting from duplication of existing capacity.

Table 3.6 shows the results of these computations for trade in manufactures Lary (1968) identified as being especially suitable for developing countries. Since the LDCs have a comparative advantage in these products, it is assumed that they could displace developed country producers if institutional constraints and other barriers were removed. The table shows both the 1975 values of LDC exports of these products to developed countries, as well as LDC imports from industrial nations. The two indices of potential intra-trade have been computed, while the projected value of intra-trade, both in total and for each product, is also shown.

The table illustrates the potential importance of intra-trade in these items. Of the 87 labour-intensive products, LDC imports exceed other LDC shipments to industrial nations in over 75 per cent of the cases. Among the key items are telecommunications equipment (SITC 724), where potential intra-trade of $1.3 billion is projected, while textile fabrics, clothing, precious stones, and thermionic valves have potential trade flows of over $500 million. Altogether, the potential LDC intra-trade in these products reaches almost $12 billion. A trade expansion of this magnitude would involve more than a doubling of actual 1978 LDC intra-trade in manufactures ($9.9 billion).

To some extent these labour-intensive product groups constitute a base for estimating potential intra-trade. Given appropriate institutional reforms, intra-trade could undoubtedly be expanded in other (non-labour-intensive) manufactures, as well as in foodstuffs and other raw materials. However, these items are less likely to be subject to elastic supply so the previous projection exercise becomes more dubious when applied outside the labour-intensive sector.

Given this qualification, equations (3–1) and (3–2) were again applied in an effort to simulate potential intra-trade for: all manufactures (SITC 6 through 8), crude materials and foods (SITC 0, 1, 2, and 4), chemicals (SITC 5), and all items excluding fuels. The results from these simulations suggest that total potential intra-trade may be more than four times the actual 1975 value with the manufacture component having the greatest potential for trade expansion.

## PREFERENTIAL TRADE RELATIONS: THE UNCTAD APPROACH

Given the importance of expanded intra-trade in the collective self-reliance concept, UNCTAD has proposed general principles for the creation of preferences for this exchange. To achieve maximum effectiveness, UNCTAD (March 1976) suggests that all items of current or potential export interest to developing countries should have preferences since broad product coverage is required for extensive LDC participation. Developing countries often produce few manufactures, with their exports consisting largely of primary products. If the benefits are to be extensive, the industrialised LDCs must offer access for such products which are as liberal as possible.

As a result of the diversity of LDC protective measures, the preferential system must provide for the reduction of both tariffs and nontariff barriers. Concerning the former, experience in GATT or regional negotiations shows that the product-by-product approach reduces the number of items for which tariff concessions are made since it focuses on vested interests. To avoid limits on the system's coverage, UNCTAD recommends that the LDCs first agree to inclusion of as many industrial and agricultural items as possible before considering concessions. General tariff reduction formulas must also account for differences in countries' economic development, as well as differences in the systems of protection. Tariff reductions by nations relying on import duties must be balanced by reductions in NTBs in nations employing these restraints.

The role of the least developed countries and whether they should also be expected to provide concessions must be considered. UNCTAD suggests that these nations should grant favourable treatment to other LDCs where possible but they would need longer lists of exceptions and may have to grant smaller preferential margins. In some cases, advanced developing nations should extend preferences unilaterally in favour of least developed countries.

As noted, trade restraints differ widely between developing countries. While some LDCs employ tariffs as the main instruments of protection, others rely on nontariff measures. For this reason, preferential relaxation or removal of NTBs must be negotiated in parallel with the tariff reductions. However, most nontariff barriers are not quantitatively defined and their true restrictive effects are often subject to debate. This factor, combined with the variety of nontariff restraints, may present special difficulties. One solution would be to establish codes of conduct for nontariff barriers which allow for differential treatment for intra-trade.

Other administrative features of the proposed preferences for intra-trade could draw on elements of the Generalized System of Preferences (GSP) operated by industrial countries. For example, rules of origin would be needed since there must be guarantees that only goods originating in developing countries themselves receive preferential treatment. The system should also provide for safeguards to prevent serious injury to domestic industry which could occur as a result of the concessions.

It is obviously not possible to predict the final form that the preferences will take as these details will have to be negotiated among the developing countries themselves. However, in such existing arrangements as the *Protocol Relating to Trade Negotiations Among Developing Countries* a foundation has been laid upon which a more comprehensive system could be based.

*An alternative approach to preferences*

For several reasons, prospects for creation of a trade preference system along the lines envisaged by UNCTAD face several difficult problems. Firstly, there is the problem of a lack of a data base for the negotiations. As noted, tariff negotiations among the industrial countries are greatly facilitated by the centralised records maintained by GATT. However, in the case of the LDCs no such records are available so the basic input for establishing preferences is not available. Furthermore, given the existing resources at the international agencies the prospects for compiling such records are not especially bright. Secondly, the diversity of vested interests in the LDCs makes it unlikely that general agreement can be achieved on preferential tariffs for a large number of products if the procedures normally used in multilateral trade negotiations are employed. Witness the problems that have been experienced in the Kennedy and Tokyo Round negotiations where a considerably smaller number of countries with closer commercial contacts are involved. What is needed is some approach that could be more easily adopted by developing countries.

The preference-creating system proposed here is based on the proposition that developing countries are often at a transport cost disadvantage in intra-trade, and on the following observations,

—Almost all LDCs employ a cost-insurance-freight (c.i.f.) valuation base for tariff assessment.

—Tariffs in the developing countries are generally much higher than in developed countries and may range from 20 to 200 per cent or more (see Table 3.2).

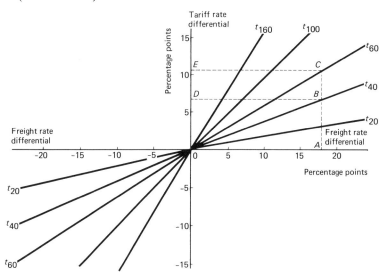

FIGURE 3.2 Diagrammatic Analysis of the Relation Between Freight and Tariff Differentials Under a Cost-Insurance-Freight Valuation Base

From the above, it can be demonstrated that the normal c.i.f. tariff base often has a potentially important *discriminatory* effect on intra-trade. Specifically, if customs duties are applied to an unfavourable transport margin, the tariff system will normally result in a higher duty collected on intra-trade than on shipments from developed countries.

Figure 3.2 illustrates this *interaction* between freight rates and the c.i.f.

tariff valuation system. The horizontal axis measures various possible freight rate differentials facing developing countries on intra-trade, while the vertical axis shows associated tariff differentials. As such, observations in the upper-right quadrant match *adverse* developing country freight margins with adverse tariff differentials. The lines in the figure, such as $t_{20}$, trace out the relation between tariff and freight rate differentials at various tariff levels.[8] For example, a freight rate differential of 18 per cent ($OA$) in connection with a 60 per cent tariff rate would produce an adverse tariff margin of over 10 percentage points ($OE$). Figure 3.2 also shows that the c.i.f. system *may* produce a tariff differential in favour of developing countries. While available evidence suggests this is an exception, some countries, such as neighbours, may have lower transport costs than those involved in trade with developed nations. Situations in which freight and tariff margins work in favour of LDC intra-trade are shown in the lower left-hand quadrant of the figure.

While one potential solution to the tariff discrimination problem might suggest removal of the transport cost component from the valuation base, i.e., apply customs duties on a f.o.b. basis, there are situations where this may have some localised unfavourable effects. Specifically, transport costs between some neighbouring countries may be lower than on shipments between the LDCs and industrial nations. Even though these situations are not likely to occur with a high frequency, adoption of a strict f.o.b. valuation base could alter the tariff system in favour of developed countries in these instances.

As an alternative, a dual import valuation system could be employed which would *always* generate trade preferences in favour of LDCs as a group. Specifically, if imports from developing countries were valued using a f.o.b. tariff base (such as that employed in the United States), while imports from developed countries were taxed under a c.i.f. procedure (used by the EEC and Japan), this two-tier system will always favour LDC intra-trade as a whole.[9] Aside from the preference-generating ability of such a proposal, another attraction is that it removes the adverse tariff effects associated with the present c.i.f. system. As such, the two-tier system is more effective than other plans which might be considered (such as linear cut to establish preferential margins), since these alternative proposals fail to do away with the detrimental effects of the *interaction* of c.i.f. tariffs and freight costs.

*Economic consequences of the valuation base*
The preceding discussion suggested that there are benefits associated with the establishment of a two-tier tariff valuation system (f.o.b. versus

c.i.f.) based on country of origin. One body of information is available to test the effects of a two-tier valuation procedure on LDC trade. Specifically, in 1974 the United States began to tabulate imports, by-product-by-country, on a joint 'free-alongside-ship' (f.a.s.) and c.i.f. basis. According to this practice, the f.a.s. valuation includes the purchase price plus all charges incurred in placing merchandise alongside the vessel at the port of exportation. The c.i.f. valuation measures the value of imports at the port of entry in the United States and includes all freight, insurance and other charges (excluding import duties) incurred in bringing the merchandise from the country of exportation and placing it alongside the vessel at the port of entry. Taking the ratio of the c.i.f. to the f.a.s. value thus provides a measure of the *ad valorem* incidence of international transport and insurance charges.

Since the United States import statistics permit separate estimation of international transportation and insurance costs, these data were used to approximate the tariff effects associated with a two-tier tariff valuation base. In these simulations, an attempt was made to estimate the effects on LDCs in six geographic regions: the Near East, Central Asia, South America, East and North Africa. *Ad valorem* freight rates for exports from Israel, India, Philippines and Brazil were employed as proxies for the first four regions, while Kenya or Ethiopia were used for East Africa, and Tunisia or Egypt used for North Africa. However, the limited range of exports from the African countries necessitated substitutions in some cases. Since the present study is interested in the use of a two-tier system to establish preferential margins for LDCs, cost-insurance-freight tariffs were also calculated for the industrial countries as a group.

Before proceeding, several points should be noted concerning the results from these simulations. First, US tariffs are now generally quite low after the Kennedy Round cuts and average about 7 to 8 per cent for manufactures. Since Figure 3.2 shows that the size of the tariff margin is related to the level of the tariff applied, this would be a factor tending to produce small preferential tariff differentials in the United States simulations. In LDCs where tariffs may range to several hundred per cent, the preferential margins would be considerably larger. A second factor is that developing country transport costs to the United States may be lower than freight rates for most intra-trade, partieularly on an inter-regional level. One factor which would tend to produce such a result is that established liner routes generally tie the United States to all parts of the world, with the result that costly transhipment is not

TABLE 3.7  Analysis of the Preference Creating Effects of a Free-on-Board as Opposed to a Cost-Insurance-Freight Valuation Base. All Figures in Percentage Points

| SITC | Description | East Africa | | North Africa | | Near East | | Central Asia | | South Asia | | South America | | Developed country c.i.f. Tariff |
|---|---|---|---|---|---|---|---|---|---|---|---|---|---|---|
| | | c.i.f. Tariff | f.o.b. Margin | c.i.f. Tariff | f.o.b. Margin | c.i.f. Tariff | f.o.b. Margin | c.i.f. Tariff | f.o.b. Margin | c.i.f. Tariff | f.o.b. Margin | c.i.f. Tariff | f.o.b. Margin | |
| 005.3 | Canned fruits and vegetables | 14.2 | 1.8 | 14.6 | 2.2 | 15.4 | 3.0 | 14.9 | 2.5 | 14.9 | 2.5 | 14.4 | 2.0 | 13.5 |
| 005.5 | Dehydrated fruits | 13.2 | 3.0 | 11.7 | 1.5 | 13.0 | 1.8 | 12.6 | 2.4 | 11.9 | 1.7 | 12.4 | 2.2 | 11.0 |
| 006.2 | Confectionery | 17.4 | 5.0 | — | — | 14.5 | 2.1 | 14.0 | 2.0 | 14.3 | 2.3 | 14.3 | 2.3 | 13.8 |
| 122.1 | Cigars | — | — | 37.3 | 5.9 | 41.0 | 9.6 | 55.7 | 24.3 | 34.1 | 3.1 | 34.4 | 3.0 | 33.2 |
| 243.3 | Hardwood flooring | — | — | 10.4 | 2.5 | — | — | 9.2 | 1.3 | 11.2 | 3.3 | 10.5 | 2.6 | 9.0 |
| 631.0 | Veneers and plywood | — | — | 14.3 | 4.5 | 12.0 | 2.2 | 13.4 | 3.6 | 13.0 | 3.2 | 12.5 | 2.7 | 11.8 |
| 632.0 | Prefabricated structures | 9.8 | 2.1 | 10.3 | 2.9 | 8.3 | 0.6 | 9.9 | 2.2 | 9.5 | 1.8 | 9.0 | 1.3 | 8.6 |
| 642.1 | Nontextile bags and boxes | — | — | — | — | — | — | 15.3 | 2.2 | 28.2 | 15.1 | 16.9 | 3.8 | 14.6 |
| 653.2 | Broad woven wool mills | 23.9 | 3.9 | 27.8 | 7.8 | 22.5 | 2.5 | 22.8 | 2.8 | 21.3 | 1.3 | 21.5 | 1.5 | 22.2 |
| 653.5 | Broad woven fabrics | — | — | 17.0 | 1.0 | 17.5 | 1.5 | 18.4 | 2.4 | 20.0 | 4.0 | 16.9 | 0.9 | 17.0 |
| 654.0 | Narrow fabric mills | — | — | 13.8 | 1.0 | 13.9 | 1.1 | 14.0 | 1.2 | 16.3 | 3.5 | 14.4 | 1.6 | 13.6 |
| 655.5 | Lace goods | 21.0 | 1.9 | 23.3 | 5.2 | 22.8 | 3.7 | 22.5 | 3.4 | 21.2 | 2.1 | 20.1 | 1.0 | 20.0 |
| 655.6 | Cordage | 14.6 | 1.3 | 17.2 | 3.9 | — | — | 17.7 | 4.4 | 14.8 | 1.5 | 14.0 | 0.7 | 13.8 |
| 656.1 | Textile bags | 16.7 | 3.4 | — | — | — | — | 19.1 | 2.7 | 27.9 | 11.5 | 17.0 | 0.6 | 16.8 |
| 656.9 | Tyre cord | 26.5 | 6.2 | 23.5 | 3.2 | 21.8 | 1.5 | 23.6 | 3.3 | 24.1 | 3.8 | 21.9 | 1.6 | 21.4 |
| 693.0 | Fabricated wire products | — | — | — | — | 7.9 | 0.5 | 8.4 | 1.0 | 8.1 | 0.7 | 8.5 | 1.1 | 7.8 |

| | | | | | | | | | | | | | | |
|---|---|---|---|---|---|---|---|---|---|---|---|---|---|---|
| 698.1 | Hardware, n.e.c. | — | — | 15·6 | 1·8 | 14·6 | 0·8 | 15·5 | 1·7 | 15·3 | 1·5 | 15·3 | 1·5 | 14·2 |
| 719.6 | Other machinery | — | — | — | — | 8·6 | 0·2 | 10·6 | 2·2 | 9·3 | 0·9 | 9·2 | 0·8 | 8·8 |
| 723.2 | Porcelain electric supplies | — | — | — | — | — | — | 13·3 | 3·7 | 10·7 | 1·1 | 10·2 | 0·6 | 10·0 |
| 725.0 | Electric housewares | 9·4 | 1·1 | 18·6 | 5·0 | 9·9 | 1·6 | 9·4 | 1·1 | 9·2 | 0·9 | 10·5 | 2·2 | 9·0 |
| 812.4 | Lighting fixtures | 14·7 | 1·1 | 10·5 | 1·4 | 14·4 | 0·8 | 16·9 | 3·3 | 17·6 | 4·0 | 20·8 | 7·2 | 14·2 |
| 821.0 | Wood furniture | 10·3 | 1·2 | 14·2 | 1·4 | 10·3 | 1·2 | 12·8 | 3·7 | 13·8 | 4·7 | 10·5 | 1·4 | 10·1 |
| 831.0 | Luggage | 15·8 | 3·0 | — | — | 14·0 | 1·2 | 15·0 | 2·2 | 15·2 | 2·4 | 13·9 | 1·1 | 13·5 |
| 841.1 | Men's suits and coats | 23·1 | 5·1 | 20·9 | 2·9 | 19·8 | 1·8 | 20·7 | 2·7 | 19·5 | 1·5 | 19·8 | 1·8 | 19·1 |
| 841.3 | Leather gloves | — | — | — | — | — | — | 31·2 | 7·8 | 25·9 | 2·5 | 25·0 | 1·6 | 24·5 |
| 841.4 | Robes and dressing gowns | 23·5 | 5·5 | 21·2 | 3·2 | 19·6 | 1·6 | 20·9 | 2·9 | 20·4 | 2·4 | 20·2 | 2·2 | 19·2 |
| 851.0 | Rubber footwear | — | — | — | — | 18·4 | 3·5 | 16·8 | 1·9 | 17·4 | 2·5 | 16·7 | 1·8 | 16·1 |
| 861.2 | Ophthalmic goods | — | — | — | — | 17·1 | 1·1 | 20·1 | 4·1 | 17·4 | 1·4 | 17·6 | 1·6 | 17·1 |

required. Secondly, due to the size of the US market, shipments may be larger and more systematic. As argued previously, this could also result in lower freight costs. As Figure 3.2 shows, low freight costs would be an additional factor producing smaller US tariff margins than those experienced in intra-trade. Finally, the United States is now one of the few countries which currently apply tariffs to f.o.b. valuations. However, since this country also values imports on a cost-insurance-freight basis, the statistics can be used to test the effects of the two-tier tariff base.[10]

Employing a sample of 35 four-digit SITC manufactured goods, Table 3.7 examines the preferences generated through application of a f.o.b. tariff base for LDCs while a c.i.f. procedure is used for the industrial country products. The items were drawn from a list of manufactures whose production characteristics make them especially suitable for export by developing countries.

The entries in Table 3.7 show the *ad valorem* tariffs facing LDC exports from each of the six geographic regions, and the reduction associated with application of a f.o.b. valuation base for the LDCs. These simulations bear out each point concerning the advantages of a two-tier valuation base. Due to generally adverse transport cost profiles, the c.i.f. tariffs on LDC exports are almost always higher than on goods shipped from industrial nations. For common products, the industrial country c.i.f. tariff averages 15.2 per cent while the average for the developing countries is almost two points higher. Of the six geographic regions, Central Asia experiences the most unfavourable differentials as its c.i.f. tariffs average 17.6 per cent as opposed to a 15.1 per cent rate for developed nations. East Africa also experiences an adverse average differential of over 2 percentage points, while the other LDCs have adverse differentials of one to two points. Thus, these simulations support the contention that a cost-insurance-freight valuation results in *systematic discrimination* against products originating in developing countries.

A second fact emerging from the table is that the f.o.b. valuation base produces sizeable reductions in tariffs LDCs would face under a c.i.f. system. For countries in Central Asia, a f.o.b. valuation system lowers average import duties by 3.5 percentage points, while the reduction for East Asia is 3 points. The size of this cut can be appreciated by noting that the Kennedy Round reduced industrial country tariffs by about 4 percentage points. As mentioned earlier, the magnitude of the tariff margins generated under the two-tier system would be even larger in developing countries where tariffs are much higher than in the United

States, and the adverse freight rate differentials are probably greater. However, even in the case of the United States the simulations show the preferential margin generated by the two-tier base is sufficient to reduce LDC import duties below the c.i.f. tariff rate facing industrial nations. Thus, such a system does produce the desired tariff margins in favour of the developing countries and deserves serious consideration as a means of expanding intra-trade.[11]

*Other institutional reforms*

While the preceding discussion focused on preferences as a means of stimulating intra-trade, a wide range of supplementary institutional changes will also be required to facilitate this exchange. In effect, these measures will need to embrace all aspects of LDC commercial policy and be designed to ensure that developing countries can avail themselves of the newly created trade opportunities. For example, transport systems will have to be restructured to accommodate the increased flow of goods between developing countries. In large part, this will involve the adoption of policies to increase the size of LDC fleets and their shipping capacity. New measures will also be needed to ease financial problems associated with intra-trade since this exchange is often constrained by a variety of balance of payments problems. In intra-trade, LDCs will also have to initiate a variety of measures to increase their involvement in marketing and distribution functions. Reforms of a different nature are needed in the level and structure of protectionism in the LDCs themselves. Too often, existing patterns of protection are the result of pressures by vested interests, and are not in harmony with overall trade and industrialisation objectives. However, a comprehensive approach must be taken toward these needed reforms. Given the nature and scope of these protection, shipping, financial, marketing and distribution changes, and their overall importance in the collective self-reliance strategy, implementation of these structural reforms will undoubtedly be one of the leading issues for the 1980s.

# 4 Trade in Commodities: the Integrated Programme

A major debate in the fourth meeting of the United Nations Conference on Trade and Development centred on the need for basic reforms in the commodity trade of developing countries. The proposed measures, discussed under the general title of an 'integrated programme' for commodities, covered all aspects of LDCs' commodity trade ranging from price formation, to market access, as well as questions concerning marketing and distribution arrangements. According to UNCTAD (May 1976), a primary objective of the programme is to maintain commodity prices at levels which are equitable to consumers and remunerative to producers. These price maintenance policies recognise the need to provide incentives for adequate investment in commodity production, compensate producers for the depletion of non-renewable resources such as ores, and keep prices of natural commodities competitive with synthetics. Special importance is also attributed to the need to reduce excessive fluctuations in LDC commodity export prices and earnings.

Aside from measures dealing with price formation, other issues and policy proposals are included in the integrated programme. A major concern is to guarantee liberalised market access, especially for processed commodities, since previous empirical studies show that tariffs and nontariff barriers have an important limiting effect on these exports. Related proposals aim at promoting commodity processing in developing countries since processed products may have more stable prices, as well as more favourable terms-of-trade. In addition, processing activities may be an effective way of absorbing some of the surplus labour that exists in developing countries. Since empirical studies also show that unit values for LDC commodity exports are often less than half the consumer price in importing industrial nations, reforms have been proposed for marketing, distribution, and transport systems which have the objective of securing higher revenues for developing countries.

Any evaluation of the integrated programme must recognise that a

62

key element centres on the establishment of a common fund for influencing both the level and stability of prices. UNCTAD argues that the need for a fund stems from a lack of stabilising factors to offset random supply fluctuations and cyclical changes in demand. Experience during the 1970s clearly demonstrated the need for such counter-cyclical measures, as fluctuations in commodity prices had serious disequilibrating effects on both developed and developing countries. For example, between 1971 and 1974 the UNCTAD index of agricultural raw materials prices rose more than 100 points, from a base of 111 to a peak of 236, and then began a descent which brought it close to earlier levels. Mineral prices experienced even wider fluctuations, rising from 131 to over 400 points, and then dropping almost as sharply. These rapid run-ups in commodity prices were serious inflationary influences in developed economies, and also resulted in excess investment in productive capacity in some commodity sectors which has had a protracted depressant effect on prices and export revenues. By modifying these disequilibrating price cycles, the common fund's operations could have important beneficial effects for both developed and developing countries.

## COMMODITY TRADE AND DEVELOPING COUNTRIES

To appreciate the importance UNCTAD attaches to the integrated programme, the role of commodities in the overall trade structure of LDCs must be examined. For such an assessment, Table 4.1 shows the value and share of these items in total exports of 50 developing countries. A further breakdown for four major commodity groups; foods, agricultural raw materials, fuels, ores and metals, is also given. The table shows that in 22 of the 50 cases, commodities account for over 90 per cent, while in 36 instances they comprised 80 per cent or more of total exports. Several countries actually have commodity export ratios of at least 98 per cent, including Bolivia (primarily tin), Cuba (sugar), Ghana (cocoa), Liberia (iron ore), Panama (bananas), Peru (fish meal and copper), Somalia (foodstuffs), Sudan (cotton), Uganda (coffee), and Zambia (copper). For the 50 developing countries combined, the share of commodities in total exports averages 89 per cent. In contrast, these items accounted for only 18 per cent of the exports of the Federal Republic of Germany, 19 per cent for Japan, and 21 per cent for the United Kingdom.

*Trade and Development Policies*

*Instability in commodity prices*
Given the dominant position of commodities in developing country exports, there is no question of the importance of factors which influence this trade. Key issues centre on the instability in commodity prices and export revenues, as well as means for improving the secular trend in these prices.

TABLE 4.1 The Share and Composition of Commodities in Total Exports of Selected Developing Countries

| Exporting country | Foods | Share in total exports | | | Share of all commodities | Total value of exports ($ mill) |
| | | Agricultural materials | Fuels | Ores and metals | | |
| --- | --- | --- | --- | --- | --- | --- |
| Afghanistan | 43·9 | 31·5 | 14·0 | 0·1 | 89·5 | 230·5 |
| Argentina | 68·9 | 5·9 | 0·5 | 1·1 | 76·4 | 2961·3 |
| Bolivia | 3·8 | 5·3 | 17·3 | 72·5 | 98·9 | 240·4 |
| Brazil | 54·1 | 3·9 | 2·3 | 14·3 | 74·6 | 8669·5 |
| Burma | 52·7 | 31·4 | 1·1 | 7·6 | 92·8 | 193·4 |
| Cameroon | 66·8 | 14·7 | 0·3 | 7·6 | 89·4 | 446·3 |
| Chad | 19·2 | 66·9 | 9·7 | 0·3 | 96·1 | 35·1 |
| Chile | 4·5 | 4·2 | 0·8 | 86·2 | 95·7 | 2480·6 |
| Colombia | 64·7 | 7·0 | 7·2 | 0·5 | 79·4 | 1464·9 |
| Costa Rica | 73·1 | 0·5 | 0·1 | 0·9 | 74·6 | 494·1 |
| Cuba | 83·7 | 0·0 | 0·0 | 14·9 | 98·6 | 837·9 |
| Dominican Republic | 79·8 | 0·1 | 0·0 | 17·7 | 97·6 | 636·8 |
| Ethiopia | 76·2 | 19·2 | 1·8 | 0·6 | 97·8 | 262·4 |
| Gambia | 97·1 | 0·4 | 0·0 | 0·0 | 97·5 | 42·1 |
| Ghana | 77·8 | 9·7 | 2·8 | 8·2 | 98·5 | 728·2 |
| Guadeloupe | 94·6 | 0·2 | 0·5 | 0·1 | 95·4 | 90·0 |
| Guyana | 64·1 | 1·1 | 0·0 | 32·4 | 97·6 | 352·9 |
| Honduras | 58·4 | 15·5 | 4·2 | 11·3 | 89·4 | 293·3 |
| India | 37·8 | 4·0 | 0·9 | 15·0 | 57·7 | 4354·8 |
| Ivory Coast | 62·5 | 19·5 | 5·7 | 0·8 | 88·5 | 1181·6 |
| Jordan | 29·0 | 0·5 | 0·7 | 49·9 | 80·1 | 125·6 |
| Kenya | 46·0 | 20·9 | 19·0 | 1·3 | 87·2 | 456·2 |
| Laos | 2·6 | 81·5 | 0·0 | 11·9 | 96·0 | 11·3 |
| Liberia | 4·7 | 20·6 | 0·1 | 73·2 | 98·6 | 399·8 |
| Madagascar | 69·2 | 6·8 | 9·6 | 5·1 | 90·7 | 244·2 |
| Malaysia | 23·2 | 34·1 | 10·9 | 14·0 | 82·2 | 3846·6 |
| Mauritius | 92·3 | 0·1 | 0·0 | 0·0 | 92·4 | 135·7 |
| Mexico | 33·5 | 7·4 | 4·2 | 18·9 | 64·0 | 2957·2 |
| Morocco | 24·5 | 2·7 | 0·7 | 60·9 | 88·9 | 1773·5 |
| Mozambique | 66·8 | 20·0 | 5·9 | 0·1 | 92·8 | 175·0 |
| Nicaragua | 51·4 | 29·5 | 0·4 | 2·6 | 83·9 | 371·5 |
| Niger | 34·0 | 3·9 | 0·0 | 50·1 | 88·0 | 52·6 |
| Pakistan | 24·7 | 18·8 | 1·1 | 0·5 | 45·1 | 1031·3 |
| Panama | 78·6 | 0·5 | 17·8 | 1·3 | 98·2 | 121·1 |
| Paraguay | 71·9 | 17·2 | 0·2 | 0·0 | 89·3 | 86·2 |
| Peru | 50·3 | 5·9 | 0·6 | 41·9 | 98·7 | 892·9 |
| Philippines | 56·6 | 11·3 | 0·7 | 18·8 | 87·4 | 2701·2 |

Table 4.1 (*Contd.*)

| Exporting country | Foods | Share in total exports | | | Share of all commodities | Total value of exports ($ mill) |
| | | Agricultural materials | Fuels | Ores and metals | | |
|---|---|---|---|---|---|---|
| Reunion | 84·3 | 0·1 | 0·3 | 0·7 | 85·4 | 94·0 |
| Senegal | 36·5 | 2·4 | 19·8 | 19·8 | 78·5 | 657·7 |
| Somalia | 88·5 | 9·1 | 0·1 | 0·6 | 98·3 | 54·2 |
| Sri Lanka | 63·8 | 19·5 | 0·1 | 5·3 | 88·7 | 557·7 |
| Sudan | 42·5 | 53·1 | 3·6 | 0·6 | 99·8 | 424·0 |
| Thailand | 58·2 | 11·4 | 0·5 | 7·1 | 77·2 | 2331·0 |
| Togo | 19·2 | 0·8 | 0·0 | 76·7 | 96·7 | 189·1 |
| Uganda | 80·2 | 13·6 | 0·0 | 6·0 | 99·8 | 315·4 |
| Republic of Tanzania | 41·3 | 40·7 | 5·2 | 0·4 | 87·6 | 355·2 |
| Upper Volta | 74·8 | 18·6 | 0·0 | 0·3 | 93·7 | 43·5 |
| Uruguay | 51·7 | 36·1 | 0·0 | 0·4 | 88·2 | 214·1 |
| Zaire | 12·0 | 2·8 | 0·2 | 80·1 | 95·1 | 1381·5 |
| Zambia | 1·4 | 0·1 | 0·3 | 97·6 | 99·4 | 805·1 |

*Source*: United Nations Conference on Trade and Development, *Handbook of International Trade and Development Statistics: Supplement 1977* (Geneva: United Nations, 1978). Trade data are for the most recent year shown in the Supplement – generally 1974 or 1975.

*Note*: Product groups are defined as follows: Foods include SITC $0 + 1 + 22 + 4$; Agricultural materials SITC $2 - 22 - 27 - 28$; Fuels SITC 3; Ores and metals include SITC $27 + 28 + 67 + 68$.

For an initial assessment of the instability issue, Table 4.2 examines the variation in 35 primary commodity prices over 1970–6. Shown here is the 1970 price of each item, the price range over the interval, and the average year-to-year price fluctuation. These data demonstrate the magnitude of the problems LDCs face in attempting to rationalise planning expenditures when a key element hinges on stable export earnings and prices. During 1970–6, the 35 commodities experienced an average deviation of over 200 per cent between their high and low prices, with the peak generally coming in 1974. The table also shows that the average annual price change was over 30 per cent, but some individual items experienced considerably higher fluctuations. Sugar had the highest variation in year-to-year prices (67 per cent), but copra, palm kernels, palm kernel oil, sisal, and phosphate rock all experienced annual changes of 50 per cent or more. It should also be noted that no consistent trend is apparent as prices generally rose during 1972–4, reaching a peak in the latter year, and then declined to levels below those in 1970–2.

### Commodity terms-of-trade

Aside from instability in prices and earnings, changes in the commodity terms-of-trade are of considerable importance to LDCs. The net bar-

TABLE 4.2 Analysis of Price Changes for Primary Commodities of Export Interest to Developing Countries over the Period 1970 to 1976

| | Price in dollars per metric ton | | | | 1970 to 1977 |
| | | Range over 1970 to 1976 | | | Average annual |
| Commodity | 1970 | Low | High | Difference (per cent) | price change (per cent) |
|---|---|---|---|---|---|
| Wheat | 55 | 55 | 181 | 229 | 31 |
| Maize | 73 | 71 | 159 | 123 | 19 |
| Rice | 143 | 130 | 542 | 317 | 45 |
| Sugar* | 81 | 81 | 655 | 708 | 67 |
| Coffee (Colombian Mild)* | 1249 | 1080 | 3478 | 222 | 44 |
| Cocoa* | 754 | 591 | 2416 | 309 | 44 |
| Tea* | 1093 | 1051 | 1537 | 46 | 8 |
| Beef | 1304 | 1304 | 2011 | 54 | 18 |
| Bananas | 144 | 136 | 218 | 60 | 10 |
| Pepper | 1274 | 1111 | 1971 | 77 | 14 |
| Soybean | 121 | 121 | 274 | 126 | 20 |
| Soybean oil | 290 | 238 | 863 | 263 | 43 |
| Sunflower oil | 331 | 327 | 983 | 201 | 46 |
| Groundnuts | 228 | 228 | 603 | 164 | 25 |
| Groundnut oil | 361 | 361 | 1058 | 193 | 32 |
| Copra | 223 | 143 | 664 | 364 | 57 |
| Coconut oil | 379 | 254 | 973 | 283 | 49 |
| Palm kernels | 168 | 116 | 469 | 304 | 51 |
| Palm kernel oil | 367 | 219 | 1040 | 375 | 58 |
| Palm oil | 260 | 217 | 672 | 209 | 35 |
| Olive oil | 645 | 645 | 1965 | 205 | 30 |
| Cotton* | 676 | 676 | 1755 | 160 | 25 |
| Wool | 1962 | 1786 | 6989 | 291 | 44 |
| Sisal* | 156 | 156 | 1079 | 592 | 56 |
| Abaca | 307 | 288 | 741 | 157 | 27 |
| Rubber* | 408 | 331 | 783 | 137 | 33 |
| Manganese ore | 53 | 53 | 142 | 168 | 20 |
| Iron ore | 9 | 9 | 19 | 111 | 19 |
| Aluminium | 614 | 590 | 890 | 51 | 9 |
| Copper* | 1415 | 1071 | 2058 | 92 | 27 |
| Lead | 304 | 253 | 593 | 134 | 26 |
| Zinc | 296 | 296 | 1240 | 318 | 41 |
| Tin* | 3675 | 3503 | 8190 | 133 | 23 |
| Tungsten | 7760 | 3904 | 11483 | 194 | 34 |
| Phosphate rock | 12 | 12 | 68 | 467 | 60 |

\* Designated by UNCTAD as one of the 'core' commodities whose market characteristics make it especially suitable for international stocking schemes.

*Source*: Adapted from free market price information published in United Nations Conference on Trade and Development, *Handbook of International Trade and Development Statistics: Supplement 1977* (Geneva: United Nations, 1978), pp 45–51.

ter terms-of-trade measures the price ratio of exports to imports, while changes in the terms-of-trade reflect movements in these price relatives over some time period. If the change exceeds unity, the implications are favourable since this indicates a nation's commodity export prices have risen relative to prices for their imports.

While the theoretical approach appears straightforward, several problems make practical applications difficult. Firstly, terms-of-trade measurement may be very sensitive to changes in the time periods chosen for comparison. Shifting the base by even a few years may reverse the indicated directional movement. Another difficulty is that these calculations employ unit values as proxies for transactions prices. It is recognised that unit values are often unable to distinguish true price movements from quality or product-mix changes. Index number problems common to any intertemporal price comparisons can cause problems. If the composition of a country's trade changes, the index may be sensitive to the system of weights used. There is also the problem of distinguishing cyclical movements in the terms-of-trade from more important secular changes.

In spite of these difficulties, economists often suggest that long-run changes in the terms-of-trade have generally been unfavourable to commodities. A number of factors contribute to this result. For example, raw material production is generally thought to be characterised by diminishing returns of the supply side, and low price elasticities of demand. Working in tandem, these factors would tend to lower primary producers' margins over time. Estimates of the income elasticities for commodities are also low, so their long-term demand prospects relative to manufactures are not favourable. The result is that LDCs could not count on stable or growing real foreign exchange earnings from commodity exports.

This pessimistic outlook for long-term commodity terms-of-trade has led UNCTAD to incorporate proposals for supporting prices in the integrated programme. These supports are to be achieved by three different courses of action: agreement is to be sought on limiting the use and competition from synthetics; producer cartels and export controls are planned to restrict output in periods of slack demand, and centralised agencies are to be used for disposal of LDC exports. This later measure is intended to provide developing countries with a degree of countervailing power, thereby improving their bargaining position *vis-à-vis* the industrial countries. Thus, the elements of unequal exchange and corrective measures are incorporated in specific proposals concerning the integrated programme. Finally, enactment of the integrated programme's proposals for improved market access would be a factor leading to increased demand and higher prices for processed commodities.


## ELEMENTS OF THE INTEGRATED PROGRAMME

Due to the importance of commodities in the trade of many developing countries, UNCTAD has formulated a comprehensive strategy for improving terms of LDC commodity trade. Essentially, this programme is aimed at stabilising and raising prices by concentrated action in four areas:

1. Internationally owned commodity stocks are to be established, while a common financial fund is to be created to make resources available for the acquisition of stocks;

2. Medium to long-term commitments to purchase or sell commodities at agreed prices. Purchases would be timed to offset demand shortfalls, while sales would offset irregular supply deficiencies;

3. Provision of compensatory financing to cover export earnings shortfalls; and

4. The initiation of measures to liberalise trade barriers facing primary and processed commodities, and to encourage local commodity processing.

Given these objectives, the following sections discuss specific points relating to the operation of the integrated programme.

### Commodity coverage
In principle the integrated programme is open ended, but will initially concentrate on 17 commodities which represent about 75 per cent of the LDCs' nonpetroleum mineral and agricultural exports. Ten 'core' commodities are distinguished; cocoa, coffee, cotton, copper, jute, rubber, sisal, sugar, tea, and tin, since they possess characteristics suitable for price stabilisation through stocking schemes. The remaining items—wheat, rice, bananas, beef and veal, wool, bauxite, and iron ore—are not included in these arrangements, but are covered by other aspects of the integrated programme such as measures to improve market access or to stimulate local processing.

Several performance statistics indicate why special importance is attached to these commodities. For example, seven of the ten core commodities, coffee, cocoa, tea, cotton, rubber, jute, and sisal, had a zero or negative trend in real value of shipments over 1953–72, while sugar showed an unimpressive increase of 2 percentage points per annum and that for copper was only slightly higher. Several of the core commodities were also among those exhibiting the widest annual price fluctuations over 1953–72.

## The common fund

The key element in the integrated programme's commodity price stabilisation objectives is a common fund. Specific aspects of the fund's financial requirements, sources of finance, mode of operations, and management remain to be decided in detail, but its main purpose is to finance buffer stocks. Additions and deletions to these stocks are to be timed to offset irregular movements in commodity prices.

According to UNCTAD's reasoning, a primary attraction of a 'common' fund is that commodity agreements would be less costly if financed jointly, partly because the fund could utilise what may be different financial flows into and out of individual commodity accounts, and also because it could be in a position to obtain better terms in capital markets. UNCTAD also suggests the fund would stimulate other international commodity agreements. Finally, the management would be in a far better position to facilitate lending from one commodity account to another which would facilitate the operations and credit-worthiness of the fund.

Through a simulation exercise, UNCTAD established that the fund's capital requirements for the ten core commodities would be approximately $6 billion, $3 billion of which would be in readily available funds. Of this latter total, one third would be in the form of paid-up risk capital and the rest would be loans. It is also proposed that governments undertake a further commitment of $3 billion, again with one third in paid-up capital and the rest as loans, to be on call if needed. Thus, the major portion of the fund's capital would be in the form of interest-bearing loans since the operation is considered to be self-financing.

Apart from disagreements concerning the required size of the fund,[1] concerns have been expressed that its resources might be depleted by a few problem commodities. This latter issue is of special concern since the fund is to serve as a vehicle for transferring liquidity from one commodity account to another. However, at the first preparatory meeting of the common fund in November 1976, limits on such transfers were proposed that would avoid the danger of excessive concentration on a few commodities.

Another controversial proposal relating to the fund's proposed operations deals with the establishment of a 'second window' to provide financial support for modernising production methods for certain commodities. UNCTAD has suggested that approximately $500 million be devoted to such improvements for jute, hard fibres, tea, bananas, and rubber. While the desirability of such investments has not generally been challenged, critics suggest that more appropriate sources of finance exist such as the World Bank.

*Compensatory financing*

It is an UNCTAD contention that the price and earnings stabilisation operations of the fund will need to be supplemented by arrangements to offset export *earnings* fluctuations. This proposal recognises that more stable prices need not stabilise earnings if a country's exports are adversely affected by uncontrolled variations in output.

For several reasons, UNCTAD (October 1975) suggests that existing International Monetary Fund arrangements for such financing have been inadequate. However, four basic reforms are proposed that would make the IMF facility suitable for stabilisation of export earnings:

1. The special importance of LDC commodity sectors require that compensation be available for *either* shortfalls in commodity export earnings, or for all merchandise exports.

2. Shortfalls in real export earnings should be the basis for compensation, thereby smoothing the trend of exports' purchasing power.

3. The nature of the problems which lead to the need to utilise financing warrant provisions for more liberal terms than are normally provided by the IMF. One possible improvement is the incorporation of a grant element into compensatory financing arrangements, and linking repayment of loans to recovery in export returns.

4. Qualification for compensatory financing should not be tied rigidly to a balance of payments test, but should also consider such factors as the importance of earnings changes on the growth and industrialisation prospects of the developing country.

Estimates by UNCTAD for a compensatory financing scheme fulfilling these four requirements indicate that the total payments over 1965–74 would have averaged between $700 and $850 million annually.

## INSTABILITY, GROWTH AND DEVELOPMENT

Given the importance of commodities in LDC exports, several procedures have been employed for evaluating the influence of these products' price and export revenue instability on development objectives. One approach utilises theoretical models to investigate ties between instability, industrialisation and growth. However, in spite of an extensive analysis, the conclusions from these models remain uncertain and subject to debate. In large part, the conflicting results are due to the nature of the assumptions which must be made concerning supply and demand schedules, as well as the nature of the interactions in the model. Variations in these parameters, or changes in specification, may lead to very different conclusions concerning the influence of price and revenue instability. Critics also maintain that a failure to account for some potential benefits of stable prices, such as a possible increase in LDC market position where commodities compete with synthetics, invalidates many conclusions of the theoretical exercises.

However, there is one point associated with the theoretical models on which there is general agreement: price stability benefits both importing and exporting countries by reducing uncertainty, thus lowering the risk premium for new investment. A lower risk premium will increase investment in production capacity and lead to a larger output, i.e., it would result in a rightward shift of the supply curve. However, this result need not be favourable for LDCs since the supply shift might result in lower prices if demand is sufficiently inelastic with respect to income.

Theoretical analyses have also been useful for analysing cases in which price stabilisation need not stabilise export earnings. While the result depends in part on the price elasticity of demand, the supply function is also of key importance since revenue stabilisation requires an infinitely elastic supply curve. While this may be a fairly reasonable approximation for some minerals and metals (so long as surplus production exists), Cuddy (1978) notes it is less plausible for agricultural raw materials, and patently absurd for the food and beverage crops where output is heavily dependent upon weather and other natural factors. In these cases, LDC export earnings may be destabilised even if prices remain more or less fixed. Liberalised compensatory financing arrangements will be needed to compensate for earnings fluctuations in these situations.

Practical attempts to project equilibrium commodity prices pose a major difficulty for stabilisation objectives. For example, commodity supply and demand may be influenced by a number of random factors which cause price fluctuations. A key question centres on how to distinguish short-term from secular price changes. If fund managers incorrectly conclude a random movement represents a secular change, they may attempt to stabilise prices along an inappropriate trend. This could have serious detrimental effects on commodity production, investment, and demand. If prices were stabilised at too high a level, investment in synthetic substitutes might be encouraged which could have a long-term depressant influence on prices. If an 'inappropriate' stabilisation policy were followed, market forces could build up to the point where they endanger fund operations. In discussions of the potential benefits associated with price stabilisation, these practical problems of implementation have not been given the full attention they deserve.[2]

While the results have been contested, there have been attempts to use theoretical models to quantitatively assess the consequences of price and earnings stabilisation. Using 'reasonable' estimates for supply and demand parameters, MacAvoy analysed potential benefits from a stabilisation programme for the core commodities. Laursen (1978) summarised these results by noting:

> . . . the effects of stabilising the prices of the ten core commodities do not provide a very convincing case (for the common fund). The net global benefits, counting the interest on buffer stocks and other storage costs, will be negative by more than $500 million per year. Stated differently, producers gain $250 million per year, most of which will go to middle-income countries, and consumers about $75 million, but given the interest and storage cost of about $900 million, the total operation will result in a global loss. But, taking account of long-run effects for consumers and producers and generally for the world economy will change the picture. By how much and for the benefit of whom is where opinions differ. Consumers will gain, but producers may actually lose as increased investment in response to reduced risks leads to lower prices. All in all, the price stabilisation issue remains open.

*Criticisms of the theoretical approach*
The utility of the theoretical analyses has been contested on several points, including the neglect of certain benefits from price stabilisation. Specifically, less volatile commodity prices could facilitate stabilisation of the world economy at higher levels of activity. This proposition assumes that large changes in raw material prices have a dampening effect on business activity. When commodity prices rise, the increase is incorporated in final product prices, and then wages through cost-of-living adjustments—the so-called ratchet effect. Since these events may

cause governments to adopt contractionary fiscal and monetary policies, stable commodity prices could remove a factor resulting in restrictionist economic policies, lower output, demand, and employment.

Aside from a failure to consider links between commodity prices and national economic policies, Dragaslov Avramovic (1978) launched a broad attack on opponents of the common fund. In part, Avramovic's criticisms centre on the restrictive assumptions employed in assessing the effects of stabilisation policies. For example, production or export controls have not been incorporated in these simulations, although they are included in proposals for the integrated programme. Such controls strengthen prices and revenues over the short and medium term compared to free market situations. Avramovic also notes that no account is made for the likely competitive improvement of natural products *vis-à-vis* synthetics resulting from price stabilisation, or the associated increase in demand and export revenues. No allowance has been made for more efficient investment and production scheduling, nor has any account been taken of the fact that all commodity agreements operate within a price range, rather than at a fixed price so the potential for destabilising export revenues is reduced. Above all, Avramovic argues that previous analyses disregard what he sees as the primary reason for stabilisation, i.e., the protection it offers low income countries thereby allowing them to time sales properly and improve their bargaining strength relative to buyers.[3]

*Empirical analyses of instability and growth*
Given the failure of theory to provide definitive insights into the instability–growth relationship, empirical analyses of this association have been undertaken to fill the void. However, the results from these studies are generally as inconclusive as those from the theoretical approach.

Earlier investigations by MacBean (1966) and Coppock (1962) concluded that no statistical evidence exists to support the hypothesis that export instability has an important detrimental effect on LDC growth. However, subsequent studies by Massel (1970), Glezakos (1973), and Leith (1971) reach opposite conclusions. Perhaps the real insight gained from these empirical analyses is that the results depend on the time-period chosen, countries studied, or statistical methods employed. However, neither theory nor empirical analyses provide conclusive evidence of an adverse relation between instability and growth.

Without doubt, the failure to clearly establish a causation between instability and growth is disturbing given the finances proposed for the common fund, and the importance that the South attaches to this issue. However, there is justification for believing that the failure to identify clear links between instability and growth is due to deficiencies in the state of economic theory, or the fact that previous empirical research has been too general. Specific country examples and arguments advanced by Avramovic go a considerable way toward justifying the operations of the fund and its stabilisation objectives. Avramovic also convincingly argues and illustrates that the detrimental effects of instability and a lack of LDC 'staying power' are readily evident upon examination of the effects on an individual country basis.

The fact that industrial countries have found it necessary to adopt internal price support and stabilisation policies for domestic producers of agricultural raw materials and other commodities works strongly in favour of the common fund and its policy objectives. Recent empirical studies by Sampson and Yeats (1976; 1977) show how these systems work to elevate and stabilise prices in Sweden and the EEC, while Wipf (1971) conducted a similar investigation for the United States. The fact that equity considerations dictate that commodity producers in poorer countries should have the same type of protection enjoyed by their counterparts in the North is an argument that should be adopted by the LDCs. However, the fact that local governments are often unable to offer this protection, for various economic reasons, makes a compelling case why such operations should be borne by the international community through the functioning of the common fund.

## MARKET ACCESS AND DOMESTIC PROCESSING

Aside from the influence of export instability, market access is also a vital issue for commodities. For example, UNCTAD (April 1976) states that 'the problem of tariff and nontariff barriers restricting the commodity exports of developing countries is no less important than depressed and fluctuating commodity prices and earnings. These trade restrictions are reflected in the systems of agricultural protection in developed countries, and the complex array of tariffs, quotas, variable levies, subsidies, and other barriers which severely curtail potential LDC export earnings.'

There are two major concerns involving market access for LDC commodity exports. These reflect the *structure* and *level* of protection

TABLE 4.3 Comparison of Post-Kennedy Round Nominal Tariffs on Primary and Final Products in Processing Chains for Major Exports of Developing Countries

| | Post-Kennedy nominal tariff | | | | | | | | |
| | USA | | | EEC | | | Japan | | |
| Processing chain components | Primary inputs | Final good | Change | Primary inputs | Final good | Change | Primary inputs | Final good | Change |
|---|---|---|---|---|---|---|---|---|---|
| Fresh meat—meat preparations | 4·6 | 5·9 | 1·3 | 18·8 | 19·5 | 0·7 | 6·2 | 17·9 | 11·7 |
| Fresh fish—fish preparations | 1·3 | 6·0 | 4·7 | 14·9 | 21·5 | 6·6 | 5·3 | 13·6 | 8·3 |
| Fresh fruit—preserved fruit | 5·6 | 14·8 | 9·2 | 13·9 | 20·5 | 6·6 | 14·0 | 18·5 | 4·5 |
| Fresh vegetables—preserved vegetables | 8·9 | 8·0 | -0·9 | 9·9 | 14·8 | 4·9 | 8·1 | 20·0 | 11·9 |
| Cocoa beans—Chocolate | 0·0 | 4·8 | 4·8 | 3·2 | 18·0 | 14·8 | 3·0 | 35·0 | 32·0 |
| Hides and skins—leather goods | 1·1 | 11·3 | 10·2 | 0·0 | 9·6 | 9·6 | 0·0 | 17·4 | 17·4 |
| Groundnuts—groundnut oil | 25·7 | 27·1 | 1·4 | 0·0 | 11·2 | 11·2 | 20·0 | 23·6 | 3·6 |
| Copra—coconut oil | 0·0 | 17·7 | 17·7 | 0·0 | 12·5 | 12·5 | 0·0 | 10·0 | 10·0 |
| Palm kernel—palm kernel oil | 0·0 | 2·8 | 2·8 | 0·0 | 11·5 | 11·5 | 0·0 | 7·3 | 7·3 |
| Natural rubber—rubber products | 0·0 | 4·6 | 4·6 | 0·0 | 7·9 | 7·9 | 0·0 | 6·4 | 6·4 |
| Rough wood—wood manufactures | 0·0 | 6·7 | 6·7 | 1·0 | 8·7 | 7·7 | 0·0 | 11·5 | 11·5 |
| Pulpwood—paper articles | 0·0 | 2·5 | 2·5 | 0·0 | 6·1 | 6·1 | 0·0 | 7·7 | 7·7 |
| Raw wool—wool fabrics | 9·7 | 20·7 | 11·0 | 0·0 | 16·0 | 16·0 | 0·0 | 10·0 | 10·0 |
| Raw cotton—cotton clothing | 6·2 | 18·3 | 12·1 | 0·0 | 14·7 | 14·7 | 0·0 | 15·0 | 15·0 |
| Raw jute—jute sacks and bags | 0·0 | 3·6 | 3·6 | 0·0 | 15·5 | 15·5 | 0·0 | 12·5 | 12·5 |
| Raw sisal—cordage | 0·0 | 3·6 | 3·6 | 0·0 | 10·3 | 10·3 | 0·0 | 9·6 | 9·6 |
| Iron ore—special steel products | 0·0 | 4·0 | 4·0 | 0·0 | 7·5 | 7·5 | 0·0 | 7·8 | 7·8 |
| Copper ores—wrought copper | 0·1 | 4·2 | 4·1 | 0·0 | 8·0 | 8·0 | 0·0 | 17·8 | 17·8 |
| Bauxite—wrought aluminium | 0·0 | 5·9 | 5·9 | 0·0 | 12·8 | 12·8 | 0·0 | 13·6 | 13·6 |
| Lead ores—wrought lead | 6·0 | 10·3 | 4·3 | 0·0 | 6·6 | 6·6 | 0·0 | 14·9 | 14·9 |
| Zinc ores—wrought zinc | 12·0 | 3·0 | -9·0 | 0·0 | 8·3 | 8·3 | 0·0 | 14·9 | 14·9 |
| Average | 3·6 | 8·8 | 5·2 | 2·9 | 12·4 | 9·5 | 2·7 | 14·5 | 11·8 |

against primary and processed commodities. Regarding structural factors, a tendency for industrial country tariffs to escalate or increase has been noted as one moves from primary to processed commodities. The effects of such a system are to maintain LDCs as exporters of raw materials since they are unable to overcome the higher import duties levied on processed goods.

Table 4.3 illustrates this phenomenon by showing post-Kennedy Round tariffs in the United States, EEC, and Japan for 21 commodity processing chains. These figures indicate how tariffs escalate with level of fabrication. For example, imports of fresh meat face a tariff of 6·2 per cent in Japan, but meat preparations (a processed good) are subject to a duty of 17·9 per cent. Overall, the 21 primary stage items enter Japan under an average duty of 2·7 per cent, while that on the final products is 11·8 points higher. Tariffs in the United States and EEC also show a similar tendency to escalate, but not to the same degree. Efforts to remove these discriminatory tariff structures has been, and continues to be, a long-standing UNCTAD policy objective.

While the tariffs in Table 4.3 often appear imposing, most analyses of agricultural protection conclude that import duties often constitute a minor element in total protection. Trade in agricultural goods, and other commodities, may be hampered by a complex system of quotas, variable levies, minimum import price requirements, seasonal restrictions, production subsidies, health and sanitary requirements, and other restrictions that limit imports.

Table 4.4 illustrates the potential importance of *one* of these nontariff measures, the EEC's variable levies, for food and live animals (SITC 0), and animal and vegetable oils (SITC 4). Shown here is the percentage of each two-digit component group's trade (by value) covered by levies, as well as the percentage of tariff lines subject to these charges. For comparison, both the average *ad valorem* tariff and levy rate are shown, as well as their joint protective effect. The table also indicates EEC imports from developing countries.

Perhaps the most striking feature in Table 4.4 concerns the relative magnitude of the average nominal tariff and levy. In SITC 0, a nominal tariff of 18 per cent couples with levies whose *ad valorem* equivalents are approximately three times higher. Only in SITC 06 (sugar and honey) is the incidence of levies less than that for tariffs. The primary reason for this departure are tariffs averaging over 50 per cent. The relative importance of levies is also observed in SITC 4 (animal and vegetable oils), where tariffs of approximately 8 per cent are one third the average *ad valorem* levy.

TABLE 4.4 Estimated Rates of Nominal Protection for the European Economic Community's Agricultural Products from both Tariffs and Variable Levies

| SITC | Description | EEC coverage by levies Tariff lines | 1974 Value of trade ($000) | Nominal protection (%) Tariffs | Levies | Total | 1974 Imports from LDCs ($000) |
|---|---|---|---|---|---|---|---|
| 0 | *Food and live animals* | | | | | | |
| 00 | Live animals | 33·4 | 1828 | 11·8 | 18·2 | 30·0 | 37 |
| 01 | Meat and meat preparations | 39·5 | 188887 | 18·1 | 30·4 | 48·5 | 523 |
| 02 | Dairy products and eggs | 29·4 | 892 | 18·4 | 152·9 | 171·3 | 2 |
| 03 | Fish and fish preparations | 0·0 | 0 | 12·8 | — | 12·8 | 298 |
| 04 | Cereals and cereal preparations | 41·9 | 355330 | 15·2 | 52·1 | 67·3 | 698 |
| 05 | Fruits and vegetables | 8·2 | 91936 | 16·4 | 37·1 | 53·8 | 1927 |
| 06 | Sugar and honey | 38·5 | 97075 | 53·1 | 12·0 | 65·1 | 804 |
| 07 | Coffee, tea and spices | 6·9 | 0 | 10·8 | 51·0 | 61·8 | 2834 |
| 08 | Feeding stuff for animals | 8·4 | 11 | 5·4 | 56·0 | 61·4 | 788 |
| 09 | Miscellaneous food preparations | 13·4 | 8 | 19·2 | 47·3 | 66·5 | 23 |
| 1 | *Beverages and tobacco* | | | | | | |
| 11 | Beverages | 0·0 | 0 | 27·0 | — | 27·0 | 127 |
| 12 | Tobacco manufactures | 0·0 | 0 | 61·4 | — | 61·4 | 340 |
| 4 | *Animal and Vegetable oils* | | | | | | |
| 41 | Animal oils and fats | 9·6 | 14 | 3·5 | 31·8 | 35·3 | 58 |
| 42 | Processed vegetable oils and fats | 15·8 | 16640 | 11·4 | 39·2 | 50·6 | 1111 |
| 43 | Processed animal oils and fats | 11·2 | 0 | 7·5 | 1·1 | 8·6 | 21 |

*Source:* Gary P. Sampson and Alexander J. Yeats, 'An Evaluation of the Common Agricultural Policy as a Barrier Facing Agricultural Exports to the European Economic Community', *American Journal of Agricultural Economics* (February 1977), p. 102.

A product-by-product comparison shows that nominal protection for these agricultural products is often very high. For example, when levies combine with tariffs, the nominal rate for dairy products and eggs is over 170 per cent. Cereals and preparations face combined *ad valorem* import charges averaging 67 per cent, while protection for meat and sugar ranges from 48 to 65 per cent. Although these figures pertain solely to the EEC, Sampson and Yeats (1976) show that Swedish variable levies often exceed 50 per cent for meat, dairy, and cereal products. Wipf (1971) also shows that US protection for agricultural commodities may be very high with NTBs frequently being the most important restraint.

Aside from their protective effect, Snape and Sampson (1980) show that levies are an important cause of instability in commodity markets since they move inversely with world prices. For example, when world prices are high relative to those in the EEC, levies fall to zero or even become negative. This leads to a higher EEC import demand than would occur under a fixed import charge. Higher EEC imports under these conditions causes international prices to rise even further than would be the case under a specific or *ad valorem* tariff. Conversely, when world prices fall levies rise to preserve the purchasing power of domestic producers. Increasing these import charges causes a reduction of potential demand with the result that prices fall further than they would if EEC imports were allowed to increase. Thus, while the levy system results in greater price instability for domestic producers, this is accomplished by transferring instability to world markets and the developing countries.[4] The proposed enlargement of the EEC to include Greece, Turkey, and Spain should further aggravate the problem of induced instability unless appropriate policy action is adopted.

*Trade effects of nontariff barriers*

While the problem of quantification makes empirical assessment of nontariff barriers difficult, UNCTAD and the UN Food and Agricultural Organisation (FAO) developed a model for projecting the trade effects for 10 agricultural commodities (wheat, rice, coarse grains, sugar, vegetable oils, beef and veal, mutton, pork, poultry, and milk) resulting from removal of all trade restraints. These simulations suggest that LDC exports would expand by about $17 billion per year, which represents a 20 per cent increase over 1970 levels. The UN projections also show that the United States, Australia, Canada, and New Zealand would increase export earnings by about $18 billion, while the trade of socialist countries would rise by $3 billion.

Recent studies by the World Bank are generally in agreement with these results. Assuming a 'reasonable' relaxation of existing trade barriers, the Bank estimates developed market economy imports from LDCs would rise by 25 per cent or more, with particularly strong gains projected for sugar, cereals, meat, cotton, fats and oils, and timber. A supplemental Bank (December 1978) investigation also concludes that trade barriers in developed country markets are a major limiting factor for LDC exports of processed products.[5]

While previous analyses show that NTBs are often an important factor influencing the *level* of commodity trade, an equally important consideration involves their impact on export structures. As noted, tariffs typically increase as one moves to higher levels of fabrication. However, due to problems in quantification, little empirical work has been done on NTB escalation.

A recent UNCTAD (April 1979) study provides useful insights concerning this question. The results, summarised in Table 4.5, show the frequency of application of NTBs on three categories of goods; primary commodities, semi-processed goods, and processed products in 16 industrial markets. Figures in the table indicate the percentage of tariff line items covered by NTBs in each market.

In most cases, especially in the European Economic Community, not only are the frequency indices fairly high, but increases are observed over processing stages. In France, the Federal Republic of Germany, the United Kingdom, and Denmark, the imposition of NTBs on processed products is twice that for primary forms. In the United States and Japan the NTB indices are relatively low, but also increase over processing stages. While Canada and Australia have the lowest indices for NTB application, this may be due to a smaller need for protection given these countries' comparative advantage in many commodities. While quantification of the *ad valorem* incidence of these nontariff restraints is needed, so that definite conclusions can be reached, the UNCTAD data do suggest that NTBs are more of a problem for processed commodities than for primary goods.

### Transport costs and commodity trade

All items entering international trade bear transport costs which include freight, insurance, handling and other related charges. Thus, transport costs constitute 'natural protection' for domestically produced products, just as tariffs provide artificial protection. While transport costs have received relatively little attention, compared to artificial trade barriers like tariffs, a study by Finger and Yeats (1976) indicates that

TABLE 4.5   Frequency of Import Restrictions Applied on Selected Products of Export Interest to Developing Countries by Countries Maintaining Restrictions[a]

| Countries | BTN 1–24 | | | | BTN 25–99 | | | | Total BTN 1–99 | Number of products affected |
|---|---|---|---|---|---|---|---|---|---|---|
| | Primary commodity | Semi-processed | Processed | Total BTN 1–24 | Primary commodity | Semi-manufactured | Manu-factured | Total BTN 25–99 | | |
| France | 6·7 | 9·0 | 12·5 | 9·0 | — | 5·3 | 16·7 | 6·3 | 8·3 | 38 |
| Fed. Rep. of Germany | 3·9 | 6·9 | 10·8 | 6·7 | — | 6·8 | — | 6·8 | 7·3 | 31 |
| Ireland | 6·7 | 6·9 | 10·0 | 7·7 | — | 3·0 | — | 3·0 | 6·5 | 34 |
| United Kingdom | 5·6 | 6·9 | 11·7 | 7·7 | — | 2·3 | — | 2·3 | 6·3 | 31 |
| Denmark | 5·6 | 6·9 | 10·6 | 7·4 | — | 1·5 | — | 1·5 | 5·8 | 29 |
| Italy | 5·6 | 7·6 | 7·5 | 6·8 | — | 1·5 | — | 1·5 | 5·4 | 31 |
| Benelux | 5·0 | 6·9 | 7·5 | 6·3 | — | 2·3 | — | 2·3 | 5·3 | 30 |
| Austria | 10·0 | 9·0 | 7·5 | 9·0 | — | — | — | — | 6·8 | 23 |
| Norway | 8·9 | 6·3 | 2·5 | 6·3 | — | — | — | — | 4·8 | 21 |
| Switzerland | 7·8 | 4·9 | 5·8 | 6·3 | — | — | — | — | 4·8 | 16 |
| Japan | 3·3 | 4·2 | 5·0 | 4·1 | — | — | — | — | 3·1 | 18 |
| United States | 1·7 | 1·4 | 2·5 | 1·8 | — | 2·3 | — | 2·3 | 1·9 | 10 |
| Finland | — | 1·4 | 5·0 | 1·8 | — | — | — | — | 1·4 | 6 |
| Canada | 1·1 | 2·1 | — | 1·1 | — | 3·0 | — | 3·0 | 1·5 | 9 |
| Sweden | — | 4·9 | 4·2 | 2·7 | — | — | — | — | 1·0 | 5 |
| Australia | 1·1 | — | 0·8 | 0·7 | — | — | — | — | 0·5 | 3 |

a The frequency is defined as the number of restrictions in a group as a percentage of the total number possible in the group. These calculations are based on a total of 49 products or product groups comprising 15 primary commodities; 23 processed and semi-processed commodities; and 11 manufactured products.

*Source:* UNCTAD, *The Processing Before Export of Primary Commodities* (TD/229/Supp. 2), mimeo (Geneva, April 1979), p. 39.

average *ad valorem* transport costs for US imports exceed most favoured nation tariffs.

Since the processing function often entails a reduction in the weight, volume, and stowage factor for a good, there is reason to believe that nominal freight costs should decline as a commodity moves to higher stages of fabrication. Such transport cost structures could be a factor working in favour of domestic processing of raw materials. However, if liner freight rates are based on other considerations, such as charging what the traffic will bear, these charges may differ from actual cost of carriage. As such, the *actual structure* of freight rates may not work in favour of local processing as some economists have suggested.

Using recent information on transport costs, Yeats (November 1977) examined *ad valorem* freight rates for US imports of different stages of 21 processing chains, irrespective of the countries exporting the commodities. The results showed that nominal transport costs declined in 13 processing chains while they escalated in 8 cases.

However, since transport costs for the same product will differ depending on the location of suppliers, simply calculating average *ad valorem* transport costs for imports at varying stages of fabrication need not approximate the experience of individual countries if the mix of suppliers changes. Recognising this fact, freight ratios were computed for specific exporting countries. Since many nations did not export all stages of the processing chains, this analysis could be conducted for 14 commodity groups and 40 exporting countries. The results showed 27 cases of freight rate escalation versus 13 cases where rates declined. In a similar study of India's exports, it was found that *ad valorem* transport costs clearly escalated in most processing chains. Based on these results, Yeats (October 1977) concluded that 'All in all, these data suggest that the actual behaviour of transport costs over processing chains may not serve to stimulate fabrication in developing countries. In other specific cases, the behaviour of shipping costs may serve to discourage the processing function.'

Several possible explanations for the transport cost escalation have been advanced. Firstly, some processed products are more difficult to handle, more fragile, and also subject to higher insurance costs. A high volume ratio for primary to processed goods shipments might also lead to differentials in shipping costs for some items if significant economies of scale exist. Secondly, over the last decade, dramatic advances have been made in the transport of primary commodities such as the development of bulk carriers and mechanised loading and unloading procedures, with the result that freight rates for items affected have experienced a secular decline. Finally, it is acknowledged that the structure of liner shipping charges is often arbitrary, a key element being the practice of 'charging what the traffic will bear'. This in effect subsidises shipments of primary goods through high rates on processed products. As such, the rate-making policies of liner conferences have the potential to run counter to the LDCs' trade and development objectives. Since this is an important issue, further research and policy proposals on freight rate structure are urgently needed for commodities.

*Commodity processing and price stability*

Most arguments favouring a transfer of the processing function to LDCs are framed in terms of a need to improve export revenues, absorb surplus labour, stimulate the domestic economy, or avoid deteriorating terms-of-trade. However, another potentially important factor is the link between increased processing and stabilisation of prices and export revenues. This tie has been largely ignored in the professional literature dealing with commodities.

The line of reasoning behind this argument can be illustrated through reference to a specific example. In the processing chain for iron, five stages of production exist, each of which involves a higher degree of fabrication:

> stage  1 –  iron ore (SITC 283.1)
> "      2 –  pig iron (SITC 671)
> "      3 –  steel ingots (SITC 672)
> "      4 –  steel mill products (SITC 676)
> "      5 –  other steel products (SITC 677)

while UNCTAD (April 1979) has identified similar processing stages for 27 other commodities. If time series on export prices were examined in terms of a stage of processing formulation, this could provide key insights into such policy issues as:

—Commodity price stabilisation and fluctuations in LDC export earnings. Time series price changes by processing stages could show the potential for stabilising LDC export earnings by shifting to higher levels of fabrication. For example, computation of price and revenue instability indices for iron ore, along with similiar data for pig iron, would show the potential for avoiding price and earnings instability through increased fabrication. While there are *a priori* reasons for believing price stability should increase, such an investigation would allow quantification of the benefits. It would also determine the extent to which increased processing complements the stabilisation objectives of the common fund.

—*Terms-of-trade analysis.* Computation of secular changes in unit prices by level of fabrication would be useful for examining commodity terms-of-trade at different processing stages. This exercise could show the potential to offset deteriorating conditions for primary products by shifting to higher level goods. Such an analysis could constitute a major innovation in commodity price research since a systematic examination of the terms-of-trade within a stage-of-processing framework has not yet been undertaken.

—*Interrelations between commodity price margins and retained value.* If time series show fabricated product prices moving on a different trend from primary goods, this would point to where investigations' should be undertaken to determine the reasons for such differentials and the potential for LDCs to benefit from more favourable price formation at higher stages of fabrication. Such an analysis should provide useful policy information on changes in marketing and distribution costs, margins, and price formation in different markets.

In spite of the potential benefits and insights which might follow, these lines of research have not yet been pursued. However, given the need for such information, this analysis would seem to have a very high priority for policy formulation.


## COMMODITY MARKETING AND DISTRIBUTION SYSTEMS

While it was noted that reforms are needed to correct serious problems associated with commodity price and earnings instability, as well as to liberalise market access, the integrated programme also makes specific proposals concerning marketing and distribution systems. The proposals are based on the fact that these operations often are controlled by commercial concerns in industrial nations, and the observation that LDCs often receive a small fraction of the retail consumer price for their products.

As background, UNCTAD previously initiated several studies concerning the margins absorbed in the marketing and distribution of LDC commodity exports. For example, the UN General Assembly requested the Secretary General of UNCTAD to 'prepare a preliminary study on the proportion between prices of raw materials and commodities exported by developing countries and the final consumer price, particularly in developed countries'. In response to this mandate, preliminary studies were made for iron ore, copper, aluminium, tin, coffee, tea, cocoa, groundnut oil, citrus fruit, bananas, sugar and jute. In addition, UNCTAD also investigated the marketing and distribution systems for cocoa, bananas, and leather, while a similar study has been undertaken on cotton.

One approach employed in these investigations was to take the f.o.b. export unit value as a proxy for the price received by LDCs. Next, the unit value was compared to the price for the principle form in which the commodity is consumed in the importing market, or is used in the manufacture of a different product. For coffee, tea, cocoa powder, groundnut oil, sugar, bananas, and oranges this was the retail price for the form offered for direct consumption. These consumer price data were generally available from statistics published by national agencies in the developed countries. However, for metals comparisons were made between ore prices (in terms of per-ton metal content) and the primary fabricated form in which the commodity enters wholesale trade. The latter comparisons were considered less reliable than those for foodstuffs since some processing was involved.

Table 4.6 shows average export unit values for the food items over 1967–72 and the corresponding consumer price. While an effort was made to gather as large a sample as possible, problems associated with lack of information or nonhomogeneous goods sometimes necessitated the substitution of export prices received by principle suppliers. Lack of matched wholesale or retail statistics prevented export-consumption price comparisons for some industrial countries, although this data was generally available for France, Germany, the United Kingdom and United States.

The table shows that the LDC price for coffee accounted for 43 per cent of the consumer price in the United States, 18 per cent in Germany, and 34 per cent in France. Further statistical analysis suggests the differences between export-retail margins in the United States and Europe are mainly due to internal taxes levied by Germany and France.[6] Similar taxes result in the export price of tea being only 13 per cent of the consumer price in Germany, while high packaging costs are held to be a factor lowering the export-consumer price ratio to 20 per cent in the United States.

Since reliable information for all LDCs was not available, UNCTAD compared unit values for Brazil's shipments of cocoa powder with the

TABLE 4.6 Comparisons Between the Export and Consumer Prices of Selected Commodities Exported by Developing Countries over the Interval 1967–72

| Product comparison | Country comparison | | Price comparison | Transaction price | | Exporter proportion |
|---|---|---|---|---|---|---|
| | Exporter | Consumer | | Exporter | Consumer | |
| Coffee | All LDCs | USA | $ per kilo | 0·80 | 1·86 | 43 |
| ,, | All LDCs | Germany | ,, | 0·80 | 4·44 | 18 |
| ,, | All LDCs | France | ,, | 0·80 | 2·36 | 34 |
| Tea | All LDCs | USA | $ per kilo | 0·94 | 4·91 | 19 |
| ,, | Sri Lanka | Germany | ,, | 0·93 | 7·40 | 13 |
| ,, | All LDCs | UK | ,, | 0·94 | 1·76 | 53 |
| ,, | All LDCs | Netherlands | ,, | 0·94 | 2·48 | 38 |
| Cocoa powder | Brazil | Germany | $ per kilo | 0·21 | 2·32 | 9 |
| ,, | Brazil | France | ,, | 0·21 | 2·02 | 10 |
| ,, | Brazil | UK | ,, | 0·21 | 1·40 | 15 |
| ,, | Brazil | USA | ,, | 0·21 | 0·82 | 25 |
| Groundnut oil | All LDCs | France | cents per kilo | 32·8 | 68·9 | 48 |
| ,, | All LDCs | Germany | ,, | 32·8 | 64·7 | 51 |
| Citrus fruit | Morocco | France | cents per kilo | 12·1 | 40·3 | 30 |
| ,, | Morocco | Germany | ,, | 12·1 | 41·6 | 29 |
| ,, | Tunisia | France | ,, | 12·9 | 40·3 | 32 |
| ,, | Tunisia | Germany | ,, | 12·9 | 41·6 | 31 |
| Bananas | All LDCs | USA | cents per kilo | 8·4 | 34·5 | 24 |
| ,, | All LDCs | Germany | ,, | 8·4 | 35·9 | 23 |
| ,, | All LDCs | UK | ,, | 8·4 | 40·8 | 21 |
| ,, | All LDCs | France | ,, | 8·4 | 42·8 | 20 |
| Sugar | Caribbean | Japan | cents per kilo | 8·3 | 40·4 | 21 |
| ,, | Caribbean | UK | ,, | 8·3 | 21·0 | 40 |

*Source:* Adapted from United Nations Conference on Trade and Development, *Proportion Between Export Prices and Consumer Prices of Selected Commodities Exported by Developing Countries* (Geneva: United Nations, 14 January 1976).

retail price in major markets. Table 4.6 shows that the former accounted for about 25 per cent of the US retail price, 15 per cent in the United Kingdom, and about 10 per cent in France and Germany. Export unit values for bananas ranged between 20 and 25 per cent of the retail price, and a time series analysis suggested this proportion is declining.

On average, Table 4.6 shows that an LDC exporter may receive one quarter to one third the commodities' retail price in industrial markets, with the difference absorbed by transport, marketing, distribution, or other sales functions. However, other evidence suggests that even these estimates of retained value are high. Specifically, matched export consumer price ratios may be upward biased since the former can reflect expatriated profits which accrue to foreign firms.

While published trade statistics cannot be used to determine precisely the share of the consumer price accruing to producers, UNCTAD provides estimates for bananas. Although the results are qualified, the study notes that 'the share of the domestic grower and other domestic enterprises in the final retail price can be taken as in the region of *11 or 12 per cent* [author's italics], although it may be lower in countries where transnational corporations control a substantial part of production'. Figure 4.1 provides a breakdown of the estimated margins for factors entering into retail price formation. As shown, ripeners' gross margins (19 per cent) combine with retail margins (32 per cent) to absorb over 50 per cent of consumer prices. These costs alone represent about five times the estimated returns to LDC growers.

*Improving marketing and distribution systems*

In view of the relatively low retail price share received by LDCs, the integrated programme has an obvious interest in raising this margin. However, several factors may limit alternatives for immediate corrective action. A major problem is that there are a number of links in marketing chains, and little is known about the margins absorbed or the inefficiencies that exist at different stages. Therefore, efforts to collect and assess information are required before remedial action can be prescribed.

One point emerging from previous analyses, however, is that commodity marketing and distribution operations are often highly concentrated in a relatively few transnational corporations. For example, Table 4.7 shows import shares for the largest corporations marketing bananas in developed countries. The three firm market shares reach 90 to 100 per cent in Northern America, and are only slightly lower in Europe. Highly concentrated markets are common for other

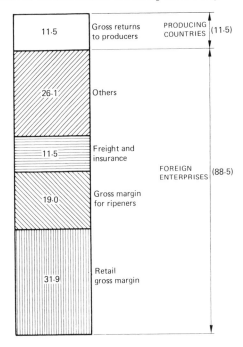

FIGURE 4.1 Estimated Cost Elements Entering into the Formation of the Average Retail Price of Bananas in 1971 (figures in per cent)

*Source*: United Nations Conference on Trade and Development, *The Marketing and Distribution Systems for Bananas* (TD/B/C.1/162) (Geneva: United Nations, 10 February 1975), p. 17

commodities as the largest firm controls between 20 and 30 per cent of world trade in cocoa beans, and the top three firms between 50 and 80 per cent. One firm accounted for one quarter of the world's tea trade and twelve firms accounted for 80 per cent of world rubber trade in the early 1970s. Imposing as these figures may seem, it should be realised that the degree of national concentration is even greater.

The message emerging from these statistics relates to the normal performance of concentrated markets as opposed to those characterised by aggressive competition. Numerous studies of domestic US markets have shown that prices and profits are consistently higher when monopoly elements exist, with weaker units experiencing the detrimental effects. Given the results of these investigations, US federal regulatory agencies often consider three-firm concentration ratios (i.e.,

TABLE 4.7 Market Shares of Transnational and Other Large Corporations in the Banana Import Trade of Selected Industrial Countries 1970–2

| Importing country | Transnational corporations | | | | | |
| | United Brands | Standard Fruit | Del Monte | Sub-total | Others | Total |
| --- | --- | --- | --- | --- | --- | --- |
| Canada | 60 | 30 | 10 | 100 | 0 | 100 |
| United States | 36 | 42 | 12 | 90 | 10 | 100 |
| Switzerland | 81 | 6 | 2 | 89 | 11 | 100 |
| Denmark | 47 | 17 | 19 | 83 | 17 | 100 |
| Sweden | 57 | 16 | 6 | 79 | 21 | 100 |
| Belgium | 47 | 25 | 6 | 78 | 22 | 100 |
| Italy | 45 | 31 | 2 | 78 | 22 | 100 |
| Norway | 54 | 17 | 3 | 74 | 26 | 100 |
| Netherlands | 41 | 21 | 10 | 72 | 28 | 100 |
| Germany, Federal Republic | 42 | 18 | 10 | 70 | 30 | 100 |
| Poland | 70 | 0 | 0 | 70 | 30 | 100 |
| Japan | 12 | 18 | 17 | 47 | 53 | 100 |
| United Kingdom | 40 | 0 | 0 | 40 | 60 | 100 |
| France | 14 | 0 | 0 | 14 | 86 | 100 |
| German Democratic Republic | 0 | 0 | 0 | 0 | 100 | 100 |
| New Zealand | 0 | 0 | 0 | 0 | 100 | 100 |
| Average | 33 | 25 | 10 | 68 | 32 | 100 |

*Source:* United Nations Conference on Trade and Development, *The Marketing and Distribution System for Bananas* (Geneva: United Nations, 24 December 1974).

the percentage of sales generated by the three largest firms) of over 50 per cent to be a *prima facie* case of monopoly control with such markets in need of corrective action. As Chapter 2 indicated, the same detrimental structure-performance relation exists in concentrated international markets. The key question, therefore, is what sort of policy alternatives are available to LDCs to insure better functioning of the commodity markets in which they operate. While several general solutions to this problem were advanced in Chapter 2, there are specific policy measures relevant to commodities.

One potential prescription which may offer LDC producers some countervailing power is government involvement in commodity trade, either individually or as a union of exporters. For example, the Indian state trading corporation negotiates terms for iron, manganese ore, and other commodity exports. Since this approach has met with some success, it may be an option for other developing countries. Given the inelastic demand for some commodities, export taxes may increase revenues. The liner conference code of conduct, with its provisions for carriage by national fleets, could also be a factor extending the LDCs' influence over the distribution of their exports. However, the use of regulatory policy to reduce multinationals' market power in marketing and distribution is one of the more promising approaches. Whether through an international code of conduct for transnationals, or by appropriate legislation on a unilateral basis, this line of action should be pursued. However, a major problem is to convince the industrial country governments that such measures work in their own national interests. In view of the importance of this latter consideration, surprisingly little relevant empirical research has been done.

In a comprehensive analysis of commodity problems, Maizels (1976) provides several specific proposals for improving the bargaining position of LDCs, or increasing their export earnings. These suggestions include,

—The establishment of an intergovernmental joint marketing agency to act as sole buyer for LDC producers, and sole seller to developed countries. Through its monopoly position, the agency would be able to raise prices where appropriate, and provide some degree of countervailing power.

—Maizels notes that certain commodities could benefit from fiscal or pricing policies such as a common minimum export price, or the adoption of a uniform *ad valorem* export tax by producers. The more elastic the aggregate supply, and the more inelastic demand, the greater will be the portion of the tax borne by consumers. This *ad valorem* export tax proposal has the attraction of avoiding classification problems for different grades of products, as well as avoiding problems in negotiating export quotas.

—Where transnationals are producers as well as traders, LDC returns may be increased through taxes on corporate operations. However, given the power imbalances which often exist, this approach may be inapplicable in cases.

Maizels also proposes action to achieve greater control over international commodity marketing and distribution systems. Where several transnationals compete in production and marketing, this might be used to bargain for better terms or the establishment of local processing facilities. Alternatively, governments might adopt measures aimed at participation in existing marketing and distribution operations, or sponsor the establishment of new facilities.

Given the market power transnationals exercise, an objective evaluation must conclude that the vertical integration of LDCs into marketing and distribution functions will not be easy. However, as Chapter 3 noted, recent thinking on development planning stressed the need to expand LDC intra-trade. Measures to encourage LDC marketing and distribution functions in this exchange could provide incentives for vertical integration. Given the experience gained in these operations, marketing and distribution operations may later be extended to industrial markets.

*Commodity problems and policies in the 1980s*

Without doubt, the key commodity policy issues during the 1970s will carry over into the next decade. A major concern will undoubtedly be the establishment and operations of the common fund, given the importance that the South attaches to commodity price and earnings stability. Compensatory financing and the need for a second window should continue to be important issues for commodities. Hopefully, a complementarity of interests, the South for remunerative and stable prices and earnings and the North's desire to secure stable sources of supply, will be the link that allows producers and consumers to arrive at mutually beneficial positions.

The issue of domestic processing of commodities should also assume increasing importance during the 1980s. As noted, local processing has the potential to absorb surplus labour that exists in most LDCs, while processed goods also seem to have better trade and earnings prospects. Since the issues involved in local processing cut across a wide variety of areas such as the removal of tariffs and NTBs to improved marketing and distribution systems, implementation of the required policy measures will undoubtedly be major factors influencing North–South relations during the 1980s.

Advances in deep-sea mining also have the potential to produce major issues for selected commodities. Specifically, it has been established that certain sections of the ocean floor contain high concentrations of manganese nodules which are rich sources of minerals such as manganese, nickle, copper, and cobalt. However, only a handful of industrial countries have the technology to extract these potentially lucrative natural resources. Given that the United Nations has declared the oceans and their resources to be 'the common heritage of mankind', ways of utilising these resources for the benefit of all nations will undoubtedly be a major issue during the 1980s.

# 5 Transnational Corporations and Developing Countries

International trade theory rests on several strict assumptions concerning the nature of this exchange and conditions in domestic and international markets. For example, the classical model of trade according to comparative advantage is based on a two-commodity, two-factor, two-country world with full employment, identical production functions, and perfect competition in both domestic and international markets. Given these conditions it was demonstrated that both countries will be better off with free trade or, at the least, one country will be better off while the other's position would not deteriorate.

Even a casual analysis quickly reveals that the postulates of classical theory are invalid. Numerous countries exist, and large numbers of goods are exchanged internationally. Less than full employment is a common occurrence in both developed and developing countries, while domestic labour, production, and capital markets often are subject to varying degrees of monopoly control. Empirical evidence also shows that international trade in some items may be dominated by a relatively small number of transnational corporations (TNCs). The market power of these organisations may be such as to bias LDC trade and other economic relations.

In spite of the controversy surrounding TNCs, there is a general lack of concrete empirical evidence concerning these organisations. This is surprising given that transnationals have been accused of charging too high a price for some LDC imports and too low a price for exports – particularly those destined for parent companies in developed countries. Such actions can reduce foreign exchange availability for capital equipment purchases or related development expenditures. Other charges levied against the TNCs range from adoption of inappropriate production technologies for developing countries, to active subversion of internal economic and social relations. On the other hand, some economists maintain that TNCs make positive contributions to LDCs' industrialisation efforts through their trade, investment and employment policies which more than offset the negative effects stressed by opponents of these organisations. In spite of the importance of these issues, the factual evidence is very sketchy and subject to a wide range of interpretations.

This chapter surveys the nature of the controversy that surrounds the transnational corporations, and the probable importance of the 'transnational issue' for the 1980s. The analysis begins with a discussion of the evolution, nature, organisational structure, and scope of TNC operations, and indicates how these factors contribute to the discord between the corporations and developing countries. The focus then shifts to an evaluation of the empirical evidence concerning the influence of these organisations on LDC pricing, technology, employment, finance and investment decisions. After an overall assessment, the discussion examines the need for further research as well as the use of 'codes of conduct' or antitrust legislation to control potential transnational abuses.

## CHARACTERISTICS OF TRANSNATIONALS

One aspect of the adverse reaction to TNCs stems from the historical role such institutions have played in key industrial and financial sectors. For example, banking has long been an international operation, given the need to finance trade, or to transfer capital to areas of relative scarcity and higher returns. Such operations have resulted in the international banker acquiring something of an unfavourable reputation since his concern and actions for capital preservation may run counter to other national interests. Secondly, resource industries such as mining have long been subject to transnational operations. These activities were viewed by many individuals as robbing the LDCs of their natural wealth and exploiting domestic labour. In the past, transnational corporations controlled the export–import trade of some LDCs. In India, Indonesia, China and Indo-China these organisations and their operations were invariably associated with colonialism.[1]

### The rationale for transnational operations
Aside from the nature of the TNCs' forerunners, other factors have contributed to a negative appraisal of these organisations. Since economic theory regards corporations as being motivated primarily by

profits, financial incentives may have a key influence on corporate actions. Given the tie between profits and corporate behaviour, TNCs will feel a need to control their business environment since variations in profits may be caused by exogenous factors. The more the firms expand internationally, and the larger their investments, the greater will be the range of exogenous factors which can influence profits and earnings. Therefore, incentives exist for TNCs to strengthen customer loyalty or protect production capacity. However, the actions needed to achieve such security may run counter to LDC industrialisation or social policies.

The importance modern corporations attach to security of operations has been the source of major problems since it can lead to direct conflicts of interests with foreign nationals. Galbraith (1978) acknowledges this aspect of corporate behaviour in observing that these organisations attempt to reduce uncertainty associated with the free play of market forces and substitute planning. However, the possibilities for eliminating this source of conflict may be limited since modern technical manufacture seems to require transnational operations. Products like foodstuffs, cotton, textiles, wool or coal, which previously were major items in international trade, required no special connections between producer and consumer since they were shipped through intermediaries. Modern industrial enterprises, in contrast, deal in products that must be marketed and these merchandising functions require well-controlled sales organisations, with complementary instruction, repair and service functions. To support these operations and the sizeable investments often required for plant and equipment, the corporations must have some power, so Galbraith argues, over developments in their respective markets. The achievement and exercise of this power is a natural development of corporate growth and the production of modern technology-based goods.

In arguing that TNCs are specialists in the production of information that is more efficiently transmitted within firms than between markets, Magee (1977) takes a somewhat similar position concerning factors leading to the development of TNCs. Transnationals generally deal with sophisticated technologies because appropriability (i.e., the ability of private originators of technological innovations to obtain the pecuniary value of the advance) is higher than for simple technology-based items. Magee also suggests that private market generation of information and production techniques functions best with concentrated industry structures and large firm size. Therefore, policy proposals aimed at increasing technological transfer by reducing TNC market power, such as regulatory action to stimulate intra-industry competition, has conflicting objectives. This point is important since such policy action has often been the focus of LDC demands concerning the transnationals.

Neither Galbraith nor Magee fail to acknowledge potential dangers associated with the concentration of power in large corporations. Galbraith specifically identifies five TNC 'danger zones' which should be avoided. These include the threat to move operations to a different country, bribery of foreign officials, currency speculation, environmental damage in host countries, and the international arms trade. Magee also notes that multinationals can create artificial and sophisticated 'masking devices' such as product differentiation, and expend resources to appropriate returns on earlier investments. Such actions can have important negative social effects. Transnationals with significant market power may also attempt to prevent or delay introduction of unskilled labour-intensive production processes if they conflict with existing technology in which they have a vested interest. This can work counter to LDC employment objectives where sizeable portions of the population may be without work. However, positive factors are also cited which may offset the negative effects. Galbraith suggests that transnationals have been an important force in favour of trade liberalisation, a lessening of international conflicts, fostering the spread of technology, and net employment creation.

On balance, Galbraith and Magee reach relatively positive overall views concerning transnationals. Compared with many developing country spokesmen, their analysis and conclusions differ on two crucial counts: the importance and degree of competition in world markets where TNCs operate, and the political power of the corporations and resulting capacity for anti-social action.

*The relation between market structure and performance*
Since economic theory and empirical research show that increases in market structure or the power of large corporations will have adverse effects on various aspects of performance (see Chapter 2), the trend toward increased industry control by fewer firms is of considerable importance to LDCs. In this respect, conventional measures of market structure often show growing industrial concentration in markets of most industrial countries. For example, the hundred largest US producers' share of value added in manufacturing rose from 23 per cent in 1947 to 30 per cent in 1958, and 33 per cent in 1966. In addition to the increasing trend, international comparisons of concentration indices show that many industries are often dominated by a relatively small

number of corporations. This observation has important implications since empirical evidence indicates that developing countries often are not able to effectively compete in export markets where they come up against oligopolistic market structures dominated by a few large firms.

As an illustration, Figure 5.1 shows the relation between market structure and the degree of LDC export penetration. The vertical axis employs the four-firm concentration ratio for selected US industries as a proxy for market structure, while the horizontal axis shows developing country import shares. The curve *LL* is based on a regression which employed over one hundred observations, and accounts for over 50 per cent of the observed variation in the data. The message that emerges from the figure is that in highly concentrated oligopolistic markets LDCs may be relegated to the role of marginal suppliers with import shares of 20 per cent or less. Furthermore, it has been alleged that these highly concentrated market structures work against developing countries in various other aspects of commercial relations.

As with other aspects of the controversy surrounding TNCs, some economists disagree with this contention and suggest that *static* concentration measures such as the four-firm ratio do not reflect the true degree of competition in national or international markets since they typically are based on short-term data. When top firm turnover is rapid, high concentration ratios may conceal the real intensity of competition since the shares of industry leaders will be lower when computed on, say, a ten-year basis than for any shorter interval. Also the measures are derived from national data and neglect the influence of foreign competition. In other words, Ford and General Motors' share in current US automobile production is larger than in the 1930s, yet the industry may be more competitive today due to greater foreign pressures. This means that LDCs may have fewer corporations to deal with in *specific* industrial nations, yet their bargaining power may have increased due to rivalry among firms headquartered in different countries. Thus, the degree and benefits of competition in LDC import or export markets may be greater than implied by short-term industry concentration data.

The contention that the rivalry between firms in different nations has led to increased international competition has been challenged by those who view this as a temporary phenomenon which will eventually lead, through mergers or market-sharing arrangements, to formation of even larger and more truly multinational organisations. However, the variety of nationalities of TNCs seems to be a positive factor for maintenance of competition. Furthermore, if the advanced semi-industrialised LDCs form their own transnationals this would heighten international

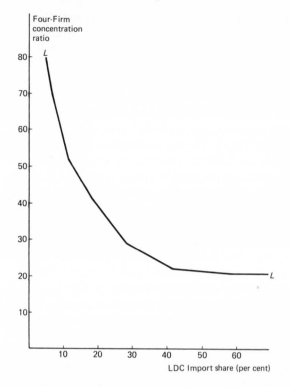

FIGURE 5.1 The Relation Between Market Structure and the Share of Developing Countries in US Imports; Based on Selected Manufacturing Industries

competition. The role of the socialist countries could be important. In areas of international commerce (particularly shipping) these nations have been major factors heightening international competition and lowering prices.

These major issues—competition, performance and developing countries—all remain subject to considerable controversy. However, a point to be noted in weighing the potential pros and cons of TNC behaviour is that industrialised countries have felt the need to enact legislation designed to curb domestic abuses of economic power, yet at the international level such regulations are often non-existent. Furthermore, national legislation often specifically exempts corporate international operations from anti-trust action, or is in conflict with other nations' laws. As a result, Diaz-Alejandro suggests that the balance between collusion and competition in international operations is tilted in the direction of the former by lack of clear anti-trust agreements.

### Multinationals and developing country exports

While the previous discussion outlined the possible influence of TNCs in world markets, specific questions may be raised concerning the influence of these organisations on the developing countries. For example, transnationals are often equipped to provide capital, technology and managerial skills which are of vital importance for LDC industrialisation programmes. However, the benefits from these operations may diminish when capital is generated in local markets, or where the imported technology is inappropriate.

Territorial production and marketing agreements sometimes used by TNCs may also influence exports. When such arrangements provide an LDC subsidiary with assured markets they can be beneficial. However, if transnationals reduce exports from subsidiaries as part of these market-sharing arrangements, this can have a negative impact on LDC production, employment, and foreign exchange earnings. One method for enforcing such restrictions has been through the patent systems which have been used by multinationals to control production and trade. This has been the source of a frequent complaint that patent systems and other limits on technological transfer constrain the ability of developing countries to secure the technology needed for industrialisation.

Partly as a result of rising domestic labour costs, transnationals have steadily increased their exports of manufactures from developing countries. This is also attributable to economies of scale associated with enlarged production facilities in LDCs, governmental pressures, and the provision of incentives for transnationals to export. These expanded trade flows are often directed to neighbouring developing countries due to their relative capital intensity (see Chapter 3), or to agreements on economic integration such as the Latin America Free Trade Area. If transnationals employ territorial and market allocation arrangements to restrict exports, they reduce benefits which accrue to the LDCs from such unions. On the other hand, promotion of exports by multinationals may have detrimental effects on the export potential of firms owned by LDC nationals which cannot compete with the international corporations.

Trade statistics show that certain manufactures which involve the assembly of foreign-produced components have been exported in rapidly increasing quantities from developing countries. TNCs have played a major role in these 'off-shore assembly' operations in which raw materials or components are sent to developing countries for assembly, with the finished products re-imported for final sale. This process is encouraged by industrial country tariff provisions which apply import duties only to the value added component of such goods. One advantage is that these activities offer access to foreign markets which might otherwise not exist, particularly when the developing countries cannot produce the components, and also may lead the TNCs to lobby against increased protectionism in home markets. However, the actual benefits to LDCs may be diminished if the final product has a high import content, which would reduce linkage effects, or if operations are confined to free-zone processing areas with little diffusion of the economic effects.

The influence of transnationals in developing country markets may be increased by the acquisition of domestic firms, particularly if such acquisitions involve established local concerns. These mergers can convey positive benefits if they lead to greater efficiency, an increased propensity to export, or greater capital availability. However, where acquisitions involve firms with considerable market power, the negative effects associated with increased market concentration may offset these benefits.

Transnationals' transfer pricing practices can also promote or impede exports since the cost of inputs or end products is artificially established. If inputs are purchased below 'arm's length' prices this should improve export prospects due to the beneficial impact on production costs, while higher relative input prices would reduce export potentials. If applied to final goods, under-pricing of exports may lower foreign exchange earnings while over-pricing can reduce total sales volume and revenues. Generalisations are difficult since the exact relation will depend on the import elasticity of demand. However, it is agreed that transfer pricing practices do have the potential to exert an important influence on developing country trade.

### Multinationals and developing country imports

The United Nations acknowledges that there are potential advantages for LDCs which obtain imports from transnationals. Specifically, UNCTAD (30 December 1975) identifies four benefits: the improved ability to obtain supplies for industrialisation, the reliability of transnationals in satisfying import requirements, the provision of products of guaranteed quality with efficient after-sales service, and sale of such goods at favourable prices and terms.

Concerning the first point, as a result of the multinationals' international operations, LDCs may experience benefits not available if foreign firms' production were primarily geared to domestic markets. TNCs may be able to design products specifically suited to developing countries, or to adapt established designs to local conditions. Due to the scale and degree of specialisation of TNC operations, efficiencies may result which would be translated into lower prices and LDC import costs. Furthermore, their capital resources and access to financial markets may enable transnationals to supply imports on more favourable credit terms.

In certain situations, TNC pricing policies may benefit developing countries since oligopolistic markets are often characterised by price rigidity, and therefore relative price stability. In periods of inflation, this could be an advantage if it restrains import costs. However, inflexible prices could mean costs might fall more slowly in a recession. Moreover, as a result of the multinationals' international pricing policies, LDCs might not benefit from currency devaluations in the producing developed country. However, when devaluations occur in the LDCs the likelihood is that prices for such imports will be increased. As in other areas regarding the TNCs, little empirical information exists on these aspects of pricing policy and this is a rich field for research.

Transnationals may exert their influence on the marketing function if they utilise narrow distribution channels for their products. For example, through exclusive dealer arrangements the parent company or a subsidiary can be given the supply rights for a LDC distributor while contractors have also been assigned sole rights for import and distribution. These formal links can be reinforced through the use of laws pertaining to patents and trademarks. As a consequence, such arrangements may reduce competition and adversely affect the supply and price of imports.

As indicated in the preceding discussion, transnationals have been credited with a wide variety of policies and practices which have either positive or negative effects on developing countries. Table 5.1 identifies some of these practices and also indicates the potential beneficial or negative influences.

The key question, which is examined in the forthcoming analysis, concerns the extent to which TNCs pursue these various lines of action.

TABLE 5.1 Possible Consequences of Transnational Corporations' Commercial Policy Actions

| Function | Negative effect | Positive effect |
|---|---|---|
| Pricing policy | Transfer pricing can increase import costs or reduce export revenues. Deviations from market prices can also lead to misallocation of resources. | Inputs purchased below market prices can stimulate exports. TNCs may also supply goods below prices of local firms due to scale of operations or related factors. |
| Financial operations | Utilisation of domestic financial markets can drain scarce capital from local firms. | Direct investment or TNC guaranteed loans can increase the supply of capital. |
| Export policy | TNCs may lobby for high protection and gear production to the domestic market. Exports may also be constrained by international cartels or market sharing arrangements. | Territorial and market sharing agreements may provide guaranteed and stable outlets which are vital for LDC production. |
| Transfer of technology | Capital-intensive techniques may be employed which are too expensive or fail to fully utilise available labour. | TNCs may be the sole source of capital equipment required for development. These goods may also be adapted to local conditions. |
| Production policy | TNCs may not utilise domestic factors but favour inputs manufactured by the parent company or another subsidiary. Production may also occur in an 'enclave' with few important general effects. | Functions such as 'off-shore assembly' can lead to production and export of certain goods which otherwise would not be possible. |
| Market entry | Acquisitions of established local firms can increase concentration and heighten monopoly influences in LDC markets. | New or 'toe-hold' entry can increase competitive pressures in local markets and also involve important plant and equipment expenditures. |
| Labour policy | Skilled and managerial functions may be reserved for foreign nationals with menial and unskilled functions assigned to the domestic work force. | On the job and other training functions can make an important contribution to improving human capital in developing countries. |

| | | |
|---|---|---|
| Political activity | TNC actions may be designed to undermine 'unfriendly' local governments or attempt to gain tax or other financial concessions which will not stimulate the development effort. | Operations may be conducted in harmony with the local government's development plan and provide a valuable supplement to industrialisation objectives. |
| Competitive policy | Predatory pricing and other forms of restrictive business practices may be followed to stamp out local competitors and achieve monopolistic control of LDC markets. | Aggressive competition between TNCs based in different countries may work to the advantage of LDCs. Longer-term competitive pressures may be greater than indicated by short-run concentration ratios. |
| Resource exploitation | Time patterns of natural resource exploitation may not coincide with those in the long-term interests of LDCs. Also, considerable environmental damage may occur if inappropriate techniques are used. | TNC resources may be the key elements required for exploitation and sale of LDC natural resources. Without these inputs commercialisation may not occur. |

## EMPIRICAL EVIDENCE ON TNC PRACTICES

The preceding discussion shows that a wide variety of practices have been attributed to transnational corporations, some of which stimulate development efforts while others have unfavourable effects. However, economic theory provides little evidence as to whether positive or negative influences will predominate. For such an evaluation recourse must be made to empirical analysis of actual TNC operations. Unfortunately, there are major gaps in the empirical evidence that does exist. Case studies have been undertaken on TNC activities in specific markets, but it is difficult to generalise from these results. The conclusions also differ due to the methodologies used, the influence of factors peculiar to specific host countries or corporations, or the time frame chosen for study.

Within the existing limits, an attempt is made to assess evidence bearing on several major areas of transnational operations: transfer of technology, transfer pricing, the influence on the level and kind of exports, and development finance. A section also assesses the importance of transnationals in world trade so the overall influence of these organisations can be evaluated.

### The role of TNCs in world trade

While statistics on intra-firm trade are very incomplete, available evidence indicates that this exchange accounts for a sizeable percentage of international trade and is increasing in importance. The most comprehensive data source is based on US Department of Commerce survey data and relates to United States transnationals. This source indicates that these organisations account for about one quarter of world exports of all types of merchandise, and for approximately 20 per cent of manufactures exports. The Commerce Department data also show that, between 1966 and 1970, total exports of US transnationals increased by 69 per cent as opposed to a 53 per cent expansion in world trade. The corporation's exports of manufactures grew by 73 per cent, which was almost 10 points above the expansion of world trade in these goods. Thus, the statistics show that the US transnationals account for a very sizeable portion of world trade, both in total and for manufactures, and this exchange has been expanding faster than world trade in general.

Information drawn from other sources suggests that corporations headquartered in other developed countries have an equally important influence on world trade. Specifically, a research project on 'Comparative Multinational Enterprise' was sponsored by the Ford

Foundation, Harvard Business School, and the Geneva Centre for Education in International Management (CEI). This project conducted a census of the foreign operations of the world's largest transnationals. The results showed that European and Japanese firms whose 1970 sales exceeded $400 million had equity ownership positions in over 5,000 foreign manufacturing subsidiaries. While direct comparisons with the US Department of Commerce data are difficult, an analysis of this census led Franko (1975) to conclude that 'despite the absence of full comparability of the samples, the gaps in dates, and the unavailability of information concerning subsidiary size, it seems nonetheless probable that non-US transnational's foreign activity *at least equalled* [author's italics] that of the United States firms'. If this proposition is correct, TNCs are involved in approximately 50 per cent of world trade. Franko also found that the Japanese transnationals were particularly active in foreign markets since over 20 per cent of the Japanese subsidiaries were export oriented and located in less developed countries.[2] In contrast, only 1 per cent of the UK's subsidiaries were so placed with the European countries' percentage reaching a maximum 7 per cent for France.[3]

Given the role of TNCs in world trade, questions arise as to which industry groups are subject to transnational activity, and what factors attract the corporations to LDC markets. Concerning the first question, it must be admitted that data on TNC industry activity are even more scarce than for world trade. However, an industry sector analysis of US corporations' activities in Brazil and Mexico provides some indication as to the role of TNCs in two developing countries.

Table 5.2 summarises the results of this investigation. Shown here are total 1960 and 1972 values of US-based transnational exports, by industry sector, as well as exports destined for parent corporations. According to the table, intra-firm trade accounted for 73 per cent of 1972 Brazilian exports while the share was almost 10 percentage points higher for Mexico. The table also shows that intra-firm trade was expanding in both countries with Mexico experiencing the largest increase (from 54 to 82 per cent).

It should be noted that wide differences exist between the intra-firm trade share on an industry sector basis. For example, transport, electrical machinery, and scientific instruments have 1972 intra-firm trade shares that range from 80 to 100 per cent, with the ratios for less capital-intensive and specialised industries like stone, glass and clay, metals, or food products being generally lower.

Analysis of the import structure of the affiliates shows that close ties

TABLE 5.2 Exports of Manufactures by US Affiliates in Mexico and Brazil in 1960 and 1972, values in $000

| Industry | Brazil 1960 Total exports | Brazil 1960 To parents | Brazil 1972 Total exports | Brazil 1972 To parents | Brazil Per cent intra-firm 1960 | Brazil Per cent intra-firm 1972 | Mexico 1960 Total exports | Mexico 1960 To parents | Mexico 1972 Total exports | Mexico 1972 To parents | Mexico Per cent intra-firm 1960 | Mexico Per cent intra-firm 1972 |
|---|---|---|---|---|---|---|---|---|---|---|---|---|
| Food | 0 | 0 | 2350 | 391 | 0 | 17 | 35 | 0 | 7093 | 5446 | 0 | 77 |
| Textiles | 0 | 0 | a | a | 0 | a | 0 | 0 | 0 | 0 | 0 | 0 |
| Paper | 0 | 0 | 2947 | 85 | 0 | 3 | 0 | 0 | 0 | 0 | 0 | 0 |
| Chemicals | 382 | 382 | 6240 | 2894 | 100 | 63 | 5102 | 2752 | 32941 | 18466 | 54 | 56 |
| Rubber | 0 | 0 | 1191 | 557 | 0 | 47 | 0 | 0 | 520 | 394 | 0 | 76 |
| Stone, glass and clay | 0 | 0 | 2663 | 0 | 0 | 0 | 0 | 0 | 1616 | 154 | 0 | 10 |
| Primary and fabricated metals | 5 | 0 | 2151 | 218 | 0 | 10 | 0 | 0 | 2361 | 1310 | 0 | 55 |
| Non-electrical machinery | 543 | 25 | 31455 | 24431 | 5 | 78 | 43 | 17 | 7320 | 5033 | 39 | 70 |
| Electrical machinery | 684 | 684 | 17533 | 13959 | 100 | 80 | 56 | 0 | 28529 | 25498 | 0 | 89 |
| Transportation | 0 | 0 | 27508 | 24247 | 0 | 89 | 0 | 0 | 48514 | 46480 | 0 | 100 |
| Instruments | 22 | 22 | 1211 | 1211 | 100 | 100 | 185 | 185 | 8989 | 8989 | 100 | 100 |
| Others | 0 | 0 | 3711 | 3644 | 0 | 98 | 0 | 0 | 1188 | 934 | 0 | 79 |
| Total | 1636 | 1113 | 98960 | 71637 | 68 | 73 | 5421 | 2954 | 139071 | 112704 | 54 | 81 |

a Trade values included in the 'others' category to avoid disclosure.

Source: Adapted from R. S. Newfarmer and W. F. Mueller, *Multinational Corporations in Brazil and Mexico: Structural Sources of Economic and Non-economic Power*, Report to the Subcommittee on Multinational Corporations, United States Congress, Senate Committee on Foreign Relations (Washington, US Government Printing Office, 1975), pp. 27, 128.

were maintained with parent companies, but the import share for intra-firm trade has declined substantially in Mexico with somewhat smaller reductions for Brazil. Even so, imports from the parent corporation still account for between 10 and 20 per cent of total material production costs, and for over 50 per cent of the affiliates' total material import requirements.

To what extent can these data on economic and trade ties be generalised to other countries? As in practically all facets of TNC activity, the scarcity of empirical information makes generalisations difficult. However, a study by C. K. Park on Japanese and US transnationals in Korea showed that more than half of the firms imported over 50 per cent of their total imports of raw materials from parent companies, or from the countries of these companies. The Park study also found that the proportion of imported intermediate inputs is high in most Korean manufacturing industries, but was particularly important for firms with sizeable foreign investment. For example, in petroleum and electronic machinery more than 60 per cent of intermediate inputs were imported in 1975, while in transport equipment, machinery, and metals the proportion ranged between 25 and 40 per cent. Thus, existing empirical evidence from three countries (Brazil, Mexico and Korea) shows that TNCs maintain very close commercial contacts with affiliates on both the import and export side.

Three points emerge from the general empirical analyses and case studies. Firstly, transnationals account for a substantial portion of world trade with some estimates ranging to 50 per cent of the total and 40 per cent for manufactures. In addition, TNC trade seems to be expanding faster than world trade in general so this exchange should assume even more important proportions in the future. Finally, several studies show that a large percentage of TNC trade occurs between related parties. Since this exchange bypasses the normal market mechanisms, the potential exists for distortions in prices, revenues or production techniques.

What are the factors that have led to the growth in the level and importance of TNC activity in foreign markets? In developing countries, obvious attractions are lower wage rates, although some LDC governments have offered special tax and financial incentives to locate certain manufacturing processes abroad. Also, if domestically produced components are assembled abroad it was noted they can be re-imported to almost all developed countries under tariffs which apply to the value added component of the final goods.

Table 5.3 illustrates the importance of this off-shore assembly

TABLE 5.3 Comparison of the Growth and Share of OAP Manufactures Exported from LDCs with the Share of US Affiliates in Total LDC Manufactured Exports, 1966–74

| Year | US imports from developing countries under OAP provisions ($ million) | | Gross value of OAP imports as a percentage of LDC manufactures exports | Share of US affiliates in LDC manufactures exports |
|---|---|---|---|---|
| | gross | dutiable | | |
| 1966 | 60·7 | 31·4 | 1.1 | 10.6 |
| 1967 | 99·0 | 42·8 | 1.6 | 11.5 |
| 1968 | 221·7 | 97·7 | 2.9 | 11.0 |
| 1969 | 394·8 | 177·3 | 4.3 | 9.2 |
| 1970 | 541·5 | 245·9 | 5.8 | 10.8 |
| 1971 | 652·5 | 314·1 | 5.9 | 9.5 |
| 1972 | 1031·7 | 531·2 | 6.6 | 8.5 |
| 1973 | 1522·9 | 827·0 | 6.3 | 8.1 |
| 1974 | 2328·8 | 1289·4 | 7.2 | 8.7 |

*Source*: 'Growing Exports of Manufactures by Multinations from LDCs', *Multinational Business* (No. 1, 1978), p. 40.

processing as part of the overall TNC operations. The first two columns of the table show gross and dutiable values of these imports in the United States, while the third gives gross value of OAP shipments as a percentage of manufactured exports from LDCs. For comparison, the share of US-controlled affiliates in total LDC manufactures (of all kinds) is also shown. Comparing column three with four shows that OAP imports in the United States are now almost equal in importance to total exports of manufactures by affiliated enterprises to all markets. Also noteworthy is the declining share of American affiliates in total manufactures exports of LDCs. This result seems largely due to an increasing share of domestic LDC enterprise in exports, and a vigorous expansion of Japanese firms.

In summary, what do the statistics concerning the extent of transnational operations show? A key element concerns the size and extent of these corporations' operations. If the organisations play a relatively minor role in world and LDC trade, this would influence the priority assigned to the TNCs as an issue for the 1980s. However, the preceding discussion has shown that transnationals' operations are extensive, perhaps involving 40 to 50 per cent of world trade. Given the extent of these operations, serious consideration must be given to how the TNCs can influence economic, social and industrialisation objectives of developing countries, and which aspects of these operations are in need of corrective action.

## Transnationals and the transfer of technology

The controversy surrounding transfer of technology is related to a shift in emphasis economists place on problems facing developing countries. While the traditional development objectives often were concerned with accelerating national income or GNP growth, in cases where such growth was achieved the benefits often were not dispersed widely through the population. This observation, coupled with rising population pressures and massive migration to urban centres, led to a shift in priorities under which alleviation of unemployment pressures was assigned a major emphasis. For example, in some LDCs unemployment exceeds one quarter of the adult population. If appropriate labour-intensive production processes were introduced it could alleviate these social problems and also be a factor for more equitable income distributions. Since TNCs often establish new manufacturing industries in developing countries, proper selection of production techniques could contribute to lowering unemployment rates.

The controversy concerning the transfer of technology centres on the contention that TNC production techniques tend to be capital-intensive and do little to alleviate unemployment pressures. It is argued that TNCs prefer capital-intensive techniques because they need not borrow at the high local market interest rates which face domestic firms, and also because commercial interests work against development of new or modified labour-intensive technologies. The technology utilised by TNCs can also displace local labour-intensive firms (in which case more jobs may be destroyed than created) or force domestic industry to use similar techniques. Technological choice of labour-intensive techniques may also be bypassed if the TNC uses its bargaining strength to secure special privileges such as high tariff protection or favourable tax status. As such, TNCs may offset market pressures for adoption of labour-intensive production which would be the natural result of low wage rates.

This purported TNC bias in favour of capital-intensive procedures can have other unfavourable effects. As these technologies are often skill-intensive, TNCs may drain limited skilled labour supplies. The fact that TNC technologies are imported may deplete foreign exchange reserves and deprive the local manufacturing sector of funds for capital equipment or modernisation. It has also been argued that sophisticated technology and product differentiation are linked so that TNCs often provide only for the special tastes of a small segment of the population. Such effects may lead to a further concentration of the LDC economic base and greater inequalities in the distribution of income or social power.

In a major discussion paper, Magee (1977) outlines an economic rationale for the transnationals' preference for technologically advanced production processes. Transnationals do not develop simple technologies, it is argued, because their appropriability is low. For example, transnationals normally cannot appropriate the return on a new superior re-arrangement of unskilled workers because such innovations are easily copied and may not be protectable by patents. Given this lack of financial incentives, Magee argues that TNCs should not be expected to provide the types of labour-intensive technologies which are appropriate for developing countries.

While there has been considerable speculation, and some theoretical analysis such as that by Magee, a key question centres on what empirical studies of technological transfer show. In this respect, there have been several general investigations and related case studies. Table 5.4 summarises results of one such study by Forsyth (1977) on the relative capital intensity (value of plant and machinery per worker) of foreign and domestically controlled firms in nine Ghanaian industries. In four

TABLE 5.4  Comparative Statistics of Technologies Employed by Transnational Corporations and Domestic Firms in Ghana

| Industry | Value of plant and machinery per operative[a] | | Ratio of skilled to total employees | |
|---|---|---|---|---|
| | Foreign | Ghanaian | Foreign | Ghanaian |
| Footwear | 3129 | 625 | 0.15 | 0.21 |
| Sawn timber | 1142 | 1121 | 0.17 | 0.14 |
| Bakery products | 442 | 1183 | 0.16 | 0.33 |
| Wood furniture | 507 | 1062 | 0.13 | 0.22 |
| Small metal fabrications | 1672 | 775 | 0.20 | 0.31 |
| Small plastic fabrications | 2237 | 1327 | 0.16 | 0.19 |
| Concrete blocks | 776 | 772 | 0.13 | 0.22 |
| Shirts | 633 | 552 | 0.14 | 0.17 |
| Blouses | 797 | 405 | 0.14 | 0.14 |

[a] Measured in Ghanaian cedis per operative.

*Source*: David J. C. Forsyth, 'Restrictions on Multinationals in the Developing World', *Multinational Business* (No. 4, 1977), p. 6.

cases (footwear, metal fabrication, plastic fabrication, and blouses) foreign firms are clearly more capital-intensive, yet in others the differences seem insignificant or in favour of greater capital intensity by domestic concerns (wood furniture and bakery products are in this class). The table also shows that foreign-owned enterprises used fewer skilled workers in 7 of the 9 industries. Thus, the TNCs appear to be making less imposing demands on this important resource than domestic concerns. Forsyth cites related studies for the Philippines and Mexico which also conclude that it is difficult to distinguish between the technologies adopted by transnationals and domestically controlled firms.[4]

An analysis of employment statistics leads Franko (1975) to conclude that transnationals probably cannot make an important contribution to reducing LDC unemployment. At the maximum, Franko notes that the world's 400 largest industrial enterprises employ 30 million people at home and abroad. Recent United Nations statistics show that unemployment in Indonesia, Bangladesh and Pakistan alone exceeds this figure. However, TNC operations involve not only the direct employment of workers, but also the 'linkage' effects. Any increase in, say, clothing production will raise demand and employment in industries supplying yarn, thread, dyes and other materials that are inputs for the manufacture of clothing. In the past, analyses of the employment effects of TNC activities have focused on the direct effects which Franko argues involve a relatively unimportant number of jobs compared to the scope of LDC unemployment problems. Unfortunately, quantification of the indirect employment effects can only be undertaken through detailed studies, so little reliable information is currently available.[5]

Other factors lead Franko to be pessimistic about the employment-creating ability of transnationals. As shown in Table 5.5, the majority of both US and other countries' foreign subsidiaries are in relatively capital-intensive industries. Thus, the TNC corporate form seems to be best suited for sectors which are capital-intensive in nature irrespective of whether the manufacturing operation occurs in a developed or developing country. The table also shows only a slight tendency for TNCs to locate a higher portion of labour-intensive industry subsidiaries in developing countries. If most transnationals are originally in sectors which employ relatively few workers, and if they locate in LDCs for reasons not connected with availability of low-cost labour, these corporations seem likely to have only a marginal role in any solution to general employment problems.

While more empirical research is needed, it appears that trans-

TABLE 5.5 Comparison of Industry Capital Intensity and the Tendency to Establish Subsidiaries in Other Developed or Developing Countries

| Principal industry of subsidiary ranked by diminishing capital intensity | Subsidiaries of | | | |
|---|---|---|---|---|
| | US parents | | Non-US parents | |
| | Total number | % in LDCs | Total number | % in LDCs |
| Chemicals | 1079 | 46 | 1238 | 42 |
| Petroleum refining | 199 | 35 | 189 | 39 |
| Food and tobacco | 503 | 44 | 673 | 42 |
| Precision goods | 74 | 26 | 78 | 16 |
| Transport equipment | 225 | 42 | 242 | 62 |
| Primary metals | 111 | 37 | 408 | 39 |
| Electrical equipment | 358 | 41 | 781 | 41 |
| Non-electric machinery[a] | 530 | 32 | 598 | 38 |
| Wood, furniture and paper | 197 | 52 | 210 | 27 |
| Rubber and tyres | 113 | 59 | 106 | 50 |
| Textiles and apparel | 102 | 47 | 270 | 69 |

[a] Includes fabricated metals.

*Source*: L. G. Franko, *Multinational Enterprise, the International Division of Labour in Manufactures, and the Developing Countries* (Geneva: Centre d'Etudes Industrielles, 1975), p. 32.

nationals do not have the capability to make a major contribution to solving third world employment problems. Firstly, the evidence that exists suggests that TNCs do not necessarily employ more capital-intensive production processes than local firms, although one must interpret such statistics with caution. Secondly, the existing employment of the world's largest corporations is a small fraction of the unemployment pool in developing countries. Estimates of linkages also suggest that these secondary effects are not likely to add much to the employment-creating potential of TNCs; an increase in jobs equal to the direct effects would seem to be a maximum. It was also observed that transnationals have generally evolved in capital-intensive production processes which would also seem to limit their potential employment-creating effects.

While the preceding observations are pessimistic about the employment-creating potential of TNCs in general, this aspect of transnational activity should not be dismissed entirely or not be subject to some review. In specific countries, size of TNC operations may make the selection of appropriate technology of considerable importance so incentives should be provided to induce adoption of labour-intensive techniques where they are substitutable for capital-intensive processes. Further research is also needed on linkage effects since so little concrete information about employment creation through these secondary influences exists.

*Transfer pricing*

As noted, price manipulation for goods traded internationally can be of considerable importance since these practices influence the volume and the value of trade, foreign exchange earnings, income or employment. The basic problem centres on the fact that 'transfer prices' involve the exchange of goods within a firm even though the units are located in different countries. Since this exchange is not subject to the influence of normal market forces, transnationals may be free to assign arbitrary prices to these transactions.

The inducement to manipulate transfer prices has various causes. Lall (1973) notes that if a parent and a subsidiary both made profits, if effective tax rates on remissible earnings (taking into account withholding taxes) were equal, there were no restrictions on remissions, and no price controls on the output in either country, import duties did not exceed the effective tax rates, the exchange rate of the two countries was stable, and there were no political or other pressures on the level of declared, present or future profits, then there would be no inducement to employ transfer prices to move profits from one country to another. However, if deviations from these conditions occur, there will be an incentive to adjust prices to offset the factors reducing profits.

UNCTAD identifies five types of incentives to employ transfer pricing:

—Transfer prices can be used to strengthen the competitive position of the company or to control competition. For example, by under-pricing raw materials, the receiving unit can produce fabricated products at lower prices and thereby increase its market share or discourage new entry.
—Corporations may try to minimise overall tax burdens by manipulating intra-firm transaction prices so as to raise profits in countries having lower taxes. TNCs may also establish affiliates in 'tax havens' with the objective of accumulating profits in that subsidiary.
—Transfer prices may be an important element in monetary and fiscal management. For example, when a devaluation is believed imminent, corporations may try to shift profits and cash balances out of the country through higher prices. Where strict exchange controls apply,

TNCs may attempt to limit profits. If these regulations constrain dividend or royalty payments, an incentive exists to raise prices on inputs from abroad to achieve a higher level of remittances.

—Controls which limit mark-ups on ex-factory or import prices make transfer price manipulation attractive. Where maximum retail prices are based on import prices or the cost of production, TNCs may increase profit margins by inflating raw material import costs.

—Transfer prices may be manipulated to disguise profit levels of a subsidiary and increase the parent company's profits where the former has local participation or ownership. Transfer prices may also be used to shift profits from subsidiaries to the parent to reduce wage pressures from labour unions, or from governments for higher local participation or even nationalisation.

While it would seem relatively simple to quantitatively assess the magnitude of the abuses associated with transfer pricing, several factors work against such evaluations and the dissemination of findings. Where such abuses are uncovered by government investigations, especially when undertaken by tax and customs authorities, the results may not be made publicly available. Considerable secrecy also surrounds the way in which transfer prices are established, while there are often difficulties in determining 'arm's length' comparison prices. However, specific studies have overcome, at least partially, these problems and provide a guide to the potential magnitude of distortions in transfer prices.

A detailed study of transfer price abuses in a developing country comes from Colombia. In 1972, the Colombian government examined transfer prices with the objective of determining if it was sufficient to control dividend and royalty remittances without some guarantee that such controls were not being circumvented. The main industries examined were pharmaceuticals, rubber, chemicals and electrical goods.

Table 5.6 summarises the results of this investigation which revealed an average over-pricing for pharmaceutical imports of 155 per cent, for electrical and rubber goods of 44 per cent, and of chemical imports of 25 per cent. Over-pricing on individual products was sometimes as high as 3000 per cent, while the overall over-pricing for the foreign firms averaged 6 times their declared royalties and 24 times their declared profits. While names of the individual firms were not disclosed, Table 5.6 shows that the pharmaceutical firm with some local ownership had the lowest transfer price margin. Further research is obviously needed, but this suggests that local participation may be a check on transfer pricing abuses.

TABLE 5.6 Estimated Over-pricing and Profitability of 14 Foreign Firms in Colombia over 1966–70 (percentages)

| Sector and firm | Proportion of imports investigated | Extent of proved over-pricing | Declared profits as percentage of net worth | Profits on proved over-pricing as percentage of net worth |
|---|---|---|---|---|
| **Pharmaceuticals** | | | | |
| 1. (A) | 52·1 | 158·3 | 7·6 | 41·5 |
| 2. (B) | 20·1 | 39·5 | 11·2 | 2·0 |
| 3. (A) | 100·0 | 56·6 | 16·5 | 19·6 |
| 4. (A) | 28·1 | 81·0 | 6·3 | 5·6 |
| 5. (A) | 32·4 | 288·9 | 6·3 | 19·2 |
| 6. (A) | 39·1 | 33·5 | 0·1 | 2·5 |
| 7. (A) | 35·2 | 33·7 | 12·4 | 3·1 |
| 8. (A) | 54·1 | 95·4 | −7·4 | 17·9 |
| 9. (A) | 48·6 | 83·7 | 42·8 | 111·7 |
| 10. (A) | 44·2 | 313·8 | 27·5 | 39·6 |
| 11. (A) | 30·9 | 138·9 | 5·9 | 9·9 |
| **Rubber** | | | | |
| 12. (B) | 60·0 | 40·0 | 8·3 | 6·1 |
| **Electrical goods** | | | | |
| 13. (A) | 22·3 | 24·1 | 8·1 | 0·3 |
| 14. (A) | 30·4 | 81·1 | 0·7 | 1·8 |

*Note:* (A) indicates that the firm is wholly foreign-owned, (B) that foreign investors hold 51–99 per cent of the equity. Individual firm names were not given to avoid disclosure.

*Source:* United Nations Conference on Trade and Development, *Dominant Positions of Market Power of Transnational Corporations* (TD/B/C.2/167) (Geneva: United Nations, 1978), p. 21.

An UNCTAD (November 1978) study of the pharmaceutical industry shows import over-pricing in a number of cases. Import prices in Chile averaged over 100 per cent of world prices for 50 goods, while much the same margins were found in Ecuador. In Peru, import prices for a sample of pharmaceutical products ranged from 5 to 300 per cent above 'world trade' prices for these goods.

Sample-survey data for Iran show that, in the late 1960s, almost 40 per cent of pharmaceutical imports involved over-pricing of intermediate drug chemicals of up to 199 per cent while 50 per cent of the shipments were 200 to 999 per cent above world prices. UNCTAD also documents claims that, in the Philippines, transnationals made up to 1000 per cent profit on finished drugs. Such distortions need not be confined to LDCs since UNCTAD (August 1978) has shown that Greece experienced over-pricing on metal imports of 5 to 88 per cent, and between 12.5 and 229 per cent on chemicals. These excess prices caused a foreign exchange loss of $8·4 million for metals, and $1·8 million for chemicals. However, if the adverse price differentials apply to all metals and chemical imports, and not just the sampled items, the foreign exchange loss would be about $60 million.

Recognising that abuses of transfer prices may be one of the most important adverse consequences of TNC operations, the question arises as to what policy actions can be initiated to correct the problem. One approach which has met with success is the establishment of a special body to continually monitor prices of major imports. Indeed, the Greek experience suggests that such an operation can achieve sizeable foreign exchange savings. Comprehensive information for standardised goods, or those of alternative suppliers, also need to be made generally available. UNCTAD or some other international body could provide an important service by collecting and disseminating such information.

*Financial aspects of TNC operations*

Available data suggest that multinationals may play only a marginal role in solving the problem of increasing financial flows to most developing countries.[6] Multinationals have typically been purveyors of capital, rarely investing their own except in petroleum and other extractive industries. For example, the US Treasury estimated that 1975 total net foreign direct investment flows from TNCs to non-petroleum-exporting countries totalled some $4 billion. This flow remained roughly constant during the 1970s and has comprised little more than 10 per cent of total financing of non-oil LDCs' current account deficits.

Despite the limited importance of TNC activities to *all* developing countries, their investments and exports have been important in some cases. For example, TNC investments and activities are concentrated in countries such as Brazil, Mexico, Argentina, Taiwan and the smaller Asian nations which have been the most active borrowers from private capital markets. Furthermore, almost two thirds of US firms' direct investment in LDC manufacturing is associated with these relatively high income countries. An even higher percentage of US affiliates' capital equipment expenditures has been concentrated in these markets: $1·2 billion in 1974 and nearly $1·4 billion in 1975.

TNC related exports of manufactures from developing countries are also highly concentrated among the wealthier, more creditworthy LDCs. Export activity of non-US transnationals (especially Japan) also appears to be centred in a handful of more advanced South East Asian and Latin American countries.

It is possible that, through export activities and access to capital markets, TNCs could generate a large percentage of future foreign exchange needed by Brazil, Mexico and other advanced developing countries to reduce foreign indebtedness. The non-petroleum-exporting LDCs which have the largest total debt service payments are largely the same as those having the highest indebtedness to private banks: Brazil, Mexico and Argentina lead both lists and Taiwan is not far behind. These countries are also largely the ones in which transnationals have invested most, and have been most influential in the export sector. According to the World Bank data, the combined debt-service payments of Brazil, Mexico, Korea, Malaysia, Singapore and Thailand totalled $4·6 billion in 1975, as opposed to a total $7 billion for 70 non-OPEC developing countries.[7] Each of these six countries was an important base for transnationals with the total volume of TNC-related exports probably about equal to total $4·6 billion of debt-service payments. Thus, for selected advanced developing countries, the export activities of transnationals, as well as their access to capital markets, seemingly has the potential to make a significant contribution to solving financial and credit problems.

It should also be noted that transnationals may contribute to solving the wealthier LDCs' financial problems by attracting some capital to their affiliates in LDCs, and may also guarantee such loans. Since the World Bank debt-recording system includes only debts owed by governments and government-owned firms in LDCs, or debts which carry a government guarantee, there is little data on the role TNC affiliates play in attracting developing country loans. One estimate could be based on the past role of external financing of US affiliates' capital expenditures. Historically, external funds have accounted for about one third of the financing of these institutions' capital expenditures. In 1975, such expenditures by US manufacturing affiliates in all LDCs were $1·8 billion, which implies that direct external borrowings may have been about $0.6 billion. Data also show that TNC affiliates' borrowings from private banks is also concentrated among the relatively advanced export-oriented developing countries. In 1975, over 70 per cent of the capital expenditures of US manufacturing TNCs' affiliates were in Brazil, Mexico, Argentina and the smaller South East Asian countries; presumably external financing followed suit.

In short, transnational corporations, like private banks and capital markets, are central to the financing plans of a few advanced developing countries. Available information also shows that transnationals, like the banks, normally play only a marginal role in financing the economic development of the less advanced nations. This observation alone should not result in transnational investments or exports being dismissed altogether by low to medium income LDCs. Marginal measures may be of particular importance in efforts to obtain foreign exchange to adjust to unforeseen economic problems or simply to tolerate low or negative growth without upheaval. Even small increases in foreign exchange availability from transnationals or other sources might help avoid overt crises.

A key question centres on whether the role of TNCs could be greater if the corporation's policy of objectives were not only to insure against unforeseen crises which influence profits and earnings, but to promote more rapid development. It is evident that, in the long term, commitments of investment capital have the potential for furthering development and for contributing to the financing of development. Where TNCs go, investment, technology, management and multinational private bank loans may follow. However, it must be acknowledged that little appropriate policy action has been proposed which would effectively attune corporate objectives to these social policy goals. If past is prologue, transnationals will continue to be of primary importance to those countries which already have access to private sources of foreign exchange, and which have established a viable export-oriented manufacturing base. Those countries now experiencing low or zero growth have been subject to little TNC on private banks interest. For the foreseeable future, their access to foreign exchange will vary with commodity earnings, prices of oil, grain, small-scale manufactures and public assistance.

## TRANSNATIONAL CORPORATIONS AND DEVELOPMENT POLICY

A key point emerging from much of the preceding discussion is that a distinct lack of empirical information exists concerning the scope and influence of transnational operations in developing countries. Also, much of the empirical information that does exist is the specific result of research aimed at uncovering negative practices. For example, several studies have specifically set out to uncover evidence of transfer pricing abuses by TNCs, but little has been done to assess how pricing practices may stimulate exports or have other beneficial effects. In spite of this deficiency, transnationals have become the focus of increasing international attention and debate. Thus, there is increasing pressure for policy action, but the design of appropriate policy is a very dubious prospect, given the gross inadequacies that exist concerning our knowledge of TNC operations.

The problem of how to design policy in the absence of required empirical information has been aptly summarised by Forsyth (1977):

> . . . the most important effect of the debate from the point of view of the TNCs is the spill-over into new restrictive, sometimes punitive, legislation which is either threatened or already actually in force in many host countries. Given the large stake that TNCs already have in manufacturing and raw material production in the Third World, and the high probability that direct investment there will continue to grow in importance, accurate evaluation of the operations of the TNCs in these areas should be an essential prerequisite for the formulation of these policies. In certain crucial areas, restrictive measures are being introduced largely in the absence of reliable information and on the basis of a vague conventional wisdom as to what TNCs are doing. Moreover, such hard evidence as has (very recently) been put together suggests that present and prospective legislation in this area may in fact be inimical to the interests not only of the TNCs, but also of the developing countries which seek to enforce it.

Thus, two key questions centre on which areas should be given priorities for research, and what policy actions can be prescribed in view of the general lack of empirical information on transnationals.

### Proposals of the Club of Rome
While there undoubtedly will be disagreement on specific proposals, the following suggestions by the Club of Rome (1977) are indicative of

measures which have been proposed to foster research on transnationals or provide guidelines for their operations:

—Governments of host countries should stress socio-economic policy considerations in negotiations with TNCs so the interests of low income groups can be given high priority. Such negotiations should aim at achieving a more equal distribution of purchasing power, thereby allowing the poorest groups to satisfy basic human needs. Formal recognition of this policy should be incorporated in an official development plan, with some legislation enacted to ensure that TNCs comply with the plan's objectives.

—The desirability of establishing limits to corporate size and concentration in international markets should be investigated with a research programme aimed at development of guidelines for these standards. Issues concerning social and public accountability of TNCs also need further study.

—In order that TNC activities result in appropriate increases in the host country's GNP, strengthen its industrial base, and maximise local value added, commercial policy decisions involving economic, financial, commercial and technological factors should be in accord with host country development policies.

—Policies to improve the bargaining power of third world countries *vis-à-vis* the TNCs should be encouraged. The position of LDCs could be enhanced through the formation of regional unions such as the Andean Group, and through producers' associations. Such unions could establish joint investment codes directed towards fostering employment, consumer protection, competition, market structure, ownership and control, financial flows, balance of payments, research and development, commercialisation of technology, transfer pricing, taxation, accounting standards and disclosure. In formulating such codes, particular attention should be given to restrictions on the use of local capital markets; measures to stimulate research and development of labour-intensive production methods, the specification of limits on direct and indirect profit remittances; the use of transnationals as consultative rather than productive entities, or as suppliers of plant and equipment under contract to state or other local concerns.

While TNCs have many common characteristics, the Club of Rome acknowledges that strict generalisations can be misleading. Individual differences exist which reflect the size and power of their country of origin, research and development policies, location, the nature of the internal decision-making process, the extent to which political pressure or illegal practices are employed, and the ability to adapt to local circumstances. This suggests that an international register should be established to distinguish positive and negative aspects of individual corporations. An international body of technical advisers could be created to compile such a register and also provide advice on other issues relating to multinationals.

Longer-term proposals concerning TNC operations should also focus on the following points:

(a) establishment of measures to harmonise TNC activities with host countries' development plans which should specify priorities such as employment creation, increasing food production, or income redistribution;

(b) agreements should be negotiated on minimum information to be supplied concerning TNC activities relating to primary employment creation, total and local capital attracted, investment per capita as well as some technological characteristics such as productivity or capital intensity;

(c) creation of a pool of technological knowledge to service third world governments in negotiations with transnationals;

(d) formulation of a *code of conduct* for TNCs dealing with such questions as ownership and control, financial flows, research and development policies, commercialisation of technology, employment and labour practices, consumer protection, competition and market structure, transfer pricing, taxation standards, accounting and disclosure, and non-interference in local politics;

(e) research on alternative ways of performing TNC functions should be encouraged, including investigation of the potential development of public international corporations. Also, increased cooperation between governments is needed to establish countervailing power, and to make tax structures more uniform.

*Policy formulation for the 1980s*

A major feature that distinguishes the 'transnational issue' from other trade and development concerns is the lack of reliable information on many important aspects of TNC behaviour. Issues concerning the role of TNCs in world trade, their pricing practices, transfer of technology, finance, and other commercial policy actions are clouded by the serious gaps which exist in our knowledge of transnationals' operations. This deficiency can only be rectified by a major international research effort.

Here, the United Nations Centre on Transnational Corporations, UNCTAD, and the International Labour Organisation could play a key role in stimulating and disseminating research findings. Given the importance attached to this issue, these agencies should have the highest possible priority for resources to carry on the work. Prospects for coordinating the individual country's legislation to control monopolistic practices, and for extending such legislation to international operations, must also be given a very high priority due to the almost complete lack of current controls.

A major problem concerns the tendency to discuss transnationals' operations as if the organisations were instruments of social change instead of corporate business forms that respond to stimuli largely connected with profits. While it is acknowledged that these corporations have important social effects due to the magnitude and nature of their activities, there is no reason for believing that these institutions should respond primarily to nonpecuniary motivations. In this respect, the policy failure involves a lack of appropriate measures to encourage TNCs to follow socially advantageous courses of action. For example, if transnationals do not transfer the appropriate type of technology to suit the industrialisation plans of LDCs it is because financial incentives are lacking. The possibility of designing such financial stimuli to encourage transnationals to follow 'socially beneficial' courses of action deserves more attention than it has been given in the past.

A major problem in the design of current policy measures *vis-à-vis* transnationals concerns actions which should be prohibited or subject to some degree of policy control. As Forsyth has indicated, this issue poses special problems since some recently enacted legislation is not producing intended effects, while some results may actually be running counter to the trade and industrialisation objectives of the countries enacting such measures. As such, a cautious approach must be advised in this area. For policy formulation, the proposals of the Club of Rome provide a useful basis for discussion since these measures recognise the need for further research as well as the differences between individual corporations. As a minimum, a code of conduct based on Galbraith's five 'danger zones', and prohibition of covert actions such as ITT pursued in Chile, would provide standards of operation that have few, if any, negative social consequences. Additions and qualifications to the code could be made as further research adds to our knowledge of TNC operations and their consequences.

# 6 Trade Relations with Socialist Countries

Andrzej Olechowski and Alexander Yeats*

In previous analyses of developing country trade relations, economists have generally focused attention on the exchange between LDCs and the developed market economy countries (DMECs). There are various reasons for this concentration of interest. Firstly, trade with the DMECs is of primary importance as these markets received 73 per cent of developing country exports in 1976 and supplied 68 per cent of imports. In contrast, the centrally planned countries (CPCs) accounted for only 4 per cent of LDC exports and 5 per cent of imports, figures which were well below corresponding ratios for LDC intra-trade. Thus, the fact that existing trade volumes are so small may be a major reason for the relative lack of attention devoted to this exchange.

Various statistical measures indicate that trade between developing and socialist countries has the potential to assume far greater proportions than suggested by existing trade flows. For example, the centrally planned countries of Europe (Albania, Bulgaria, Czechoslovakia, German Democratic Republic, Hungary, Poland, Romania and the Soviet Union) currently have a population about half that of the Organisation for Economic Cooperation and Development member states' total, while the figure is more than 30 per cent of the world total if the socialist countries of Asia (People's Republic of China, Mongolia, Democratic People's Republic of Korea, and Democratic Republic of Vietnam) are included. The European Socialist countries have a gross national product equivalent to about one quarter of the OECD total, with the proportion rising to about one third if the Asian socialist nations are included. Thus, in terms of these measures of potential market size, the socialist countries could assume far greater importance than existing trade flows indicate. Since there is some

---

* Dr Olechowski is an economist with the Foreign Trade Research Institute, Warsaw, Poland.

indication the LDCs may be straining industrial country absorptive capacities in certain sectors, the role of the socialist countries as new outlets may be of crucial importance in the 1980s.

## COMPARATIVE ANALYSIS OF SOCIALIST COUNTRY TRADE

Given the potential importance of socialist countries in the future trade relations of developing countries, an analysis of their current trade with LDCs could serve as a basis for assessing prospects for the expansion of this exchange. Aside from an examination of the level, share, and structure of trade, such an analysis should also examine the performance of individual socialist states to determine if important differences exist in trade with developing countries.

*The level and share of imports from LDCs*
For an initial evaluation of the level of imports from developing countries, the CPCs' population and gross domestic product were used as measures of potential market size. Table 6.1 relates actual 1975 imports from LDCs to each of these measures, both in total and for individual socialist countries. For comparison, similar tabulations have been made for the OECD countries. In addition, the percentage of socialist and OECD imports supplied by developing countries is also shown.

For the socialist countries as a group, the LDC market share of 10·9 per cent is 17 points below the corresponding share in OECD markets.[1] Furthermore, the inferior performance of the socialist states extends to all individual countries with Bulgaria having only 4·7 per cent of total imports from LDCs while this proportion reaches a high in the USSR at 17 per cent. In contrast, Japan has the highest LDC imports share among the OECD nations (53 per cent), although the United States receives 40 per cent of its imports from developing countries.

Relative to either population or gross national product the socialist country performance is distinctly inferior to that of the OECD nations. Overall, the former averaged $26 per capita in imports from LDCs in 1975 as opposed to more than $200 for the market economy countries. In addition, imports from developing countries constituted only about 1 per cent of the socialist states' gross national product while the corresponding figure for the OECD nations was four times higher. Thus, in terms of either measure of market size, the performance of the socialist countries, individually or as a group, is distinctly inferior to the market economy countries.[2]

TABLE 6.1 Comparative Analysis of LDC Export Performance in Socialist and Developed Market Economy Countries

| Importing country | 1975 Imports ($million) | | | LDC Imports | | Percentage change in LDC imports under alternative market criteria[a] | | |
|---|---|---|---|---|---|---|---|---|
| | LDCs | Total | LDC Share | Per capita | Share of GNP | Market share | Population | GNP |
| Socialist countries of Europe of which: | 9361 | 86178 | 10·9 | 26 | ·010 | 150 | 680 | 300 |
| Bulgaria | 255 | 5407 | 4·7 | 29 | ·014 | 480 | 590 | 170 |
| Czechoslovakia | 562 | 9105 | 6·2 | 31 | ·010 | 340 | 560 | 280 |
| German Democratic Republic[b] | 599 | 9646 | 6·2 | 36 | ·008 | 340 | 470 | 370 |
| Hungary | 545 | 7177 | 7·6 | 52 | ·021 | 260 | 290 | 90 |
| Poland | 613 | 12536 | 4·9 | 18 | ·006 | 460 | 1010 | 540 |
| Romania | 654 | 5339 | 12·2 | 31 | ·024 | 120 | 550 | 70 |
| Soviet Union | 6133 | 36968 | 16·6 | 24 | ·009 | 70 | 740 | 330 |
| All OECD countries of which: | 160205 | 584725 | 27·4 | 202 | ·039 | — | — | — |
| France | 14399 | 53606 | 26·9 | 273 | ·040 | 0 | −30 | 0 |
| German Federal Republic | 15062 | 74208 | 20·2 | 244 | ·035 | 30 | −20 | 10 |
| Italy | 11353 | 37928 | 29·9 | 203 | ·066 | −10 | 0 | −40 |
| Japan | 30841 | 57865 | 53·3 | 144 | ·020 | −50 | 40 | 90 |
| United Kingdom | 12826 | 53188 | 24·1 | 229 | ·056 | 10 | −10 | −30 |
| United States | 39045 | 96904 | 40·3 | 183 | ·026 | −30 | 10 | 50 |

a Percentage change in LDC imports if the country in question brought its LDC market share, imports per capita, or import–GNP ratio up to the OECD average. Figures rounded to the nearest 10 per cent.
b Trade figures for the German Democratic Republic are for 1974.

An important question concerns the magnitude of the trade expansion which would occur if the socialist nations brought their developing country imports up to the OECD average for these market size parameters. For example, if the socialist countries increased their import shares to the OECD average (from 10·9 to 27·4 per cent), developing country exports would increase by 150 per cent, a rise of about $14 billion. On a relative basis, the Bulgarian increase would be largest (480 per cent) with Polish imports increasing by 450 per cent. However, these increases refer solely to equalisation of import *shares* with those already achieved in the West. Considerably larger trade expansion projections result from use of the GNP and population measures of market size. If the CPCs were to equal the developed market economy country average for these ratios it would imply a trade expansion of between 300 and almost 700 per cent.

While there is variation between the trade projections depending on the statistical measures employed as guides to market size, each of the indices used suggests that the potential expansion of East–South trade is huge. Put in perspective, it should be noted that if the centrally planned countries brought their import–GNP trade ratios up to the OECD average this would imply a LDC trade gain only slightly less than current imports of France and the Federal Republic of Germany from developing countries.[3]

*The structure of developing country trade*
Aside from questions relating to aggregate trade levels or shares, economists have devoted increased attention to the structure of developing country exports. Specifically, efforts have been made to shift from exports of primary products to semi-finished or fabricated goods. The potential benefits of such a change include: improved terms-of-trade for processed products, greater price and earnings stabilisation, and the employment creation effects of domestic processing. Thus, even though the level and overall share of the socialist country trade with LDCs is inferior to that of the OECD nations, the detrimental effects may be offset if a larger proportion of imports are composed of processed goods.

Table 6.2 compares the structure of CPC imports from non-petroleum-exporting developing countries with the developed market economy countries' trade. Shown here are primary product and manufactures imports as well as import values for some of the more important component products. Since the overall values of LDC trade with the socialist and market economy countries are so different, the percentage of imports falling in each product category are shown. In this

TABLE 6.2 Comparison of the Structure of Eastern European and Developed Market Economy Imports from Developing Countries in 1975 (all values in $ billion)

| Product group | CPCs of Eastern Europe | | Developed market economies | |
|---|---|---|---|---|
| | Value | Per cent | Value | Per cent |
| *All items* | 7·65 | 100·0 | 63·00 | 100·0 |
| *Primary products* of which: | 6·40 | 83·7 | 41·00 | 65·1 |
| Foods | 4·44 | 58·0 | 19·60 | 31·1 |
| Raw materials | 1·26 | 16·5 | 4·01 | 6·4 |
| Ores and minerals | 0·58 | 7·6 | 4·89 | 7·8 |
| Fuels | 0·12 | 1·6 | 12·50 | 19·8 |
| *Manufactures* of which: | 1·25 | 16·3 | 22·00 | 34·9 |
| Nonferrous metals | 0·13 | 1·7 | 3·28 | 5·2 |
| Iron and steel | 0·05 | 0·6 | 0·59 | 0·9 |
| Chemicals | 0·16 | 2·1 | 1·45 | 2·3 |
| Wood and paper | — | 0·0 | 0·52 | 0·8 |
| Other semi- manufactures | 0·12 | 1·6 | 1·68 | 2·7 |
| Transport, machinery and appliances | 0·05 | 0·6 | 4·90 | 7·8 |
| Textiles | 0·48 | 6·3 | 1·98 | 3·2 |
| Clothing | 0·13 | 1·7 | 4·49 | 7·2 |
| Other consumer goods | 0·13 | 1·7 | 3·01 | 4·8 |

*Note*: Trade values exclude shipments from petroleum-exporting developing countries.

*Source*: Adapted from General Agreement on Tariffs and Trade, *Networks of World Trade by Areas and Commodity Classes*, Geneva, 1978.

way, the distribution of CPC and DMEC imports from developing countries can be compared directly.

While the previous analysis demonstrated that the level and aggregate share of centrally planned country imports was inferior to that of the DMECs, Table 6.2 shows that the CPCs also have an inferior import structure. For example, 84 per cent of CPC imports from non-petroleum-exporting developing countries were composed of primary products with the foods component accounting for 58 per cent of the total. In contrast, primary products constitute 65 per cent of total DMEC imports with the food share being almost 30 points below that of the socialist countries. However, this lower food percentage is undoubtedly influenced by high support prices and other trade barriers industrial nations have erected around their agricultural sectors. As

Chapter 4 indicated, these restraints frequently have a serious retardation effect on developing country trade.

With regard to manufactures, Table 6.2 shows that these items
constitute 35 per cent of the DMECs' imports whereas their share is only
16 per cent in socialist country trade. Analysis of the major group
components' shares also shows that the DMECs import a higher
percentage of each individual item with the exception of textiles. Textiles
constitute 6·3 per cent of the socialist states' imports, but only 3·2 per
cent for the developed market economy countries. Aside from this
reversal, however, DMEC trade *structures* must also (in addition to
levels and shares) be considered more in harmony with the LDCs' trade
and development objectives.

A related concern centres on the composition of goods LDCs
exchange for their exports. To investigate this question, Table 6.3

TABLE 6.3 Comparison of the Structure of Eastern European and Developed
Market Economy Exports to Developing Countries in 1975 (values in $billion)

| Product group | Eastern Europe | | Developed market economies | |
|---|---|---|---|---|
| | Value | Per cent | Value | Per cent |
| *All items* | 8·65 | 100·0 | 79·45 | 100·0 |
| *Primary products* of which: | 3·65 | 42·2 | 14·60 | 18·4 |
|    Foods | 2·10 | 24·3 | 10·56 | 13·3 |
|    Raw materials | 0·44 | 5·1 | 1·95 | 2·5 |
|    Ores and minerals | 0·05 | 0·6 | 0·75 | 0·9 |
|    Fuels | 1·06 | 12·2 | 1·34 | 1·7 |
| *Manufactures* of which: | 5·00 | 57·8 | 64·85 | 81·6 |
|    Nonferrous metals | 0·08 | 0·9 | 1·02 | 1·3 |
|    Iron and steel | 0·39 | 4·5 | 6·00 | 7·6 |
|    Chemicals | 0·56 | 6·5 | 10·46 | 13·2 |
|    Wood and paper | 0·20 | 2·3 | 1·17 | 1·5 |
|    Other semi-manufactures | 0·28 | 3·2 | 2·81 | 3·5 |
|    Transport, machinery and appliances | 2·40 | 27·7 | 38·32 | 48·1 |
|    Textiles | 0·47 | 5·4 | 2·62 | 3·3 |
|    Clothing | 0·12 | 1·5 | 0·54 | 0·7 |
|    Other consumer goods | 0·50 | 5·8 | 1·91 | 2·4 |

*Note*: Trade values exclude shipments to the petroleum-exporting developing countries.

*Source*: Adapted from General Agreement on Tariffs and Trade, *Networks of World
Trade by Areas and Commodity Classes*, Geneva, 1978.

examines the distribution of socialist and DMEC exports to developing countries. These statistics also show marked differences between the trade structures of the two groups. For example, 42 per cent of the CPC exports are primary products while the corresponding figure is 18 per cent for the market economy countries. In manufactures, the largest difference occurs for the transport and machinery component. These items comprise 48 per cent of LDC imports from the developed market economy countries and only 28 per cent for the socialist states. Thus, Tables 6.2 and 6.3 point to a basic difference in DMEC and CPC trade relations with developing countries. While the former is increasingly geared to a two-way exchange of manufactures, trade between socialist and developing countries is more concerned with a two-way flow of raw materials and commodities.

The causes of these trade differences should be noted as well as their implications for future commercial relations. A case can be made that the level, share or structure of socialist imports from LDCs are below par due to a lack of traditional contacts, inappropriate institutional arrangements, or fewer types of goods that could be beneficially exchanged. As such, developing countries are to some extent forced to turn to the DMECs to supply the types of capital equipment needed for development planning and industrialisation, or to serve as outlets for growing exports of manufactures. However, in the 1980s and beyond, centrally planned countries should be producing increasing quantities of capital goods for domestic and foreign consumption. Making these products available to developing countries could do much to stimulate trade. In addition, a variety of internal factors should contribute to a higher CPC import demand for raw materials and certain types (labour-intensive) of manufactures. As will be discussed in a later section, these basic internal forces are working in favour of increased East–South trade in the 1980s.

*Trade concentration and stability*
Before leaving the comparative analysis of East–West markets, there are two additional performance criteria (concentration and stability) that should also be examined. Specifically, analysis of international trade statistics bears out the fact that CPC trade relations with developing countries are relatively more concentrated than those of their developed market economy counterparts. For example, in 1974 the centrally planned countries maintained trade relations with almost all developing countries, yet in only a few cases did the value of this exchange exceed $10 million. Furthermore, in only 13 cases: Algeria, Argentina, Brazil, Cuba

(a COMECON member), Egypt, India, Iran, Malaysia, Morocco, Nigeria, Peru, Singapore, and Syria, did developing country exports exceed $100 million. Of the major suppliers (excluding Cuba), Egypt and India were of primary importance with exports of over $500 million.

The relative concentration of CPC trade with developing countries can be illustrated through use of the Hirschman Geographic Concentration Index. This index $(G_j)$ is defined as,

$$G_j = \left[ \sum_i x_{ij} / X_j \right]^{\frac{1}{2}} \qquad (6\text{--}1)$$

where $x_{ij}$ is the value of country $j$'s imports (or exports) from country $i$, while $X_j$ is the total value of imports. The index ranges between 0 and 1 with the higher values indicating more concentrated trade structures. As shown in Table 6.4, the Hirschman indicates that the centrally planned countries are more concentrated in both imports and exports than the major developed market economy countries. For example, the USSR has

TABLE 6.4 The Level and Concentration of Centrally Planned and Developed Market Economy Country Trade Relations with Developing Countries

| Importer | 1975 Value of LDC trade | | LDC Trade per capita | | Hirschman Concentration Index[a] | |
|---|---|---|---|---|---|---|
| | Imports | Exports | Imports | Exports | Imports | Exports |
| *Centrally planned* | | | | | | |
| Bulgaria | 255 | 486 | 29 | 55 | ·387 | ·366 |
| Czechoslovakia | 562 | 750 | 31 | 41 | ·400 | ·376 |
| German Dem. Rep.[b] | 599 | 395 | 36 | 24 | ·328 | ·332 |
| Hungary | 545 | 427 | 52 | 41 | ·433 | ·421 |
| Poland | 613 | 806 | 18 | 24 | ·368 | ·310 |
| Romania | 654 | 967 | 31 | 46 | ·360 | ·320 |
| USSR | 6133 | 4272 | 24 | 17 | ·454 | ·412 |
| *Developed market economy* | | | | | | |
| France | 14339 | 12939 | 273 | 246 | ·303 | ·299 |
| German Fed. Rep. | 15062 | 15331 | 244 | 246 | ·328 | ·332 |
| Japan | 30841 | 27458 | 144 | 128 | ·353 | ·259 |
| United Kingdom | 12826 | 11199 | 229 | 199 | ·316 | ·315 |
| United States | 39045 | 37998 | 183 | 178 | ·264 | ·284 |

[a] Computed from developing country trade data only.
[b] 1974 trade data.

*Note*: Based on trade data for the latest year available in United Nations *Yearbook of International Trade Statistics, 1976* (New York: United Nations, 1977).

the highest geographic import concentration index among the countries listed (0·454), while ratios of 0·4 or more are also recorded by Czechoslovakia and Hungary. In contrast, the indices for the DMECs are consistently lower with the Hirschman taking a value of 0·264 for the United States. A similar picture emerges on the export side as generally higher index values show that CPCs' trade with developing countries is relatively more concentrated than that of the developed market economy countries.

There are several reasons which suggest trade relations between LDCs and the centrally planned countries should be more stable than South–North trade. The fact that CPC import demand is 'planned' is important since the trading partners have predetermined targets to work with. However, the inflexibility associated with planning can lead to revenue instability. Once domestic production is established, the level of import demand becomes a fixed residual which is rigid in spite of fluctuating world prices. In other words, importation of fixed quantities, irrespective of price changes, can lead to revenue instability.

The fact that the centrally planned countries' imports may be less price responsive than those of the DMECs is one reason why the value of their imports from developing countries was more unstable over 1961–75.[4] Another factor was the concentration in food imports (39 per cent of the LDC total as opposed to 27 per cent for DMECs). Since these commodities' production functions are often unstable due to changes in natural factors such as weather, this is an additional element leading to greater overall instability of CPC imports. Low efficiency in CPC agricultural production is another factor causing unstable import demand. In the 1970s, domestic production shortfalls (particularly for grains) led the centrally planned countries to enter world markets with sizeable and irregular purchases.

## FUTURE EAST–SOUTH TRADE

While the preceding analysis examined the level, structure, and stability of CPC–LDC trade in the past, this chapter is primarily concerned with the evolution of this exchange in the future. In attempting such an assessment, it is recognised that an important factor influencing such relations will be the economic situation in the centrally planned countries during the 1980s. Concerning this question, we have assumed that internal pressures on the CPC economies will be more of a problem in several areas than in the past. A growing problem will be the coupling of the traditional capital shortage with growing labour and raw material scarcities (particularly in the area of energy).

The result of these material shortages should be increased pressure to fill the gaps through trade (particularly with raw material-producing developing countries), and to work toward more efficient use of productive factors. This attempt to increase efficiency should move in two directions:

—Since CPC production techniques employ relatively more raw materials than the western nations, a major effort will be made to improve the efficiency of operations. For example, Macieja (1978) shows that Poland used 0·23 tons of steel per $1000 of GNP while the corresponding ratio for the UK and Italy was 0·12, Germany 0·09, and France 0·07. Similarly, in the case of electric power, Poland used 2165 kWh per $1000 of GNP, the UK 1622 kWh, Italy 1190 kWh, Germany 918 kWh, and France 857 kWh. Similar adverse ratios also exist for other CPC countries and for other important raw material inputs. Growing shortages of these basic raw materials will increase pressure for improving the efficiency of their use and to trade for these items.

—It is also anticipated that an attempt will be made to increase labour efficiency (due to increased bottlenecks associated with skilled labour shortages) by shifting employment from low-skilled labour-intensive production processes and filling this demand through imports. Due to the nature of the goods involved, much of this new import demand will fall on the developing countries. (This line of reasoning is developed further in Chapter 7.)

*The balance of payments constraint*

While growing shortages of raw materials, and increased efforts to redirect domestic production away from labour-intensive industries, will be positive factors working in favour of increased developing country trade, a major constraint to this exchange is likely to be the adverse balance of payments position of the centrally planned countries. For example, the net CPC hard currency debt to the West is provisionally estimated by the United States government (January 1979) to be $55 billion at the end of 1978, up from $6·5 billion in 1970. Furthermore, yearly deficits should continue to run at least through 1985, although some observers feel they will last longer.

Two factors appear to be working against rapid improvement in the CPCs' balance of payments position which, in turn, works against expanded developing country trade. Firstly, the prolonged recession in Western markets has kept demand for socialist country tradeables at lower than potential levels. This recession may have had a pronounced effect on CPC exports of some investment (SITC 7) goods. While these items accounted for approximately 40 per cent of intra-trade, they only totalled about 9 per cent of exports to DMECs in 1975. However, it must be acknowledged that lower quality standards could be a factor accounting for the smaller proportion of SITC 7 items shipped to the West.

Without doubt, a factor working against improvement in the CPCs' balance of payments problems, and a potential expansion of trade with developing countries, is the discretionary nature of many Western country trade barriers. For example, in the United States only Romania, Poland and Hungary have been afforded MFN tariff status. As such, the import duties paid by other socialist countries may be twice the most-favoured-nation rate. This tariff differential may be insurmountable for products in which *duty free* entry is afforded developing countries under the generalised system of preferences, or among developed countries which have formed customs unions like the European Community. Another set of particularly onerous trade barriers facing the CPCs is the European Community's system of variable levies which cover a wide variety of processed and primary agricultural products. Recent studies by Sampson and Yeats (1976; 1977) show that these special import charges may have *ad valorem* equivalents of 50 to 100 per cent or more and have a strong restrictive effect on imports. Separate tabulations also show that levies are applied with a particularly high frequency to products which are of current and potential export importance to centrally planned countries.

Table 6.5 illustrates the differential incidence of nontariff trade barriers on centrally planned country exports to the EEC and the United States through the use of a trade-weighted index of NTB application. The index ($N_j$) is defined as,

$$N_j = \sum_i \frac{B_i}{T_i} \cdot \frac{m_i}{M} \qquad (6-2)$$

where $B_i$ is the number of four-digit BTNs in which at least one tariff line is subject to an NTB, $T_i$ is the total number of four-digit BTNs in product group $i$, $m_i$ is the total value of $i$'s imports, and $M$ is the total value of imports. As shown, the United States applies nontariff barriers to centrally planned country goods with twice the frequency as that for other DMEC shipments, while the CPC index value is 6 points higher in

TABLE 6.5 Analysis of the Incidence of Nontariff Trade Barriers on Exports of
Manufactures to the EEC and US

| Type of restraint | EEC Imports from | | | US Imports from | | |
|---|---|---|---|---|---|---|
| | Developed countries | LDCs | Centrally planned countries | Developed countries | LDCs | Centrally planned countries |
| Quotas | ·063 | ·095 | ·148 | ·014 | ·031 | ·009 |
| Licensing | ·045 | ·149 | ·007 | — | — | — |
| Price regulating NTBs[1] | ·007 | ·010 | ·009 | ·051 | ·037 | ·057 |
| Export restraints | ·028 | ·078 | ·051 | ·031 | ·171 | ·151 |
| Total of above | ·195 | ·339 | ·258 | ·114 | ·229 | ·235 |

[1] Includes American selling price valuation system, US trigger prices, and the EEC basic
steel price system.

the European Community. The table also shows that CPC imports are
more often subject to 'hard core' restrictions like quotas, while imports
from other countries encounter 'softer' restraints like licensing.

*Solutions to the currency constraint*
While liberalisation of trade barriers would make a positive contribution to improving the trade balance, the question remains as to what
the CPCs themselves can do to facilitate the expansion of trade with
developing countries. The most promising areas for such action include
the adoption of new international payments mechanisms that bypass
many existing currency limitations, agreement on joint ventures, or
negotiation of barter arrangements that involve payments in goods and
services instead of convertible currency.

    Concerning the adoption of new payment facilities, UNCTAD has
made several important initiatives to determine if such a system could be
established, while the report of an UNCTAD (16 December 1977) panel
of experts concluded that

> At this stage no final recommendation can be made concerning any
> single method of introducing elements of multilateralism in the
> existing systems of payments between socialist countries of eastern
> Europe and the developing countries. At the same time, in order to
> make such a system more flexible, the various multilateral elements
> and forms of payment should be used by mutual consent. The use of a
> combination of categories of payments, combining payments in

clearing with payments in convertible currencies, could be further explored.

The report also concluded that expanding payments in transferable roubles may be a promising avenue for facilitating trade between centrally planned and developing countries.

Recognising that creation of an effective international payments mechanism will require time to evolve into arrangements that meet the needs of trading partners, efforts have been made to derive more immediate CPC–LDC trade facilitation arrangements. In this area, spokesmen for both centrally planned and developing countries have advocated the adoption of compensation or other forms of buy-back agreements. One especially promising variation of this plan is for the CPCs to export domestically produced capital equipment and services to developing countries and extend future credits against the purchase of processed goods. Once the factories or other productive enterprises are established, developing country exports of goods and services can be used to settle the initial debt associated with the capital goods transfers. Such a system could bypass the payments constraint, provide the CPCs with labour- or resource-intensive goods, and also supply developing countries with capital equipment and guaranteed outlets for processed products. As such, this arrangement appears to have the potential to make a contribution to the trade and development objectives of developing countries in the 1980s.

*An agenda for the 1980s*
As indicated, the need to expand trade relations between developing and centrally planned countries is likely to assume greater importance during the 1980s. In part, increased trade will be necessitated by the growing saturation and rising protectionist pressures in Western markets, coupled with increasing production capacity in developing countries. These developments place a high priority on the search for new markets for LDC exports. Since the centrally planned countries are operating well below standards set by the DMECs, they offer considerable potential as such outlets. We have also noted that economic forces are operating within the centrally planned countries, such as increased scarcity of raw materials and an attempt to restructure industry away from labour-intensive production, which would make expanded trade contacts with LDCs of considerable benefit to the socialist countries.

While constraints such as the balance of payments problem act as limiting factors, a major stimulus to increased trade will have to come from the centrally planned countries themselves. For example, Pryor (1966) shows that trade barriers of the socialist countries of Europe against tropical foodstuffs exported by developing countries may be 100 to 200 per cent (or more) higher than in the DMECs. It has also been demonstrated that CPC–LDC trade relations are more heavily skewed in favour of 'politically allied' developing countries. Removal of trade barriers facing LDC exports, as well as a broadened base of trade contacts, must form the cornerstone of an expanded CPC trade policy.

While the details will have to be negotiated, perhaps the single most important contribution that could be made is the establishment of an international agenda or timetable for bringing the socialist countries' import performance up to internationally acceptable standards. There are several advantages to this approach: negotiated increases in imports from developing countries (at least in proportions bringing trade up to Western standards) could provide important new outlets for developing country exports in the 1980s. However, these negotiations must recognise that there are a variety of institutional constraints which work against this exchange. Efforts must be made in parallel to remove these barriers.

# 7 The Future Composition of Developing Country Exports

A factor leading to recent demands for increased protection in industrial markets is that developing countries achieved substantial export capacities in a number of industrial sectors over a remarkably short period of time, and this increase was largely unanticipated in the developed market economy countries. A further difficulty resulted from the fact that this increased capacity in sectors such as steel, shipbuilding, and electronics came 'on stream' at a time when these industries were experiencing a prolonged cyclical downturn which left demand very depressed relative to historical levels. Lack of effective demand, coupled with an inflow of goods from new foreign competitors, contributed to reduced profits and employment in the developed countries. This led to increased pressure for new protectionist measures by representatives of both labour and management, who faced the loss of domestic employment or declining profits.

To a large degree, these LDC inroads should not have been unanticipated. Developing countries have long demonstrated an ability to compete on equal terms in such sectors as shoes, textiles, and clothing, and have made important inroads into Western markets for these products over the last two decades. Developing countries have also made substantial progress in efforts to shift from the export of some primary goods such as leather, oilseeds, cocoa and wood to semifinished or processed forms of these products. In these and other goods, LDC production was stimulated by the availability of raw material inputs, ample supplies of low-cost labour, or government-sponsored incentives to encourage processing of raw materials. These latter measures ranged from export taxes on primary products to subsidies or other tax and financial incentives for the export of processed goods. Logistical considerations also have played a role in favouring production of some processed goods in developing countries.

If the current problems of market disruptions, labour redundancies and depressed manufacturing profitability are not to be repeated in the 1980s, policy-makers in both developed and developing countries will need information on products whose characteristics make them likely candidates for increased production and export by LDCs. Given such information, various measures could be initiated to facilitate the transition of productive resources to industries where the developed countries retain a comparative advantage. These adjustment assistance measures encompass policies such as educational programmes for retraining labour, fiscal incentives to stimulate private investment, or even direct government subsidisation of new industries along with the development of required infrastructure.

Given the need for information concerning the future composition of LDC trade, this chapter examines the potential use of labour intensity and the 'income composition' of exports as such a guide. By way of introduction, the theoretical underpinnings of the factor-proportions model are discussed in an attempt to clarify the basis for use of labour intensity as a predictor of the composition of trade flows. The focus then shifts to an empirical evaluation of the developing countries' export performance in labour-intensive manufactures as opposed to other types of products. Given this evaluation of the reliability of labour intensity in the past as a guide to the changing composition of LDC exports, its implications for the future are examined. Using an alternative procedure, an attempt is also made to identify the capital goods sectors which are likely to come under competitive pressure from the advanced developing countries in the 1980s.

## DETERMINANTS OF THE STRUCTURE OF TRADE

Traditional factor-proportions explanations of the determinants of trade rest on the assumption that countries with an abundance of certain production inputs will export goods which are intensive in these factors and import goods intensive in inputs which are relatively scarce. Given a two-commodity, two-factor, two-country world with full employment and perfect competition in domestic and international markets, factor-proportions explanations of trade patterns lead to definite conclusions. A poor country with a relative surplus of labour will export the labour-intensive good, while the rich country with an abundance of capital will export the good which is capital-intensive in production. While there are admittedly problems in attempting to generalise to a multi-product, multi-country world, where the assumptions of perfect competition or full employment are not operational, many economists still hold that factor proportions provide at least a partial explanation of international trading patterns. Therefore, determination of the relative proportions of labour and capital required for the manufacture of goods could provide a rough indication as to whether an item was more suitable for production in rich or poor countries.

Plausible though it may sound, the factor-proportions theory has come under considerable criticism on a number of grounds relating to its restrictive assumptions of perfect competition, full employment and constant returns to scale, or its inability to explain the occurrence of intra-industry trade due to its assumption of homogeneous goods. As a result of these deficiencies, several new explanations for the level and composition of international trade have been advanced.

*Trade and income levels*
One such alternative theory suggests that product differentiation and demand factors are key determinants of trading patterns. This explanation, as expounded by Dreze (1960) and Linder (1961), maintains that countries at roughly the same level of income will tend to trade more heavily with each other, exchanging one sort of differentiated product for another. Dreze also argued that economies of scale and barriers to trade across national borders will cause economically large countries to specialise in nationally differentiated goods when it comes to trade, while small countries will specialise in internationally standardised goods. This is related to Linder's argument that a country will tend to produce goods designed for tastes in the home market because of the need for close contact between producers and consumers. Thus, goods will be exported if there is a foreign demand for them. Since tastes are more likely to be similar in countries with similar per capita incomes, the direction and composition of trade will be influenced by this variable.

A third explanation of trade patterns has come to be known as the 'availability theory' of trade. This suggests that a country tends to import products that are unavailable at home: availability is determined by natural resources, technological progress and product differentiation. Technological progress as a trade-creating factor is examined by Posner (1961) who suggests that product innovation can create a temporary export monopoly which is gradually reduced by imitation, expiration of patents, or further product change. Hufbauer (1966) concluded that trade in synthetic materials can be explained by this model, although it cannot be clearly distinguished from explanations which centre on economies of scale in production. However, there seems to be general agreement that the 'availability theory' accounts for the influence of technology on trade flows, but it cannot account for the general increase in trade over the last two decades, particularly in some manufactured goods like motor vehicles, iron and steel, clothing, or footwear where no dramatic innovations have been made.

### Factor-intensity reversals

Aside from the implications of these alternative trade theories, factor-proportions has been called into question by empirical investigations which run counter to what theory predicts. For example, the United States employs more capital per worker than other countries, yet empirical studies show that it exports many labour-intensive goods and imports capital-intensive products. However, it is not clear to what extent these 'factor-intensity reversals' are the result of trade control measures such as tariffs, nontariff restraints, subsidies and other commercial policy devices, or a failure to properly assess the influence of human capital or natural resources on production.[1]

The conclusions which emerge from these alternative models and empirical studies is that no *one* theoretical approach can fully account for differences in the composition and level of trade flows. As such, if theory is to provide a comprehensive guide to changes in LDC exports, it must incorporate the postulates of these alternative models within a systematic framework. However, the objectives of this chapter are less ambitious than a reformulation of theory. While the potential limitations of factor-proportions are acknowledged, the present goal is to assess the predictive power of this theory in practice with particular attention devoted to the identification of product groups where labour intensity provides a reliable guide to LDC export performance as opposed to products where some alternative explanation is needed.


## TRADE IN LABOUR-INTENSIVE PRODUCTS

The problem of identifying labour-intensive products has been facilitated by drawing on the work of Hal Lary (1968) for the United States National Bureau of Economic Research. Lary's analysis employed the criterion of value added per employee, both in the United States and other countries, for identification of products which are capital- or labour-intensive. The general rule followed was to classify labour-intensive products as those which met two conditions: that value added per employee did not exceed the national average for all manufacturing by more than 10 per cent,[2] and that imports by developed countries from LDCs totalled at least $100 thousand at the three-digit level of the Standard International Trade Classification system in 1965. According to the NBER reasoning, this approach excluded the most clearly capital-intensive products while applying the test of the market (as reflected in imports) to items at or near the overall national average. The import value criterion was therefore added in recognition that value added per employee is not an infallible guide to factor intensity.

Since the National Bureau study employed 1965 trade data as a reference point, a considerable interval has elapsed in which the LDCs' export performance in labour-intensive products could be contrasted with that for other goods. Table 7.1 presents such a summary comparison for the decade 1965–75. Shown here are values of OECD member country imports, both in total (excluding fuels) and at the one-digit SITC level, while a separate breakdown shows imports from developing countries. To assist in comparing the LDCs' export perfor-mance in labour-intensive with other products, their import shares for each group are given for 1965 and 1975 along with export growth rates.

The impression which emerges from Table 7.1 is that developing countries' performance for labour-intensive products was clearly su-perior to that for other goods. Overall, the LDCs actually managed to increase their import share for labour-intensive exports by 4.4 per-centage points (from 7.8 to 12.2 per cent), while their trade shares for other products declined by almost 8 points over the decade.[3] Analysis of one-digit SITC data shows that the LDCs made their most impressive competitive gains in miscellaneous manufactures (SITC 8) where their market share for labour-intensive products increased by over 10 points. In crude materials, beverages and tobacco, and manufactured goods (SITC 6), the developing countries made positive market share gains for the labour-intensive components in spite of declining shares for other items. In the case of food and live animals (SITC 0), their important share for labour-intensive products fell by 1·6 percentage points, but this was at a lower rate than for other items in the group. All in all, the impression emerging from Table 7·1 is that labour intensity would have provided a very useful guide to products in which the LDCs made their best performance.[4]

*Comparative analysis of import markets*
Under the postulates of the factor-proportions model it could be concluded that exports of labour-intensive products should do relatively better the more capital rich is the importing country. Since the United

TABLE 7.1 Comparative Analysis of Organisation for Economic Cooperation and Development Member Country Imports of Labour-intensive and Other Products over the Period 1965 to 1975

| SITC | Description | Value of OECD Imports ($million) | | | | Growth Rate | LDCs' market share | | |
|---|---|---|---|---|---|---|---|---|---|
| | | 1965 | | 1975 | | | 1965 | 1975 | Change |
| | | LDCs | Total | LDCs | Total | | | | |
| | *All products excluding fuels* | | | | | | | | |
| | Labour-intensive products | 2571·3 | 33254·8 | 20674·7 | 169520·1 | 17·7 | 7·8 | 12·2 | 4·4 |
| | Other products | 17395·3 | 75210·6 | 42490·8 | 277528·8 | 14·0 | 23·1 | 15·3 | −7·8 |
| | Total | 19966·6 | 108465·4 | 63165·5 | 447048·9 | 15·2 | 18·4 | 14·1 | −4·3 |
| 0 | *Food and live animals* | | | | | | | | |
| | Labour-intensive products | 456·8 | 1864·0 | 1350·1 | 5886·0 | 12·2 | 24·5 | 22·9 | −1·6 |
| | Other products | 7299·9 | 18681·3 | 19216·8 | 59913·7 | 12·3 | 39·1 | 32·1 | −7·0 |
| | Total | 7756·7 | 20545·3 | 20566·9 | 65799·7 | 12·3 | 37·8 | 31·2 | −6·6 |
| 1 | *Beverages and tobacco* | | | | | | | | |
| | Labour-intensive products* | 5·9 | 38·4 | 39·0 | 196·2 | 17·8 | 15·4 | 19·8 | 4·4 |
| | Other products | 506·6 | 2137·2 | 1002·5 | 6562·2 | 11·9 | 23·7 | 15·3 | −8·4 |
| | Total | 512·5 | 2175·6 | 1041·5 | 6758·4 | 12·0 | 23·6 | 15·4 | −8·2 |
| 2 | *Crude materials* | | | | | | | | |
| | Labour-intensive products* | 188·0 | 1841·2 | 652·0 | 4170·9 | 8·5 | 10·2 | 15·6 | 5·4 |
| | Other products | 6408·1 | 17744·5 | 13454·5 | 47135·1 | 10·2 | 36·1 | 28·5 | −7·6 |
| | Total | 6596·1 | 19585·7 | 14106·5 | 51306·0 | 10·1 | 33·7 | 27·4 | −6·3 |
| 4 | *Animal and vegetable oils* | | | | | | | | |
| | Labour-intensive products | 29·6 | 139·1 | 54·1 | 210·6 | 4·4 | 21·2 | 25·7 | 4·5 |
| | Other products | 452·0 | 977·3 | 1471·5 | 3664·5 | 14·1 | 46·2 | 40·2 | −6·0 |
| | Total | 481·6 | 1116·4 | 1525·6 | 3875·1 | 13·2 | 43·1 | 39·4 | −3·7 |

| | | | | | | | | |
|---|---|---|---|---|---|---|---|---|
| **5 Chemicals** | | | | | | | | |
| Labour-intensive products** | 52·5 | 210·4 | 91·8 | 556·9 | 10·2 | 25·0 | 16·4 | −8·6 |
| Other products | 297·5 | 7154·3 | 1574·3 | 38001·1 | 18·2 | 4·2 | 4·1 | −0·1 |
| Total | 350·0 | 7364·7 | 1666·1 | 38558·0 | 18·0 | 4·8 | 4·3 | −0·5 |
| **6 Manufactured goods** | | | | | | | | |
| Labour-intensive products | 1072·6 | 10144·0 | 5456·4 | 45185·3 | 16·1 | 10·6 | 12·1 | 1·5 |
| Other products*** | 2239·9 | 15446·3 | 4502·7 | 49874·0 | 12·4 | 14·5 | 9·0 | −5·5 |
| Total | 3312·5 | 25590·3 | 9959·1 | 95059·3 | 14·0 | 12·9 | 10·5 | −2·4 |
| **7 Machinery and transport** | | | | | | | | |
| Labour-intensive products | 73·9 | 12380·1 | 3675·5 | 68919·8 | 18·7 | 0·6 | 5·3 | 4·7 |
| Other products | 116·0 | 11310·9 | 1213·2 | 67163·6 | 19·5 | 1·0 | 1·8 | 0·8 |
| Total | 189·9 | 23691·0 | 4888·7 | 136083·4 | 19·1 | 0·8 | 3·6 | 3·0 |
| **8 Miscellaneous manufactures** | | | | | | | | |
| Labour-intensive items | 692·0 | 6637·8 | 9355·8 | 44394·4 | 20·9 | 10·4 | 21·1 | 10·7 |
| Other products | 75·3 | 1758·6 | 55·3 | 5214·6 | 11·5 | 4·2 | 1·1 | −3·1 |
| Total | 767·3 | 8396·4 | 9411·1 | 49609·0 | 19·4 | 9·1 | 19·0 | 9·9 |

*   Labour-intensive products in the beverages and tobacco group fall in SITC 122.1 (cigars and cheroots), while those in crude materials include products classified in SITC 243.0 (shaped wood).
**  Items falling in SITC 551.0 (essential oils).
*** The overall developing country market performance for this group is dominated by non-ferrous metals (SITC 68). If these products were excluded, the developing countries' market share for non-labour-intensive products in SITC 6 would have fallen from 4·4 per cent in 1965 to 2·5 per cent in 1975.

TABLE 7.2  Condensed List of Manufactures Selected as Being Labour-intensive under Criteria Applied by the National Bureau of Economic Research and Selected Production and Trade Data for these Products (values in $ million)

| Product group and subgroup | Index of value added per employee* | 1965 Value of US imports | | Developing country market share | | | | | |
|---|---|---|---|---|---|---|---|---|---|
| | | Total | LDCs | US | | | Other developed countries | | |
| | | | | 1965 | 1975 | Change | 1965 | 1975 | Change |
| LABOUR-INTENSIVE MANUFACTURES, TOTAL | 75·0 | 5696·1 | 1010·4 | 17·7 | 31·0 | 13·3 | 5·7 | 8·9 | 3·2 |
| Textiles, clothing and accessories | 53·7 | 1052·8 | 286·6 | 27·2 | 65·4 | 38·2 | 9·9 | 19·3 | 9·9 |
| Yarn and thread | 60·0 | 63·6 | 5·9 | 9·3 | 16·6 | 7·4 | 2·0 | 9·6 | 7·6 |
| Cotton fabrics, woven | 61·2 | 134·5 | 61·5 | 45·7 | 60·6 | 14·9 | 19·0 | 20·1 | 1·1 |
| Other woven fabrics, excluding jute | 71·9 | 236·1 | 9·4 | 4·0 | 8·5 | 4·5 | 1·0 | 5·2 | 4·2 |
| Textile small wares | 63·2 | 67·2 | 13·0 | 19·3 | 43·3 | 24·0 | 6·3 | 9·8 | 3·5 |
| Carpets and floor coverings | 74·4 | 54·3 | 15·7 | 28·9 | 42·8 | 13·9 | 29·1 | 26·1 | -3·0 |
| Clothing and accessories | 47·4 | 497·1 | 181·1 | 36·4 | 80·1 | 43·8 | 15·0 | 30·4 | 15·4 |
| Other light manufactures, excluding food | 86·0 | 3281·5 | 269·8 | 8·2 | 24·8 | 16·6 | 1·5 | 5·0 | 3·5 |
| Footwear, rubber and plastic goods | 57·6 | 337·0 | 54·2 | 16·1 | 50·7 | 34·6 | 4·8 | 13·3 | 8·6 |
| Glassware, china and pottery | 81·4 | 111·7 | 3·2 | 2·9 | 14·3 | 11·4 | 0·6 | 2·4 | 1·8 |
| Furniture | 64·3 | 59·9 | 6·8 | 11·4 | 23·5 | 12·1 | 1·2 | 4·0 | 2·7 |
| Books and printed matter | 78·5 | 58·5 | 4·2 | 7·2 | 10·9 | 3·7 | 0·6 | 2·2 | 1·6 |
| Games, toys and sporting goods | 77·6 | 368·5 | 25·8 | 7·0 | 19·0 | 12·0 | 6·3 | 7·9 | 1·6 |
| Jewelry and silverware | 81·6 | 61·8 | 17·5 | 28·3 | 37·5 | 9·2 | 18·1 | 14·3 | -3·9 |
| Miscellaneous manufactures | 79·3 | 242·5 | 90·7 | 37·4 | 46·2 | 8·8 | 7·8 | 9·3 | 1·6 |
| Optical goods, watches and instruments | 92·9 | 200·9 | 3·2 | 1·5 | 18·1 | 16·5 | 0·8 | 4·6 | 3·8 |
| Cutlery, hardware and metal products | 91·3 | 340·4 | 14·2 | 4·2 | 11·7 | 7·6 | 0·8 | 3·2 | 2·4 |
| Electrical apparatus | 91·5 | 703·5 | 46·1 | 6·6 | 40·5 | 33·9 | 0·7 | 4·8 | 4·0 |
| Non-electrical machinery | 102·0 | 796·8 | 3·9 | 0·5 | 6·1 | 5·6 | 0·1 | 1·4 | 1·2 |

| | | | | | | | | | |
|---|---|---|---|---|---|---|---|---|---|
| Labour-intensive food manufactures | 89·7 | 268·3 | 112·4 | 41·9 | 44·3 | 2·4 | 21·4 | 20·2 | −1·2 |
| Fish and fish products | 95·5 | 124·5 | 44·6 | 35·8 | 31·9 | −3·9 | 27·4 | 27·6 | 0·2 |
| Fruits and vegetables | 90·5 | 117·3 | 65·2 | 55·6 | 58·9 | 3·3 | 19·8 | 21·8 | 2·0 |
| Misc. food products and cigars | 87·8 | 26·5 | 2·6 | 9·8 | 27·2 | 17·4 | 6·3 | 7·4 | 1·1 |
| Labour-intensive industrial materials | 66·4 | 1093·5 | 341·6 | 31·2 | 32·5 | 1·3 | 11·2 | 13·4 | 2·2 |
| Jute products and other coarse fibres | 58·5 | 238·1 | 194·6 | 81·7 | 79·5 | −2·3 | 53·4 | 41·8 | −11·6 |
| Leather and dressed fur skins | 80·6 | 78·7 | 20·5 | 26·0 | 45·1 | 19·1 | 14·4 | 17·6 | 3·2 |
| Lumber, plywood and wood products | 58·3 | 648·8 | 115·8 | 17·9 | 27·6 | 9·7 | 10·1 | 17·1 | 7·0 |
| Building materials of clay or stone | 83·8 | 127·9 | 10·7 | 8·4 | 11·2 | 2·9 | 0·3 | 1·7 | 1·4 |

* The index's value varies *inversely* with the labour intensity of each product group. If the index is over 100, this suggests that the group employs fewer workers per dollar of value added than the national average.

States is acknowledged to have the highest stocks of capital among the developed countries, labour-intensive exports to the United States should, *ceteris paribus*, outperform similar shipments to other industrial markets.[5]

To pursue this line of reasoning, Table 7.2 compares the relative performance of labour-intensive exports to the United States with similar shipments to other developed countries. The product groups shown here were employed by Lary with the exception that the trade data have been updated from 1965 to 1975. The table shows the United States value of imports, in total and from developing countries, as well as an index of value added per employee for each product group.

Overall, the figures in Table 7.2 support the contention that labour-intensive exports have done better in the United States than in other industrial countries. Import shares for these items increased by over 13 percentage points in the United States (from 17·7 to 31 per cent), while the increase for other industrial nations was only about 3 percentage points. In addition to the more favourable change in market shares, the level of penetration is considerably higher as LDCs supplied 31 per cent of the labour-intensive products in the United States, as opposed to about 9 per cent in the other developed countries. Examination of the lower-level statistics shows that the higher US import shares are a general phenomenon as the LDCs normally supply a greater proportion of each of the product groups' components.

To what extent can the pattern of results shown in Table 7.2 be explained by differences in labour intensity among the various product groups? To investigate this question, correlations were run between the level and change in LDC market shares and the index of value added per employee. The correlation between the index and the 1975 developing countries' import share in the United States ($r = -0.539$) was significant at the 95 per cent level, as was the correlation between the value added index and the LDC share in other industrial countries ($r = -0.435$). The negative sign was anticipated since the more labour-intensive items (i.e., lower value added per employee index) would be a factor leading to higher developing country market shares. Labour intensity also has considerable explanatory power in accounting for changes in the developing countries' US import shares as this correlation ($r = -0.440$) is also significant. Thus, the evidence strongly suggests that LDCs' market performance is influenced by the degree of labour intensity of individual products.

Aside from the influence of labour intensity on export performance, another interesting question centres on what the trade effects would be if other developed countries brought their market shares up to the US average. The question has potentially important policy implications for the 1980s since a partial explanation for the poorer LDC market penetration outside the United States rests on the discriminatory tariff and trade policies of the European customs unions. To examine this issue the following equation was employed,

$$\hat{P}_j = (s_{j,\,u} - s_{j,\,0})E_{j,\,0} \qquad (7\text{--}1)$$

where $\hat{P}_j$ is the projected change in LDC exports of product $j$, $s_{j,\,u}$ is the 1975 share of LDCs in exports of labour-intensive product $j$ to the United States, $s_{j,\,0}$ is the share in exports to other industrial countries, and $E_{j,\,0}$ is the 1975 value of total exports to other countries.

Overall, if the other developed nations brought their import shares up to the United States average, developing country exports of these labour-intensive products would increase by about 125 per cent, or \$28 billion above the 1975 trade base.[6] Exports of electrical apparatus and clothing accessories would rise by \$5 billion or more, while footwear, jewelry, miscellaneous manufactures and nonelectrical machinery would increase by at least \$1 billion.

### The export performance of individual products

Having once identified a product as labour-intensive, the question arises as to whether there are other useful criteria for predicting the likelihood of successful adoption in a LDC export venture. For a test, Lary's complete selection of labour-intensive products were ranked in terms of the percentage point change in developing countries' import shares. Next, the products were divided into three approximately equal groups: those in which the developing countries achieved a superior export performance, products in which the competitive performance was about average, and those in which the performance was below par. Table 7.3 lists the products in which LDCs made their most impressive competitive gains, gives import values for the United States and other developed countries, and also shows the LDC market shares in 1965 and 1975. Table 7.4 provides similar information on products in which the developing countries' market performance was the poorest among the labour-intensive items.

One fact emerging from Table 7.3 is that there seems to be a concentration of products classified in SITC 8 (miscellaneous manufactures) among the most successful of the labour-intensive export items. In umbrellas and walking sticks (SITC 899.40) and leather

TABLE 7.3 Analysis of Changes in Imports of Labour-intensive Products in which Developing Countries' Market Shares Made their Largest Increases over the Interval 1965 to 1975. (Values in $ million)

| | | 1965 Imports | | | | 1975 Imports | | | | LDCS' share in the US | | | LDCS' share in other developed | | |
|---|---|---|---|---|---|---|---|---|---|---|---|---|---|---|---|
| | | US | | Other developed | | US | | Other developed | | | | | | | |
| SITC | Description | LDCS | Total | LDCS | Total | LDCS | Total | LDCS | Total | 1965 | 1975 | Chg. | 1965 | 1975 | Chg. |
| 89940 | Umbrellas | 1·3 | 7·6 | 1·1 | 17·5 | 14·9 | 18·1 | 45·8 | 104·5 | 17·1 | 82·6 | 65·5 | 6·3 | 43·8 | 37·6 |
| 84130 | Leather clothing | 9·2 | 43·9 | 1·7 | 35·1 | 160·9 | 216·9 | 235·9 | 656·8 | 21·0 | 74·2 | 53·2 | 4·8 | 35·9 | 31·1 |
| 89910 | Carved manufactures | 0·8 | 2·6 | 1·2 | 12·7 | 9·4 | 15·3 | 23·6 | 58·3 | 30·8 | 61·5 | 30·7 | 9·4 | 40·4 | 30·9 |
| 89920 | Basketwork and brooms | 5·0 | 24·1 | 3·6 | 53·9 | 38·4 | 74·0 | 77·1 | 256·8 | 20·7 | 51·8 | 31·1 | 6·7 | 30·0 | 23·3 |
| 88100 | Travel goods | 18·6 | 50·0 | 5·9 | 91·4 | 163·2 | 217·9 | 158·6 | 612·8 | 37·2 | 74·9 | 37·7 | 6·5 | 25·9 | 19·4 |
| 84200 | Fur clothing | 0·2 | 2·0 | 0·3 | 28·7 | 8·0 | 14·8 | 75·7 | 383·5 | 10·0 | 53·9 | 43·9 | 1·0 | 19·7 | 18·7 |
| 63110 | Veneer sheets | 16·6 | 45·8 | 6·3 | 101·8 | 14·5 | 51·1 | 64·5 | 271·1 | 36·2 | 28·4 | -7·9 | 6·2 | 23·8 | 17·6 |
| 71420 | Calculating machines | 0·2 | 53·7 | 0·1 | 347·1 | 111·7 | 339·4 | 161·1 | 982·4 | 0·4 | 32·9 | 32·5 | 0·0 | 16·4 | 16·4 |
| 72420 | Radio receivers | 19·8 | 149·0 | 8·2 | 201·3 | 294·2 | 661·0 | 278·1 | 1365·1 | 13·3 | 44·5 | 31·2 | 4·1 | 20·4 | 16·3 |
| 84110 | Clothing, not knitted | 100·5 | 214·2 | 104·7 | 611·3 | 830·1 | 1022·5 | 1852·5 | 5566·9 | 46·9 | 81·2 | 34·3 | 17·1 | 33·8 | 16·1 |
| 63120 | Plywood | 56·0 | 124·9 | 27·7 | 191·4 | 208·7 | 262·1 | 212·4 | 717·1 | 44·8 | 79·6 | 34·8 | 14·5 | 29·6 | 15·1 |
| 3200 | Canned fish | 20·0 | 83·6 | 36·6 | 304·6 | 44·9 | 165·7 | 223·4 | 842·6 | 23·9 | 27·1 | 3·2 | 12·0 | 26·5 | 14·5 |
| 65560 | Cordage | 19·0 | 48·7 | 2·5 | 42·1 | 73·0 | 123·4 | 42·0 | 205·8 | 39·0 | 59·1 | 20·1 | 5·9 | 20·4 | 14·4 |
| 65100 | Knitted accessories | 64·2 | 221·5 | 94·7 | 631·0 | 932·0 | 1123·0 | 1240·6 | 4327·7 | 29·0 | 83·0 | 54·0 | 15·0 | 28·7 | 13·7 |
| 63200 | Wood products, n.e.s. | 9·1 | 77·4 | 4·4 | 144·7 | 77·4 | 204·9 | 127·5 | 780·2 | 11·8 | 37·8 | 26·0 | 3·0 | 16·3 | 13·3 |
| 89990 | Other manufactures, n.e.s. | 55·8 | 81·7 | 11·7 | 50·9 | 84·3 | 94·2 | 62·7 | 180·0 | 68·3 | 89·5 | 21·2 | 23·0 | 34·8 | 11·8 |
| 84120 | Clothing accessories | 15·5 | 48·4 | 11·5 | 127·9 | 79·3 | 139·2 | 99·0 | 516·8 | 32·0 | 57·0 | 25·0 | 9·0 | 19·2 | 10·2 |
| 84150 | Headgear | 0·9 | 13·0 | 0·9 | 45·6 | 18·0 | 34·5 | 19·3 | 158·5 | 6·9 | 52·4 | 45·4 | 2·0 | 12·2 | 10·2 |
| 89720 | Imitation jewelry | 5·0 | 17·5 | 3·5 | 32·4 | 50·1 | 81·8 | 38·8 | 186·6 | 28·6 | 61·3 | 32·7 | 10·8 | 20·8 | 10·0 |
| 61200 | Leather manufactures | 1·7 | 10·2 | 2·4 | 45·8 | 18·0 | 32·5 | 33·1 | 226·5 | 16·7 | 55·5 | 38·9 | 5·2 | 14·6 | 9·4 |
| 86410 | Watches | 0·8 | 79·3 | 0·7 | 141·0 | 98·9 | 298·1 | 87·5 | 914·1 | 1·0 | 33·2 | 32·2 | 0·5 | 9·6 | 9·1 |
| 86140 | Photographic cameras | 1·1 | 37·4 | 1·6 | 101·7 | 22·8 | 175·3 | 66·5 | 624·5 | 2·9 | 13·0 | 10·0 | 1·6 | 10·6 | 9·1 |
| 69600 | Cutlery | 1·5 | 43·1 | 3·2 | 110·3 | 16·7 | 119·5 | 45·9 | 412·7 | 3·5 | 13·9 | 10·5 | 2·9 | 11·1 | 8·2 |
| 72930 | Thermionic materials | 9·2 | 63·2 | 0·8 | 375·2 | 729·9 | 910·7 | 223·4 | 2738·3 | 14·6 | 80·2 | 65·6 | 0·2 | 8·2 | 7·9 |
| 65100 | Textile yarn | 5·9 | 63·6 | 21·1 | 1035·1 | 21·7 | 130·4 | 386·9 | 4030·3 | 9·3 | 16·6 | 7·4 | 2·0 | 9·6 | 7·6 |
| 65350 | Synthetic fabrics | 0·6 | 28·1 | 1·6 | 239·0 | 13·9 | 172·8 | 164·5 | 2018·6 | 2·1 | 8·0 | 5·9 | 0·7 | 8·1 | 7·5 |
| 69700 | Household equipment | 4·8 | 33·2 | 3·4 | 175·7 | 56·6 | 135·6 | 67·7 | 767·5 | 14·5 | 41·7 | 27·3 | 1·9 | 8·8 | 6·9 |
| 24300 | Shaped wood | 25·3 | 375·2 | 162·7 | 1466·0 | 55·4 | 792·2 | 596·6 | 3378·7 | 6·7 | 7·0 | 0·3 | 11·1 | 17·7 | 6·6 |

| Code | Product | | | | | | | | | | | | | |
|---|---|---|---|---|---|---|---|---|---|---|---|---|---|---|
| 63180 | Simply worked wood | 8·6 | 20·7 | 0·3 | 18·5 | 22·1 | 46·7 | 39·8 | 501·2 | 41·5 | 47·4 | 5·8 | 1·6 | 7·9 | 6·3 |
| 89110 | Tape recorders | 0·0 | 100·6 | 0·2 | 211·6 | 76·6 | 603·3 | 76·9 | 1228·1 | 0·0 | 12·7 | 12·7 | 0·1 | 6·3 | 6·2 |
| 73310 | Bicycles and parts | 0·3 | 30·9 | 0·1 | 42·7 | 23·6 | 136·6 | 18·6 | 309·6 | 1·0 | 17·3 | 16·3 | 0·2 | 6·0 | 5·8 |
| 61100 | Leather | 20·4 | 67·5 | 73·6 | 313·9 | 44·4 | 89·2 | 324·5 | 1110·7 | 30·2 | 49·8 | 19·6 | 23·4 | 29·2 | 5·8 |
| 85100 | Footwear | 10·6 | 159·9 | 26·6 | 367·9 | 545·1 | 1301·4 | 334·2 | 2612·8 | 6·6 | 41·9 | 35·3 | 7·2 | 12·8 | 5·6 |
| 61300 | Tanned fur skins | 0·1 | 11·2 | 1·8 | 105·5 | 0·7 | 10·5 | 27·2 | 377·3 | 0·9 | 7·1 | 6·2 | 1·7 | 7·2 | 5·5 |
| 89710 | Gold Jewelry | 1·1 | 15·8 | 3·8 | 115·8 | 38·5 | 128·1 | 50·3 | 5766·0 | 7·0 | 30·0 | 23·1 | 3·3 | 8·7 | 5·4 |
| 66130 | Building stone | 0·4 | 15·1 | 0·7 | 42·9 | 2·4 | 32·8 | 17·0 | 248·7 | 2·6 | 7·3 | 4·6 | 1·6 | 6·8 | 5·2 |
| 65360 | Other fabrics | 0·7 | 25·0 | 2·5 | 334·7 | 0·6 | 12·7 | 34·0 | 680·3 | 2·8 | 4·4 | 1·6 | 0·7 | 5·0 | 4·2 |
| 65400 | Tulle or lace | 2·2 | 16·5 | 2·6 | 153·1 | 6·7 | 19·6 | 17·5 | 303·4 | 13·3 | 34·1 | 20·8 | 1·7 | 5·8 | 4·1 |
| 89100 | Musical instruments | 1·9 | 56·0 | 0·7 | 166·3 | 112·8 | 782·8 | 107·9 | 2423·8 | 3·4 | 14·4 | 11·0 | 0·4 | 4·4 | 4·0 |
| 41110 | Oils of fish | 0·7 | 6·0 | 28·9 | 133·1 | 0·2 | 3·2 | 53·9 | 210·6 | 11·7 | 4·8 | −6·9 | 21·7 | 25·6 | 3·9 |
| 65600 | Made-up textile fabrics | 6·5 | 34·8 | 31·8 | 198·3 | 53·7 | 98·3 | 198·8 | 1007·0 | 18·7 | 54·6 | 36·0 | 16·0 | 19·7 | 3·7 |
| 89400 | Sporting goods | 23·6 | 140·6 | 40·1 | 363·6 | 297·2 | 636·0 | 293·7 | 1990·9 | 16·8 | 46·7 | 29·9 | 11·0 | 14·8 | 3·7 |
| 86420 | Clocks | 0·0 | 20·9 | 0·4 | 110·7 | 38·4 | 128·2 | 17·6 | 454·4 | 0·0 | 29·9 |  | 0·4 | 3·9 | 3·5 |
| 71730 | Sewing machines | 0·1 | 71·2 | 0·6 | 133·7 | 13·8 | 187·2 | 17·5 | 448·8 | 0·1 | 7·4 | 7·2 | 0·4 | 3·9 | 3·5 |
| 65500 | Special textile fabric | 4·3 | 15·9 | 1·3 | 212·5 | 83·8 | 215·1 | 57·4 | 1473·3 | 27·0 | 39·0 | 11·9 | 0·6 | 3·9 | 3·3 |
| 71490 | Office machines | 1·1 | 31·2 | 0·3 | 360·1 | 99·5 | 449·4 | 60·9 | 1958·8 | 3·5 | 22·1 | 18·6 | 0·1 | 3·1 | 3·0 |
| | Total | 551·2 | 2882·7 | 740·4 | 10146·1 | 5707·1 | 12507·9 | 8458·3 | 51201·2 | 19·1 | 45·6 | 26·5 | 7·3 | 16·5 | 9·2 |

TABLE 7.4 Analysis of Changes in Imports of Labour-intensive Products in which Developing Countries' Market Shares Fell or Showed Only Slight Increases over the Interval 1965 to 1975. (Values in $ million)

| SITC | Description | 1965 Imports US LDCS | 1965 Imports US Total | 1965 Imports Other developed LDCS | 1965 Imports Other developed Total | 1975 Imports US LDCS | 1975 Imports US Total | 1975 Imports Other developed LDCS | 1975 Imports Other developed Total | LDCS' share in the US 1965 | LDCS' share in the US 1975 | LDCS' share in the US Chg. | LDCS' share in other developed 1965 | LDCS' share in other developed 1975 | LDCS' share in other developed Chg. |
|---|---|---|---|---|---|---|---|---|---|---|---|---|---|---|---|
| 66700 | Precious stones | 16.4 | 46.0 | 38.4 | 117.2 | 329.2 | 851.5 | 628.6 | 4190.3 | 35.7 | 38.7 | 3.0 | 32.8 | 15.0 | -17.7 |
| 8140 | Fish or meat meal | 23.9 | 34.9 | 127.9 | 267.8 | 17.7 | 27.8 | 116.7 | 373.9 | 68.5 | 63.7 | -4.8 | 47.8 | 31.2 | -16.6 |
| 41100 | Fish oils | 0.7 | 6.0 | 28.9 | 133.1 | 0.2 | 12.5 | 54.7 | 555.7 | 11.7 | 1.2 | -10.5 | 21.7 | 9.9 | -11.9 |
| 55100 | Essential oils | 18.8 | 45.6 | 33.7 | 164.8 | 30.5 | 77.7 | 61.3 | 479.2 | 41.2 | 39.3 | -1.9 | 20.4 | 12.8 | -7.7 |
| 65610 | Textile bags | 0.4 | 0.7 | 50.4 | 74.2 | 0.7 | 1.2 | 63.3 | 103.7 | 57.1 | 54.6 | -2.6 | 67.9 | 61.0 | -6.9 |
| 65340 | Woven jute fabrics | 174.0 | 186.7 | 55.9 | 76.5 | 123.2 | 124.1 | 66.9 | 97.3 | 93.2 | 99.3 | 6.1 | 73.1 | 68.8 | -4.3 |
| 65700 | Floor coverings | 15.7 | 54.3 | 120.7 | 415.1 | 45.4 | 106.0 | 465.8 | 1787.0 | 28.9 | 42.8 | 13.9 | 29.1 | 26.1 | -3.0 |
| 81240 | Lighting fixtures | 4.8 | 33.0 | 8.0 | 108.1 | 19.2 | 59.3 | 27.5 | 533.1 | 14.5 | 32.4 | 17.8 | 7.4 | 5.2 | -2.2 |
| 63300 | Cork manufactures | 0.1 | 3.9 | 2.4 | 43.9 | 0.0 | 10.3 | 3.8 | 102.0 | 2.6 | 0.4 | -2.2 | 5.5 | 3.7 | -1.8 |
| 66180 | Cement building material | 1.0 | 5.8 | 0.8 | 46.0 | 2.6 | 6.8 | 0.8 | 180.0 | 17.2 | 38.6 | 21.4 | 1.7 | 0.4 | -1.3 |
| 63140 | Improved wood | 0.1 | 0.8 | 0.6 | 53.5 | 0.0 | 4.3 | 1.1 | 366.2 | 12.5 | 0.0 | -12.5 | 1.1 | 0.3 | -0.8 |
| 89960 | Orthopedic goods | 0.3 | 3.1 | 0.4 | 26.4 | 0.9 | 15.5 | 2.0 | 245.8 | 9.7 | 5.7 | -4.0 | 1.5 | 0.8 | -0.7 |
| 62100 | Rubber materials | 0.0 | 0.0 | 2.3 | 119.6 | 0.0 | 0.4 | 8.0 | 554.3 | 0.0 | 2.1 | 2.1 | 1.9 | 1.4 | -0.5 |
| 5500 | Prepared vegetables | 23.1 | 45.3 | 52.6 | 238.6 | 78.7 | 183.8 | 250.6 | 1164.8 | 51.0 | 42.8 | -8.1 | 22.0 | 21.5 | -0.5 |
| 65370 | Knitted fabrics | 0.1 | 9.4 | 3.2 | 169.2 | 1.3 | 49.1 | 12.4 | 891.5 | 1.1 | 2.6 | 1.5 | 1.9 | 1.4 | -0.5 |
| 65330 | Linens | 0.0 | 0.0 | 0.2 | 16.0 | 0.0 | 0.0 | 0.6 | 57.9 | 0.0 | 0.0 | 0.0 | 1.2 | 1.0 | -0.3 |
| 6200 | Sugar confectionery | 0.4 | 16.6 | 1.3 | 58.3 | 15.0 | 79.6 | 8.5 | 373.2 | 2.4 | 18.9 | 16.5 | 2.2 | 2.3 | 0.0 |
| 65190 | Textile yarns, n.e.s. | 1.2 | 2.0 | 13.2 | 35.5 | 6.6 | 7.3 | 16.6 | 44.4 | 60.0 | 90.2 | 30.2 | 37.2 | 37.3 | 0.1 |
| 71980 | Mechanical goods, n.e.s. | 0.3 | 55.6 | 0.4 | 447.0 | 18.3 | 316.6 | 5.4 | 2303.0 | 0.5 | 5.8 | 5.2 | 0.1 | 0.2 | 0.1 |
| 84160 | Rubber clothing | 0.0 | 0.0 | 0.1 | 9.9 | 0.0 | 0.0 | 0.7 | 60.2 | 0.0 | 0.0 | 0.0 | 1.0 | 1.2 | 0.2 |
| 89950 | Toilet articles | 0.7 | 8.7 | 2.1 | 57.2 | 1.7 | 26.9 | 8.1 | 210.0 | 8.0 | 6.2 | -1.9 | 3.7 | 3.9 | 0.2 |
| 71200 | Agricultural machines | 0.5 | 194.5 | 0.1 | 935.7 | 9.7 | 872.1 | 8.1 | 3698.8 | 0.3 | 1.1 | 0.9 | 0.1 | 0.2 | 0.2 |
| 71520 | Metal working machines | 0.0 | 7.4 | 0.1 | 145.2 | 0.8 | 41.2 | 1.7 | 715.4 | 0.0 | 1.8 | 1.8 | 0.1 | 0.2 | 0.2 |
| 71830 | Food processing machines | 0.1 | 14.7 | 0.2 | 90.0 | 1.8 | 49.1 | 1.6 | 418.6 | 0.7 | 3.7 | 3.0 | 0.2 | 0.4 | 0.2 |
| 89930 | Candles and matches | 0.8 | 19.2 | 2.0 | 60.0 | 9.1 | 60.2 | 11.9 | 322.5 | 4.2 | 15.1 | 10.9 | 3.3 | 3.7 | 0.3 |
| 71810 | Paper mill machinery | 0.0 | 22.4 | 0.1 | 173.9 | 0.6 | 83.9 | 2.6 | 761.7 | 0.0 | 0.7 | 0.7 | 0.1 | 0.3 | 0.3 |
| 71710 | Textile machinery | 0.0 | 81.4 | 0.3 | 547.5 | 2.2 | 329.3 | 8.8 | 1990.2 | 0.0 | 0.7 | 0.7 | 0.1 | 0.4 | 0.4 |
| 71960 | Machines, n.e.s. | 0.1 | 17.9 | 0.5 | 307.9 | 6.1 | 104.1 | 8.8 | 1596.1 | 0.6 | 5.8 | 5.3 | 0.2 | 0.5 | 0.4 |

| | | | | | | | | | | | | | | |
|---|---|---|---|---|---|---|---|---|---|---|---|---|---|---|
| 73100 | Railway vehicles | 0·0 | 7·4 | 0·2 | 114·5 | 3·4 | 90·6 | 2·9 | 488·0 | 0·0 | 3·8 | 3·8 | 0·2 | 0·6 | 0·4 |
| 73290 | Motorcycles and parts | 0·0 | 141·0 | 0·0 | 77·6 | 4·6 | 744·4 | 3·6 | 658·3 | 0·0 | 0·6 | 0·6 | 0·0 | 0·5 | 0·5 |
| 71950 | Power tools, n.e.s. | 0·1 | 34·3 | 0·2 | 261·8 | 8·1 | 220·1 | 7·6 | 1338·5 | 0·3 | 3·7 | 3·4 | 0·1 | 0·6 | 0·5 |
| 71992 | Taps and valves | 0·2 | 12·2 | 0·5 | 309·1 | 11·7 | 167·9 | 11·0 | 1756·6 | 1·6 | 7·0 | 5·3 | 0·2 | 0·6 | 0·5 |
| 65310 | Silk fabrics | 2·3 | 29·7 | 2·5 | 45·5 | 1·6 | 16·7 | 15·4 | 251·4 | 7·7 | 9·4 | 1·7 | 5·5 | 6·1 | 0·6 |
| 65390 | Woven fabrics, n.e.s. | 1·5 | 37·4 | 0·2 | 16·4 | 3·6 | 21·7 | 0·3 | 18·9 | 4·0 | 16·4 | 12·4 | 1·2 | 1·8 | 0·6 |
| 72940 | Automotive equipment | 0·0 | 9·1 | 0·7 | 142·0 | 22·7 | 112·2 | 8·8 | 837·1 | 0·0 | 20·2 | 20·2 | 0·5 | 1·0 | 0·6 |
| 71510 | Machine tools | 0·3 | 56·1 | 0·5 | 684·1 | 7·9 | 326·5 | 15·3 | 2360·7 | 0·5 | 2·4 | 1·9 | 0·1 | 0·6 | 0·7 |
| 69890 | Metal articles, n.e.s. | 3·3 | 41·4 | 1·6 | 206·3 | 20·1 | 272·0 | 18·7 | 1243·0 | 8·0 | 7·4 | −0·6 | 0·8 | 1·5 | 0·8 |
| 71430 | Statistical machines | 0·0 | 4·2 | 4·0 | 264·0 | 1·2 | 129·0 | 86·4 | 3794·3 | 0·0 | 0·9 | 0·9 | 1·5 | 2·3 | 0·8 |
| 73280 | Motor vehicle bodies | 0·7 | 157·6 | 1·0 | 1770·0 | 97·1 | 2507·2 | 82·6 | 9706·8 | 0·4 | 3·9 | 3·4 | 0·1 | 0·9 | 0·8 |
| 86160 | Photographic apparatus | 0·0 | 4·3 | 0·6 | 119·8 | 0·7 | 25·1 | 17·1 | 1201·2 | 0·0 | 2·7 | 2·7 | 0·5 | 1·4 | 0·9 |
| 86170 | Medical instruments, n.e.s. | 0·2 | 13·2 | 0·8 | 89·2 | 7·1 | 99·9 | 14·0 | 772·7 | 1·5 | 7·1 | 5·6 | 0·9 | 1·8 | 0·9 |
| 69080 | Misc. metal articles | 1·1 | 3·9 | 0·3 | 72·4 | 4·1 | 40·4 | 4·5 | 341·7 | 28·2 | 10·1 | −18·1 | 0·4 | 1·3 | 0·9 |
| 71920 | Pumps | 0·2 | 34·7 | 0·9 | 643·8 | 7·3 | 344·3 | 42·2 | 3655·8 | 0·6 | 2·1 | 1·6 | 0·1 | 1·2 | 1·0 |
| 66300 | Mineral products, n.e.s. | 3·9 | 16·6 | 0·9 | 240·9 | 9·6 | 83·2 | 15·7 | 1119·9 | 23·5 | 11·5 | −12·0 | 0·4 | 1·4 | 1·0 |
| 66400 | Glass | 2·4 | 56·6 | 0·4 | 278·4 | 6·3 | 119·3 | 12·1 | 1015·9 | 4·2 | 5·3 | 1·0 | 0·1 | 1·2 | 1·0 |
| | Total | 299·7 | 1575·6 | 562·1 | 10273·9 | 938·3 | 8821·0 | 2204·7 | 54731·2 | 19·0 | 10·6 | −8·4 | 5·5 | 4·0 | −1·4 |

clothing (SITC 841.30), the developing countries increased their US market shares by more than 50 percentage points, while their percentage of the market rose by over 30 points in other developed countries. Among the 10 products in which the LDCs achieved their best export performance, 7 were classified in SITC 8. To put this figure in perspective, only about 30 per cent of the labour-intensive items in Lary's selection came from this group. Thus, a highly disproportionate number of the successful LDC export products came from SITC 8. Another factor relating to the LDCs' superior performance for these items is that not one SITC 8 item was among the 10 worst performing exports listed in Table 7.4.

While SITC 8 products dominate the highly successful labour-intensive products, Table 7.4 seemingly suggests that the relatively poor export performers are concentrated in SITC 6 and 7. Precious stones (SITC 667) experienced the highest erosion of competitive position over 1965–75 with the developing countries' import share falling by 18 points outside the United States. Table 7.4 shows that 7 of the 10 poorest performers came from SITC 6, and also indicates a high concentration of SITC 7 (machinery and transport) products immediately after the ten poorest performers. A further analysis shows that, while they constitute only 25 per cent of the total NBER selection, 36 per cent of these products came from SITC 7. In contrast, the proportion of SITC 6 items in the poor performance group (39 per cent) is exactly the same as their appearance in Lary's overall labour-intensive selection. Thus, Table 7.3 and 7.4 show that the products falling in SITC 8 have a disproportionate representation in the *most successful* products (44 per cent as opposed to 27 per cent in the NBER selection), while SITC 7 products have a disproportionate representation in the *poor performance* group.

There are several possible explanations as to why LDCs do less well with SITC 7 exports than for other items. Firstly, these products are generally among the least labour-intensive of all items. For example, of the two main sub-groups of SITC 7 products, electrical apparatus has an index of labour intensity (91·5) which places it 50 per cent above most of the products in the textile group. With an index value of 102, nonelectrical machinery is even less labour-intensive, as most of these items are at the US national average. Since SITC 7 items are about average in labour intensity, they do not enjoy the competitive advantage that products like yarn, footwear, cotton fabrics, or textile small wares have. As the previous correlation tests show, there is a direct relation between a product's labour intensity and the export performance of developing countries.

*Recent trends in labour-intensive production*

Since the previous analysis demonstrated that labour intensity provides a useful measure for identifying successful LDC export products, the question arises as to which goods will be manufactured by labour-intensive processes in the future. For a first test, the 1965 National Bureau indices of value added per employee were updated to identify products which were becoming (relatively) more or less labour-intensive. These indices were derived using a US Department of Commerce (1978) *Survey of Manufactures* which gave detailed information on industry production, employment and value added over 1972–6.

Table 7.5 presents information on the relative labour intensity of each of the broad product groups employed by Hal Lary. Here, the National Bureau's 1965 indices of labour intensity are reproduced along with similar statistics for 1972 and 1976. Changes from the 1965 level are also given so one can easily judge the directional movement of each product group's relative labour intensity. Thus, a negative entry in the differences column indicates that the industry was becoming more labour-intensive relative to US manufacturing processes in general.

The impression which emerges from Table 7.5 is that most of the groups previously identified by the National Bureau as being labour-intensive have become even more so over the interval 1965–76. All of the textile, clothing and accessories group became more labour-intensive, with the exception of small textile wares which declined in labour intensity (i.e., rose in relative value added per employee) by almost 2 percentage points. Much the same pattern is repeated for the 'other light manufactures' group as the relative labour intensity for all products except furniture, nonelectrical machinery and miscellaneous manufactures increased. Thus, the conditions favouring production of these items in developing countries have been maintained, or even increased, over the interval 1965–76.

While Table 7.5 shows that textiles and other light manufactures have become more labour-intensive, the situation is reversed in the foods and industrial materials groups. Processed foods have moved from about 10 points below the national average in labour intensity to about average (100·9) in 1976, while the labour intensity index for industrial raw materials rose by 5 points. However, in only one case (fish and fish products) has a group moved outside the limit set by Lary as a boundary between labour- and capital-intensive production. Therefore, one must conclude that the general supply characteristics which favoured production of these items in developing countries are still similar to those of 1965.

TABLE 7.5 Analysis of Changes in Labour Intensity in the Condensed List of Manufactures Selected by the National Bureau as Being Suitable for Production in Developing Countries

| Product group and subgroup | Indices of value added per employee (all mfg. = 100) | | | | | |
| --- | --- | --- | --- | --- | --- | --- |
| | Annual level | | | Change | | |
| | 1965 | 1972 | 1976 | 65–72 | 72–76 | 65–76 |
| Textiles, clothing and accessories | 53·7 | 54·8 | 49·8 | 1·1 | −5·0 | −3·9 |
| Yarn and thread | 60·0 | 54·6 | 50·4 | −5·4 | −4·2 | −9·6 |
| Cotton fabrics, woven | 61·2 | 54·7 | 52·6 | −6·5 | −2·1 | −8·6 |
| Other woven fabrics, excluding jute | 71·9 | 68·2 | 59·8 | −3·7 | −8·4 | −12·1 |
| Textile small wares and specialities | 63·2 | 63·5 | 64·9 | 0·3 | 1·4 | 1·7 |
| Carpets and other floor coverings | 74·4 | 78·4 | 60·4 | 4·0 | −17·9 | −14·0 |
| Clothing and accessories | 47·4 | 50·3 | 44·7 | 2·9 | −5·6 | −2·7 |
| Other light manufactures, excluding food | 86·0 | 87·9 | 84·9 | 1·9 | −2·9 | −1·1 |
| Footwear, leather, rubber and plastic goods | 57·6 | 60·0 | 45·5 | 2·4 | −14·6 | −12·2 |
| Glassware, China and pottery | 81·4 | 88·8 | 85·1 | 7·4 | −3·6 | 3·7 |
| Furniture | 64·3 | 64·6 | 56·7 | 0·3 | −7·9 | −7·6 |
| Books and other printed matter | 78·5 | 86·7 | 74·2 | 8·2 | −12·5 | −4·3 |
| Games, toys and sporting goods | 77·6 | 79·1 | 76·6 | 1·5 | −2·5 | −1·0 |
| Jewelry and silverware | 81·6 | 81·5 | 72·2 | −0·1 | −9·2 | −9·4 |
| Miscellaneous manufactures | 79·3 | 90·5 | 93·2 | 11·2 | 2·6 | 13·9 |
| Optical goods, watches and instruments | 92·9 | 95·4 | 90·2 | 2·5 | −5·2 | −2·7 |
| Cutlery, hardware and metal products | 91·3 | 91·3 | 87·4 | 0·0 | −3·9 | −3·9 |
| Electrical apparatus | 91·5 | 89·6 | 88·9 | −1·9 | −0·7 | −2·6 |
| Non-electrical machinery | 102·0 | 105·7 | 102·9 | 3·7 | −2·8 | 0·9 |

| | | | | | |
|---|---|---|---|---|---|
| Labour-intensive food manufactures | 89·7 | 91·7 | 100·9 | 2·0 | 9·2 | 11·2 |
| Fish and fish products* | 95·5 | 78·2 | 142·9 | −17·3 | 64·8 | 47·4 |
| Fruits and vegetables | 90·5 | 92·8 | 101·1 | 2·3 | 8·3 | 10·5 |
| Misc. food products and cigars | 87·8 | 93·1 | 94·0 | 5·3 | 0·9 | 6·2 |
| Labour-intensive industrial materials | 66·4 | 80·4 | 74·7 | 14·0 | −5·7 | 8·3 |
| Jute products and other coarse fibres | 58·5 | 51·9 | 64·7 | −6·6 | 12·8 | 6·2 |
| Leather and dressed furskins | 80·6 | 73·0 | 78·3 | −7·6 | 5·3 | −2·3 |
| Lumber, plywood and wood products | 58·3 | 77·4 | 71·2 | 19·1 | −6·2 | 12·9 |
| Building materials of clay and stone | 83·8 | 90·9 | 83·5 | 7·1 | −7·4 | −0·3 |

* The 1976 index places this product outside the range of labour-intensive products established by the National Bureau. Therefore, on the basis of 1976 production information, it would be classified as capital-intensive and no longer suitable for general production in developing countries.

Aside from the question of how the original NBER selection changed in labour intensity over 1965–75, it is important to inquire if other items outside the original list became significantly more labour-intensive. If so, products not included in the original NBER selection may now become suitable candidates for production and export by developing countries. However, a detailed analysis of US production data suggests there are few, if any, products which would be added to the labour-intensive group. Thus, the conclusion which emerges is that Lary's original list of labour-intensive items still remains a very valid guide to the products in which LDCs will apply heavy competitive pressure on industrial countries during the 1980s.

## TRADE IN TECHNOLOGY-RELATED GOODS

One of the important unresolved questions stemming from any analysis of labour intensity undoubtedly concerns the future developing country export performance in the machinery and capital equipment group. Over 1965–75, it was shown that LDCs made few competitive gains in these products, seemingly because many of these items were at or near the national average in labour intensity. However, several advanced developing countries such as Korea, Brazil, Taiwan, Hong Kong, Argentina, India, or Singapore, appear to have reached a stage of industrialisation where they should begin a transition from labour- to semi-intensive production. Given the intermediate values of the labour intensity indices for many machinery products, these items now appear likely to come under increased competitive pressure from the industrialised developing countries. Therefore, a question which has key policy implications for the 1980s concerns which of the capital-intensive goods are likely to come under increased competitive pressure from the more advanced developing countries.

### On the income composition of exports
A recent study by Michael Michaely (1978) has produce important new data which provide insights into this question. Michaely's approach is based on the observation that certain goods, such as advanced technology based items, are primarily exported by richer developed countries, while the poorer LDCs are heavily concentrated in the production and export of simpler goods such as shoes and textiles. Between these two extremes, there exists a wide range of products whose individual characteristics make them more or less likely to be manufac-

tured in developed or developing countries. If some measure of these production characteristics could be derived, this could be employed to determine the likelihood of future production and export of the good by a given group of countries. In particular, such a measure would be useful for identifying items whose characteristics were just above current production thresholds for the advanced developing countries, but which should be attainable in the near future.

The Michaely approach starts by defining the income level of world exports of good $i$ by the index $y_i^x$:

$$y_i^x = \sum_j y_j (X_{ij}/X_i) \qquad (7\text{--}2)$$

where:  $X_{ij}$ – is the value of good $i$ exported by country $j$
$X_i$ – is the value of world exports of good $i$
$y_j$ – is the index of country $j$'s income level.

The latter term is defined as

$$y_j = 100(Y_j/Y_u) \qquad (7\text{--}3)$$

where:  $Y_j$ – is the per capita GNP of country $j$
$Y_u$ – is the per capita GNP for the United States.

This *product-export* index $(y_i^x)$ is therefore defined as a trade-weighted average of the income levels of countries exporting the good. A country's 'richness' or 'poorness' is defined by its per capita GNP, which Michaely acknowledges is still the best possible single measure despite its well-known shortcomings. The income level $(y_j)$ is presented as an index by showing it as a ratio to the US per capita income, which was the world's highest at the time (1973) Michaely conducted his analysis. The highest possible level for the *product-export* index is 100, which would occur if the good were solely exported by the United States. The lower boundary is the relative income level of the poorest country which engages in international trade.

Aside from the income index for individual *goods*, Michaely developed a companion measure which relates to the income-export level of individual *countries*. This index $y_j^x$ is defined as,

$$y_j^x = \sum_i y_i^x (X_{ij}/X_j) \qquad (7\text{--}4)$$

where:  $X_{ij}$ – is the value of good $i$ exports by country $j$
$X_j$ – is the total value of exports by country $j$
$y_i^x$ – is the index of income level for exports of good $i$.

On average for all countries, the income level of a country's exports must be equal to the country's level of per capita income. In individual cases, however, this equality need not hold. Some countries export goods above their actual income level. These nations will, therefore, have an income index of exports which is higher than their actual per capita income levels, while other countries may have export income indices below their actual income level.

Michaely made one further adjustment to the country export-income index. Essentially, this involved running a linear regression,

$$\bar{y}_j^x = 38 \cdot 11 + 0 \cdot 287 y_j \qquad R^2 = 0 \cdot 37 \qquad (7\text{--}5)$$

where: $\bar{y}_j^x$ – is the expected income level of country $j$'s exports

$y_j$ – is the per capita income level of country $j$ measured as a percentage of United States income.

If the actual income level of a country's exports ($y_j^x$) is equal to that predicted from the regression, the nation is said to be exporting at its per capita income level. Likewise, a country is said to be exporting above (or below) its actual income, if its income index of exports is higher (or lower) than the value predicted by equation (7–5).

Before proceeding with the analysis, a numerical example can be useful in illustrating the characteristics of Michaely's indices. Table 7.6 depicts a hypothetical situation in which the United States, Italy and India export three goods: machinery, wheat and textiles. The United States specialises in machinery exports, a high income content good, while India concentrates on textiles. Italy, which has a per capita income between the United States and India, strikes a balance between machinery and textiles, and also exports some wheat.

TABLE 7.6 Hypothetical Example Illustrating the Computation of Michaely's Product and Country Income Export Indices

| Exporter | *Income values* | | *Value of exports* | | | |
|---|---|---|---|---|---|---|
| | GNP per capita | Income index* | Machinery | Wheat | Textiles | Total |
| United States | 2400 | 100 | 500 | 400 | 100 | 1000 |
| Italy | 1200 | 50 | 400 | 200 | 400 | 1000 |
| India | 600 | 25 | 100 | 400 | 500 | 1000 |
| Total | | | 1000 | 1000 | 1000 | 3000 |

* The income index represents the per capita income of each country as a ratio to that of the United States. This figure is then multiplied by 100.

Using equation (7–2) in connection with the income relatives derived from equation (7–3), shows that the product-income index for machinery is,

$$Y^x_{machinery} = 100(500/1000) + 50(400/1000) + 25(100/1000)$$
$$= 72\cdot5 \tag{7-6}$$

Similar calculations show that wheat has an income index of 60, while that for textiles is 42·5. Machinery, therefore, has the highest *product-income* index since its exports are concentrated in the richest country (United States), while textiles have a low index value due to the importance of India in this trade. Thus, these product-income indices map out the relation between individual goods and the income levels of countries primarily responsible for their export. As a supplement, equation (7–4) computes the country-export indices. For the United States this index value is,

$$Y^x_{US} = 72\cdot5(500/1000) + 60(400/1000) + 42\cdot5(100/1000)$$
$$= 64\cdot5 \tag{7-7}$$

while similar calculations show Italy has an export index of 58, and that for India is 52·5. Thus, these *country-export-income* indices show the relative income level of the basket of goods exported by each nation.

Equation (7–5) would be employed to determine if a country were exporting above or below its actual income level. Since Italy has an actual per capita income which is 39·5 per cent of that for the United States, its *projected* export income level is 49·4. Since the actual value of its income-export index is 58, Italy is said to be exporting above its income level.

*Future LDC capital goods exports*
Figure 7.1 illustrates how the concept of income-export indices for goods and countries can be combined to yield insights into the probable future composition of LDC trade flows. Per capita income levels, expressed as a percentage of that for the United States, are measured on the horizontal scale, while the position of selected developed and developing countries are shown below the axis to serve as benchmarks. The left-hand vertical scale measures the projected income-export level for individual countries, while the line *PP* shows the expected income values derived through use of equation 7–5. The dashed lines on either side of *PP* indicate a confidence interval based on one standard error. The right-most vertical scale records the product income indices, which are matched against the country index data (left scale). The actual

*Trade and Development Policies*

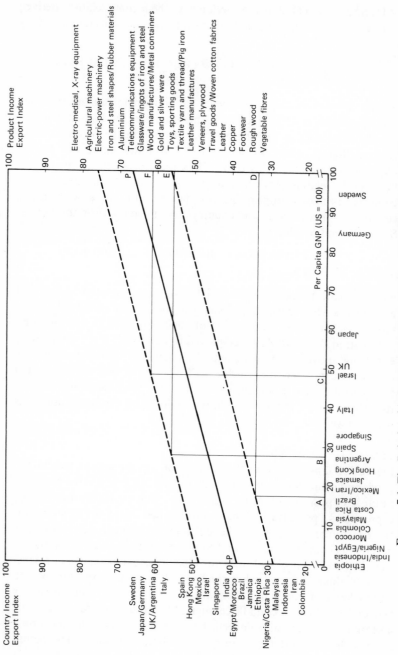

FIGURE 7.1  The Relationship Between per capita GNP and the Income Level of Exports

positions of selected products and countries have also been shown on the vertical scales to assist the reader in making comparisons.

On the horizontal axis, the interval *AB* designates the approximate range in per capita incomes for countries which are presently the major LDC exporters of manufactures. Tracing the perpendicular lines from *AB* up to the confidence interval boundaries identifies the range of products (*DE*) whose export-income characteristics make them suitable for developing countries who are now important exporters of manufactures, or by countries like Malaysia, Costa Rica, or Brazil whose incomes fall short of *OA* at present, but are likely to move across this threshold in the near future. Thus, these *Group I* products such as leather manufactures, plywood and veneers, and footwear have characteristics which are now suitable for the industrialised LDCs, or for those developing countries which will move into this income range.

Aside from this application, the major use of Figure 7.1 lies in the identification of products whose characteristics place them at the threshold of concentrated export by the industrialised developing countries. In identifying these *Group II* items extrapolations of past growth trends of developing countries' gross national products relative to that of the United States have been used, as well as estimates of future GNP published by the United Nations. These figures suggest that the frontier for the industrialised developing countries (relative to the United States) will increase from *OB* to *OC* by 1990. This projected increase in income levels (*BC*) indicates that the new product-income frontier for the industrialised developing countries is mapped out by a region such as *EF*. Items falling in this range, like wood manufactures, metal containers, pig iron, and sporting goods, have characteristics which make them candidates for concentrated future export by the industrialised developing countries.

Table 7.7 summarises the implications of the line of analysis concerning the future composition of LDC trade. Shown here is a tabulation of three-digit SITC manufactured products which are classified as either Group I or Group II items. A third classification (Group III) is used for products whose characteristics seem generally beyond the concentrated export capacity of industrialised developing countries in the 1980s. The table also gives product-income indices Michaely calculated for these items so the 'sensitivity' of each individual product's classification to the position of the boundaries used to distinguish between the groups can be assessed.[7]

Table 7.7 identifies products likely to come under increased competitive pressure from presently industrialised developing countries in

TABLE 7.7 Tabulation of Three-Digit SITC Products by Income-Export Level and the Likelihood of Concentrated Future Export by Developing Countries

| SITC | Description* | SITC | Description* |
|------|-------------|------|-------------|
| **Group I Products** | | | |
| 611 | Leather (45) | 842 | Fur Clothing (57) |
| 631 | Plywood and veneers (51) | 863 | Developed cinema film (56) |
| 633 | Cork manufactures (31) | 864** | Watches and clocks (80) |
| 652 | Woven cotton fabrics (47) | 891** | Musical instruments (67) |
| 656 | Textile products, n.e.s. (40) | 892** | Printed matter (67) |
| 661 | Cement building products (47) | 894 | Sporting goods (58) |
| 682 | Copper products (43) | 897 | Gold and silver jewelry (61) |
| 687 | Tin products (19) | 899 | Other manufactures (56) |
| 831 | Travel goods and handbags (46) | | |
| 841 | Clothing, except fur (45) | **Group III Products** | |
| 851 | Footwear (41) | 621 | Rubber products (72) |
| | | 641 | Paper and paperboard (77) |
| **Group II Products** | | 663 | Non-metal mineral mfgs (71) |
| 612 | Leather manufactures (56) | 664 | Glass (71) |
| 613 | Dressed furskins (64) | 673 | Iron and steel shapes (71) |
| 629 | Rubber articles, n.e.s. (66) | 674 | Iron and steel plates (68) |
| 632 | Wood manufactures, n.e.s. (64) | 675 | Iron and steel hoop (75) |
| 642** | Paper articles (69) | 677 | Iron and steel wire (72) |
| 653 | Woven non-cotton fabrics (57) | 679 | Iron and steel castings (75) |
| 654 | Lace and ribbons (65) | 683 | Nickle products (74) |
| 655** | Special textile products (68) | 684 | Aluminium products (70) |
| 657 | Floor coverings (56) | 691 | Metal structures (69) |
| 662 | Clay building products (62) | 695 | Tools (75) |
| 665 | Glassware (66) | 711 | Non-electric machines (77) |
| 666 | Pottery (62) | 712 | Agricultural machines (76) |
| 671 | Pig iron (57) | 714 | Office machines (76) |
| 672** | Iron and steel ingots (67) | 715 | Metal working machines (77) |
| 676 | Steel rails (65) | 717 | Textile machinery (75) |
| 678** | Iron and steel tubes (70) | 718 | Special industry machines (78) |
| 681 | Silver and platinum products (62) | 719 | Non-electric machines, n.e.s. (76) |
| 685 | Lead products (58) | 722 | Electric power machines (75) |
| 686 | Zinc products (65) | 725 | Domestic electric machines (67) |
| 689 | Non-ferrous metal products (63) | 726 | Electro-medical equipment (80) |
| 692 | Metal containers (64) | 729 | Electrical machines, n.e.s. (73) |
| 693 | Non-electric wire products (65) | 731 | Railway vehicles (70) |
| 694** | Nails and screws (71) | 732 | Road Motor vehicles (76) |
| 696 | Cutlery (62) | 734 | Aircraft (88) |
| 697 | Base metal household equipment (58) | 812 | Household fixtures (68) |
| 698** | Metal manufactures, n.e.s. (70) | 821 | Furniture (68) |
| 723 | Electric distribution machinery (66) | 861 | Scientific instruments (75) |
| 724** | Telecommunications equipment (68) | 862 | Photographic supplies (76) |
| 733** | Road non-motor vehicles (67) | 893 | Plastic articles (68) |
| 735** | Ships and boats (67) | 895 | Office supplies (73) |

\* Product-income indices are shown in parentheses.

\*\* Moved from Group III to Group II on the basis of market share and labour intensity criteria.

the 1980s. This tabulation shows that, of the 82 industries analysed through use of Michaely's indices, 38 fall in the range that the advanced developing countries should achieve within a decade. Comparisons of the characteristics of these Group II items reveals several interesting similarities. Firstly, a number of products represent different sectors of the metals trade. Specifically, of the 38 Group II items, 14 are manufactured of finished metals. The potential magnitude of the adjustment problems associated with extensive LDC competition in these industries can be appreciated by noting current market disruptions in iron and steel, coupled with chronic overcapacity, resulted in the imposition of several protectionist measures such as the US trigger price mechanism or nationalisations in France. Further erosion of the industrial countries' competitive position in metals might provoke additional protectionist measures similar to those employed for the steel industry.

A second potentially important factor is that 19 of the 38 products have income indices which are concentrated in the higher range (65 and above) of the Group II items. This finding has two important implications. Firstly, if the GDP projections err on the high side, the LDCs may not reach the income range associated with concentrated export of these products during the 1980s. However, even if delayed by a few years, the fact that many Group II products are clustered in a relatively narrow range (i.e., product index values of 65 to 70) suggests that the competitive pressures from LDCs are not likely to fall evenly on one industry after another. Rather, the pattern reflected in the income-indices suggests that the competitive pressures may be concentrated on a wide range of diversified industries within a rather narrow time frame. Intense competition from LDCs across a broad front, in a narrow time span, would appear likely to generate more intense demands for increased protection than a situation in which one industry after another experiences increased import competition.

Table 7.7 also shows that there are a number of industries which appear relatively safe from extensive competition from developing countries. In large part, these Group III products are composed of specialised machinery items, or other manufactured goods which are highly capital-intensive in production. In fact, high capital intensity seems to be a common characteristic of most of these 'safe' manufactures.[8] For example, calculations suggest that these Group III products generally have a value added per employee ratio which is at least 30 to 40 per cent above the average for all US manufacturing industries. This observation is important since any policy measures aimed at assisting industries which come under pressure from LDC exports (Group II) should be designed to encourage the flow of resources toward these specialised products in which the developed countries retain a comparative advantage.

One further point emerges from the analysis of the export-income indices. While it seems unlikely developing countries will move into highly capital-intensive industries, Table 7.7 shows they should begin to export some semi-capital-intensive goods during the next decade. For example, Group II products such as iron and steel tubes, metal containers, nonferrous metal products, and metal manufactures have value added per employee ratios in the intermediate range based on comparisons with US manufacturing data. As such, the income indices suggest that the 1980s will be a transitional period in which the currently industrialised LDCs shift into some relatively sophisticated ·manufactured goods.[9]

*Developing country exports in the 1980s*
Using special income indices for countries and goods as well as measures of labour intensity, this chapter identified products which are likely items for concentrated production and export by developing countries. While an analysis of this sort is admittedly subject to uncertainties associated with technological change, changes in protection, or variation in relative wages and prices, it is thought that the methodology provides a useful way of summarising and evaluating the implications of present production and market forces. The results suggest that developing countries will move into a wide range of diversified industries over the next decade, but two important points also emerge. Firstly, many of these advances seem likely to occur in the metals trade where the industrialised developing countries should emerge as important exporters of many ferrous and nonferrous metals products. A second point is that competitive pressures do not appear likely to fall evenly on one industry after another, but should occur in a number of diversified sectors in a short time span. Such an occurrence seems likely to produce more strident demands for protection than a situation where foreign competition is brought to bear more evenly over an extended interval.

This chapter also produced evidence suggesting that some future LDC exports will shift from a concentration in labour-intensive items to some capital-intensive goods. For example, several products which appeared to be likely future export items; iron and steel tubes, containers, nonferrous metal products, and metal manufactures, are more capital-intensive than the United States average for all manufacturing. Thus, the new development for the 1980s will be the application of competitive pressures on two broad classes of goods. While Western markets have been subject to competition from LDC exports of labour-intensive products, the range of items should be broadened in the 1980s to include capital goods. However, many of the very specialised or highly technical machinery manufactures seem safe from serious export pressures from LDCs in the 1980s.

In evaluating the potential disruptive effect of exports, it must be recognised that other LDCs such as India, Pakistan, Kenya, Brazil, Sri Lanka and the Philippines are likely to become important exporters of manufactured products over the next decade. These 'second wave' producers may bring more intense competitive pressures to bear on labour-intensive manufactured goods industries which now face competition from the industrialised developing countries. In other words, the fact that Hong Kong, Singapore, Korea, or Taiwan may move out of some labour-intensive product lines does not mean that these items will experience declining competitive pressures from developing countries. What seems likely is that one group of LDCs will supplant another. As such, there is a need to evaluate the probable magnitude and composition of exports from this 'second wave' of developing country producers. Also, this chapter has shown that a pressing need exists to formulate plans and adopt measures to facilitate the restructuring of many industrial nations' industries to meet new and broadened competitive pressures from developing countries.

This chapter closes with a call for further research concerning the factors which will shape the future composition of developing country exports. It is acknowledged that in relating export structures to relative income levels, Michaely has made an important pioneering contribution to our understanding of factors which influence the composition of international trade. However, it should be noted that the Michaely approach can be generalised to include other explanatory factors such as population, natural resource endowments, capital, etc. Efforts in this direction deserve a high priority given the potential policy applications of such information.

# Appendix
# General Assembly of the United Nations, Declaration and Programme of Action for the Establishment of a New International Economic Order

RESOLUTIONS ADOPTED ON THE REPORT OF THE *AD HOC* COMMITTEE OF THE SIXTH SPECIAL SESSION

**3201 (S.VI).  Declaration on the Establishment of a New International Economic Order**

*The General Assembly*
*Adopts* the following Declaration:

DECLARATION ON THE ESTABLISHMENT OF A NEW INTERNATIONAL ECONOMIC ORDER

*We, the Members of the United Nations,*
*Having convened* a special session of the General Assembly to study for the first time the problems of raw materials and development, devoted to the consideration of the most important economic problems facing the world community,

*Bearing in mind* the spirit, purposes and principles of the Charter of the United Nations to promote the economic advancement and social progress of all peoples,

*Solemnly proclaim* our united determination to work urgently for THE

ESTABLISHMENT OF A NEW INTERNATIONAL ECONOMIC ORDER based on equity, sovereign equality, interdependence, common interest and cooperation among all States, irrespective of their economic and social systems which shall correct inequalities and redress existing injustices, make it possible to eliminate the widening gap between the developed and the developing countries and ensure steadily accelerating economic and social development and peace and justice for present and future generations, and, to that end, declare:

1. The greatest and most significant achievement during the last decades has been the independence from colonial and alien domination of a large number of peoples and nations which has enabled them to become members of the community of free peoples. Technological progress has also been made in all spheres of economic activities in the last three decades, thus providing a solid potential for improving the well-being of all peoples. However, the remaining vestiges of alien and colonial domination, foreign occupation, racial discrimination, *apartheid* and neo-colonialism in all its forms continue to be among the greatest obstacles to the full emancipation and progress of the developing countries and all the peoples involved. The benefits of technological progress are not shared equitably by all members of the international community. The developing countries, which constitute 70 per cent of the world's population, account for only 30 per cent of the world's income. It has proved impossible to achieve an even and balanced development of the international community under the existing international economic order. The gap between the developed and the developing countries continues to widen in a system which was established at a time when most of the developing countries did not even exist as independent States and which perpetuates inequality.

2. The present international economic order is in direct conflict with current developments in international political and economic relations. Since 1970, the world economy has experienced a series of grave crises which have had severe repercussions, especially on the developing countries because of their generally greater vulnerability to external economic impulses. The developing world has become a powerful factor that makes its influence felt in all fields of international activity. These irreversible changes in the relationship of forces in the world necessitate the active, full and equal participation of the developing countries in the formulation and application of all decisions that concern the international community.

3. All these changes have thrust into prominence the reality of interdependence of all the members of the world community. Current events have brought into sharp focus the realisation that the interests of the developed countries and those of the developing countries can no longer be isolated from each other, that there is a close interrelationship between the prosperity of the developed countries and the growth and development of the developing countries, and that the prosperity of the international community as a whole depends upon the prosperity of its constituent parts. International cooperation for development is the shared goal and common duty of all countries. Thus the political, economic and social well-being of present and future generations depends more than ever on cooperation between all the members of the international community on the basis of sovereign equality and the removal of the disequilibrium that exists between them.

4. The new international economic order should be founded on full respect for the following principles:

(*a*) Sovereign equality of States, self-determination of all peoples, inadmissibility of the acquisition of territories by force, territorial integrity and non-interference in the internal affairs of other States;

(*b*) The broadest cooperation of all the States members of the international community, based on equity, whereby the prevailing disparities in the world may be banished and prosperity secured for all;

(*c*) Full and effective participation on the basis of equality of all countries in the solving of world economic problems in the common interest of all countries, bearing in mind the necessity to ensure the accelerated development of all the developing countries, while devoting particular attention to the adoption of special measures in favour of the least developed, land-locked and island developing countries as well as those developing countries most seriously affected by economic crises and natural calamities, without losing sight of the interests of other developing countries;

(*d*) The right of every country to adopt the economic and social system that it deems the most appropriate for its own development and not to be subjected to discrimination of any kind as a result;

(*e*) Full permanent sovereignty of every State over its natural resources and all economic activities. In order to safeguard these resources each State is entitled to exercise effective control over them and their exploitation with means suitable to its own situation, including the right to nationalisation or transfer of ownership to its nationals, this right being an expression of the full permanent sovereignty of the State. No State may be subjected to economic, political or any other type of coercion to prevent the free and full exercise of this inalienable right;

(*f*) The right of all States, territories and peoples under foreign occupation, alien and colonial domination or *apartheid* to restitution and full compensation for the exploitation and depletion of, and damages to, the natural resources and all other resources of those States, territories and peoples;

(*g*) Regulation and supervision of the activities of transnational corporations by taking measures in the interest of the national economies of the countries where such transnational corporations operate on the basis of the full sovereignty of those countries;

(*h*) The right of the developing countries and the peoples of territories under colonial and racial domination and foreign occupation to achieve their liberation and to regain effective control over their natural resources and economic activities;

(*i*) The extending of assistance to developing countries, peoples and territories which are under colonial and alien domination, foreign occupation, racial discrimination or *apartheid* or are subjected to economic, political or any other type of coercive measures to obtain from them the subordination of the exercise of their sovereign rights and to secure from them advantages of any kind, and to neo-colonialism in all its forms, and which have established or are endeavouring to establish effective control over their natural resources and economic activities that have been or are still under foreign control;

(*j*) Just and equitable relationship between the prices of raw materials, primary commodities, manufactured and semi-manufactured goods exported by developing countries and the prices of raw materials, primary commodities, manufactures, capital goods and equipment imported by them with the aim of bringing about sustained improvement in their unsatisfactory terms of trade and the expansion of the world economy;

(*k*) Extension of active assistance to developing countries by the whole international community, free of any political or military conditions;

(*l*) Ensuring that one of the main aims of the reformed international monetary system shall be the promotion of the development of the developing countries and the adequate flow of real resources to them;

(*m*) Improving the competitiveness of natural materials facing competition from synthetic substitutes;

(*n*) Preferential and non-reciprocal treatment for developing countries, wherever feasible, in all fields of international economic cooperation whenever possible;

(*o*) Securing favourable conditions for the transfer of financial resources to developing countries;

(*p*) Giving to the developing countries access to the achievements of modern science and technology, and promoting the transfer of technology and the creation of indigenous technology for the benefit of the developing countries in forms and in accordance with procedures which are suited to their economies;

(*q*) The need for all States to put an end to the waste of natural resources, including food products;

(*r*) The need for developing countries to concentrate all their resources for the cause of development;

(*s*) The strengthening, through individual and collective actions, of mutual economic, trade, financial and technical cooperation among the developing countries, mainly on a preferential basis;

(*t*) Facilitating the role which producers' associations may play within the framework of international cooperation and, in pursuance of their aims, *inter alia* assisting in the promotion of sustained growth of the world economy and accelerating the development of developing countries.

5. The unanimous adoption of the International Development Strategy for the Second United Nations Development Decade[1] was an important step in the promotion of international economic cooperation on a just and equitable basis. The accelerated implementation of obligations and commitments assumed by the international community within the framework of the Strategy, particularly those concerning imperative development needs of developing countries, would contribute significantly to the fulfilment of the aims and objectives of the present Declaration.

6. The United Nations as a universal organisation should be capable of dealing with problems of international economic cooperation in a comprehensive manner and ensuring equally the interests of all countries. It must have an even greater role in the establishment of a new international economic order. The Charter of Economic Rights and Duties of States, for the preparation of which the present Declaration will provide an additional source of inspiration, will constitute a significant contribution in this respect. All the States

Members of the United Nations are therefore called upon to exert maximum efforts with a view to securing the implementation of the present Declaration, which is one of the principal guarantees for the creation of better conditions for all peoples to reach a life worthy of human dignity.

7. The present Declaration on the Establishment of a New International Economic Order shall be one of the most important bases of economic relations between all peoples and all nations.

*2229th plenary meeting*
*1 May 1974*

**3202 (S.VI). Programme of Action on the Establishment of a New International Economic Order**

*The General Assembly*
*Adopts* the following Programme of Action:

## PROGRAMME OF ACTION ON THE ESTABLISHMENT OF A NEW INTERNATIONAL ECONOMIC ORDER

### INTRODUCTION

1. In view of the continuing severe economic imbalance in the relations between developed and developing countries, and in the context of the constant and continuing aggravation of the imbalance of the economies of the developing countries and the consequent need for the mitigation of their current economic difficulties, urgent and effective measures need to be taken by the international community to assist the developing countries, while devoting particular attention to the least developed, land-locked and island developing countries and those developing countries most seriously affected by economic crises and natural calamities leading to serious retardation of development processes.

2. With a view to ensuring the application of the Declaration on the Establishment of a New International Economic Order,[2] it will be necessary to adopt and implement within a specified period a programme of action of unprecedented scope and to bring about maximum economic cooperation and understanding among all States, particularly between developed and developing countries, based on the principles of dignity and sovereign equality.

I. FUNDAMENTAL PROBLEMS OF RAW MATERIALS AND PRIMARY COMMODITIES AS RELATED TO TRADE AND DEVELOPMENT

## 1. *Raw materials*

All efforts should be made:

(*a*) To put an end to all forms of foreign occupation, racial discrimination, *apartheid*, colonial, neo-colonial and alien domination and exploitation through the exercise of permanent sovereignty over natural resources;

(*b*) To take measures for the recovery, exploitation, development, marketing and distribution of natural resources, particularly of developing countries, to serve their national interests, to promote collective self-reliance among them and to strengthen mutually beneficial international economic cooperation with a view to bringing about the accelerated development of developing countries;

(*c*) To facilitate the functioning and to further the aims of producers' associations, including their joint marketing arrangements, orderly commodity trading, improvement in the export income of producing developing countries and in their terms of trade, and sustained growth of the world economy for the benefit of all;

(*d*) To evolve a just and equitable relationship between the prices of raw materials, primary commodities, manufactured and semi-manufactured goods exported by developing countries and the prices of raw materials, primary commodities, food, manufactured and semi-manufactured goods and capital equipment imported by them, and to work for a link between the prices of exports of developing countries and the prices of their imports from developed countries;

(*e*) To take measures to reverse the continued trend of stagnation or decline in the real price of several commodities exported by developing countries, despite a general rise in commodity prices, resulting in a decline in the export earnings of these developing countries;

(*f*) To take measures to expand the markets for natural products in relation to synthetics, taking into account the interests of the developing countries, and to utilise fully the ecological advantages of these products;

(*g*) To take measures to promote the processing of raw materials in the producer developing countries.

## 2. *Food*

All efforts should be made:

(*a*) To take full account of specific problems of developing countries, particularly in times of food shortages, in the international efforts connected with the food problem;

(*b*) To take into account that, owing to lack of means, some developing countries have vast potentialities of unexploited or under-exploited land which, if reclaimed and put into practical use, would contribute considerably to the solution of the food crisis;

(*c*) By the international community to undertake concrete and speedy measures with a view to arresting desertification, salination and damage by locusts or any other similar phenomenon involving several developing countries, particularly in Africa, and gravely affecting the agricultural production capacity of these countries, and also to assist the developing countries affected by any such phenomenon to develop the affected zones with a view to contributing to the solution of their food problems;

(*d*) To refrain from damaging or deteriorating natural resources and food resources, especially those derived from the sea, by preventing pollution and taking appropriate steps to protect and reconstitute those resources;

(*e*) By developed countries, in evolving their policies relating to production, stocks, imports and exports of food, to take full account of the interests of:

(i) Developing importing countries which cannot afford high prices for their imports;

(ii) Developing exporting countries which need increased market opportunities for their exports;

(*f*) To ensure that developing countries can import the necessary quantity of food without undue strain on their foreign exchange resources and without unpredictable deterioration in their balance of payments, and, in this context, that special measures are taken in respect of the least developed, land-locked and island developing countries as well as those developing countries most seriously affected by economic crises and natural calamities;

(*g*) To ensure that concrete measures to increase food production and storage facilities in developing countries are introduced, *inter alia*, by ensuring an increase in all available essential inputs, including fertilizers, from developed countries on favourable terms:

(*h*) To promote exports of food products of developing countries through just and equitable arrangements, *inter alia*, by the progressive elimination of such protective and other measures as constitute unfair competition.

### 3. *General trade*

All efforts should be made:

(*a*) To take the following measures for the amelioration of terms of trade of developing countries and concrete steps to eliminate chronic trade deficits of developing countries:

(i)   Fulfilment of relevant commitments already undertaken in the United Nations Conference on Trade and Development and in the International Development Strategy for the Second United Nations Development Decade;[3]

(ii)  Improved access to markets in developed countries through the progressive removal of tariff and non-tariff barriers and of restrictive business practices;

(iii) Expeditious formulation of commodity agreements where appropriate, in order to regulate as necessary and to stabilise the world markets for raw materials and primary commodities;

(iv)  Preparation of an over-all integrated programme, setting out guidelines and taking into account the current work in this field, for a comprehensive range of commodities of export interest to developing countries;

(v)   Where products of developing countries compete with the domestic production in developed countries, each developed country should facilitate the expansion of imports from developing countries and provide a fair and reasonable opportunity to the developing countries to share in the growth of the market;

(vi)  When the importing developed countries derive receipts from customs duties, taxes and other protective measures applied to imports of these products consideration should be given to the claim of the developing countries that these receipts should be reimbursed in full to the exporting developing countries or devoted to providing additional resources to meet their development needs;

(vii) Developed countries should make appropriate adjustments in their economies so as to facilitate the expansion and diversification of imports from developing countries and thereby permit a rational, just and equitable international division of labour;

(viii) Setting up general principles for pricing policy for exports of commodities of developing countries, with a view to rectifying and achieving satisfactory terms of trade for them;

(ix) Until satisfactory terms of trade are achieved for all developing countries, consideration should be given to alternative means, including improved compensatory financing schemes for meeting the development needs of the developing countries concerned;

(x) Implementation, improvement and enlargement of the generalised system of preferences for exports of agricultural primary commodities, manufactures and semi-manufactures from developing to developed countries and consideration of its extension to commodities, including those which are processed or semi-processed; developing countries which are or will be sharing their existing tariff advantages in some developed countries as the result of the introduction and eventual enlargement of the generalised system of preferences should, as a matter of urgency, be granted new openings in the markets of other developed countries which should offer them export opportunities that at least compensate for the sharing of those advantages;

(xi) The setting up of buffer stocks within the framework of commodity arrangements and their financing by international financial institutions, wherever necessary, by the developed countries and when they are able to do so, by the developing countries, with the aim of favouring the producer developing and consumer developing countries and of contributing to the expansion of world trade as a whole;

(xii) In cases where natural materials can satisfy the requirements of the market, new investment for the expansion of the capacity to produce synthetic materials and substitutes should not be made;

(b) To be guided by the principles of non-reciprocity and preferential treatment of developing countries in multilateral trade negotiations between developed and developing countries, and to seek sustained and additional benefits for the international trade of developing countries, so as to achieve a substantial increase in their foreign exchange earnings, diversification of their exports and acceleration of the rate of their economic growth.

#### 4. *Transportation and insurance*

All efforts should be made:

(*a*) To promote an increasing and equitable participation of developing countries in the world shipping tonnage;

(*b*) To arrest and reduce the ever-increasing freight rates in order to reduce the costs of imports to, and exports from, the developing countries;

(*c*) To minimise the cost of insurance and reinsurance for developing countries and to assist the growth of domestic insurance and reinsurance markets in developing countries and the establishment to this end, where appropriate, of institutions in these countries or at the regional level;

(*d*) To ensure the early implementation of the code of conduct for liner conferences;

(*e*) To take urgent measures to increase the import and export capability of the least developed countries and to offset the disadvantages of the adverse geographic situation of land-locked countries, particularly with regard to their transportation and transit costs, as well as developing island countries in order to increase their trading ability;

(*f*) By the developed countries to refrain from imposing measures or implementing policies designed to prevent the importation, at equitable prices, of commodities from the developing countries or from frustrating the implementation of legitimate measures and policies adopted by the developing countries in order to improve prices and encourage the export of such commodities.

## II. INTERNATIONAL MONETARY SYSTEM AND FINANCING OF THE DEVELOPMENT OF DEVELOPING COUNTRIES

### 1. *Objectives*

All efforts should be made to reform the international monetary system with, *inter alia*, the following objectives:

(*a*) Measures to check the inflation already experienced by the developed countries, to prevent it from being transferred to developing countries and to study and devise possible arrangements within the International Monetary Fund to mitigate the effects of inflation in developed countries on the economies of developing countries;

(*b*) Measures to eliminate the instability of the international monetary system, in particular the uncertainty of the exchange rates, especially as it affects adversely the trade in commodities;

(*c*) Maintenance of the real value of the currency reserves of the developing countries by preventing their erosion from inflation and exchange rate depreciation of reserve currencies;

(*d*) Full and effective participation of developing countries in all phases of decision-making for the formulation of an equitable and durable monetary system and adequate participation of developing countries in all bodies entrusted with this reform and, particularly, in the proposed Council of Governors of the International Monetary Fund;

(*e*) Adequate and orderly creation of additional liquidity with particular regard to the needs of the developing countries through the additional allocation of special drawing rights based on the concept of world liquidity needs to be appropriately revised in the light of the new international environment, any creation of international liquidity should be made through international multilateral mechanisms;

(*f*) Early establishment of a link between special drawing rights and additional development financing in the interest of developing countries, consistent with the monetary characteristics of special drawing rights;

(*g*) Review by the International Monetary Fund of the relevant provisions in order to ensure effective participation by developing countries in the decision-making process;

(*h*) Arrangements to promote an increasing net transfer of real resources from the developed to the developing countries;

(*i*) Review of the method of operation of the International Monetary Fund, in particular the terms for both credit repayments and 'stand-by' arrangements, the system of compensatory financing and the terms of the financing of commodity buffer stocks so as to enable the developing countries to make more effective use of them.

## 2. *Measures*

All efforts should be made to take the following urgent measures to finance the development of developing countries and to meet the balance-of-payment crises in the developing world.

(*a*) Implementation at an accelerated pace by the developed countries of the time-bound programme, as already laid down in the International Development Strategy for the Second United Nations Development Decade, for the net amount of financial resource transfers to developing countries, increase in the official component of the net amount of financial resource transfers to developing countries so as to meet and even to exceed the target of the Strategy.

(*b*) International financing institutions should effectively play their role as development financing banks without discrimination on account of the political or economic system of any member country, assistance being untied;

(c) More effective participation by developing countries, whether recipients or contributors in the decision-making process in the competent organs of the International Bank for Reconstruction and Development and the International Development Association, through the establishment of a more equitable pattern of voting rights;

(d) Exemption, wherever possible, of the developing countries from all import and capital outflow controls imposed by the developed countries;

(e) Promotion of foreign investment, both public and private, from developed to developing countries in accordance with the needs and requirements in sectors of their economies as determined by the recipient countries;

(f) Appropriate urgent measures, including international action, should be taken to mitigate adverse consequences for the current and future development of developing countries arising from the burden of external debt contracted on hard terms;

(g) Debt renegotiation on a case-by-case basis with a view to concluding agreements on debt cancellation, moratorium, rescheduling or interest subsidisation;

(h) International financial institutions should take into account the special situation of each developing country in reorienting their lending policies to suit these urgent needs; there is also need for improvement in practices of international financial institutions in regard to, *inter alia*, development financing and international monetary problems;

(i) Appropriate steps should be taken to give priority to the least developed, land-locked and island developing countries and to the countries most seriously affected by economic crises and natural calamities, in the availability of loans for development purposes which should include more favourable terms and conditions.

## III. INDUSTRIALISATION

All efforts should be made by the international community to take measures to encourage the industrialisation of the developing countries, and to this end:

(a) The developed countries should respond favourably within the framework of their official aid as well as international financial institutions, to the requests of developing countries for the financing of industrial projects;

(*b*) The developed countries should encourage investors to finance industrial production projects, particularly export-oriented production, in developing countries, in agreement with the latter and within the context of their laws and regulations;

(*c*) With a view to bringing about a new international economic structure which should increase the share of the developing countries in world industrial production, the developed countries and the agencies of the United Nations system, in cooperation with the developing countries, should contribute to setting up new industrial capacities including raw materials and commodity-transforming facilities as a matter of priority in the developing countries that produce those raw materials and commodities;

(*d*) The international community should continue and expand, with the aid of the developed countries and the international institutions, the operational and instruction-oriented technical assistance programmes, including vocational training and management development of national personnel of the developing countries, in the light of their special development requirements.

## IV. TRANSFER OF TECHNOLOGY

All efforts should be made;

(*a*) To formulate an international code of conduct for the transfer of technology corresponding to needs and conditions prevalent in developing countries;

(*b*) To give access on improved terms to modern technology and to adapt that technology, as appropriate, to specific economic, social and ecological conditions and varying stages of development in developing countries;

(*c*) To expand significantly the assistance from developed to developing countries in research and development programmes and in the creation of suitable indigenous technology;

(*d*) To adopt commercial practices governing transfer of technology to the requirements of the developing countries and to prevent abuse of the rights of sellers;

(*e*) To promote international cooperation in research and development in exploration and exploitation, conservation and the legitimate utilisation of natural resources and all sources of energy.

In taking the above measures, the special needs of the least developed and land-locked countries should be borne in mind.

## V. Regulation and Control over the Activities of Transnational Corporations

All efforts should be made to formulate, adopt and implement an international code of conduct for transnational corporations;

(a) To prevent interference in the internal affairs of the countries where they operate and their collaboration with racist régimes and colonial administrations;

(b) To regulate their activities in host countries, to eliminate restrictive business practices and to conform to the national development plans and objectives of developing countries, and in this context facilitate, as necessary, the review and revision of previously concluded arrangements;

(c) To bring about assistance, transfer of technology and management skills to developing countries on equitable and favourable terms;

(d) To regulate the repatriation of the profits accruing from their operations, taking into account the legitimate interests of all parties concerned;

(e) To promote reinvestment of their profits in developing countries.

## VI. Charter of Economic Rights and Duties of States

The Charter of Economic Rights and Duties of States, the draft of which is being prepared by a working group of the United Nations and which the General Assembly has already expressed the intention of adopting at its twenty-ninth regular session, shall constitute an effective instrument towards the establishment of a new system of international economic relations based on equity, sovereign equality, and interdependence of the interests of developed and developing countries. It is therefore of vital importance that the aforementioned Charter be adopted by the General Assembly as its twenty-ninth session.

## VII. Promotion of Cooperation among Developing Countries

1. Collective self-reliance and growing cooperation among developing countries will further strengthen their role in the new international economic order. Developing countries, with a view to expanding cooperation at the regional, subregional and interregional levels, should take further steps, *inter alia*;

(*a*) To support the establishment and or improvement of an appropriate mechanism to defend the prices of their exportable commodities and to improve access to and stabilise markets for them. In this context the increasingly effective mobilisation by the whole group of oil-exporting countries of their natural resources for the benefit of their economic development is to be welcomed. At the same time there is the paramount need for cooperation among the developing countries in evolving urgently and in a spirit of solidarity all possible means to assist developing countries to cope with the immediate problems resulting from this legitimate and perfectly justified action. The measures already taken in this regard are a positive indication of the evolving cooperation between developing countries;

(*b*) To protect their inalienable right to permanent sovereignty over their natural resources;

(*c*) To promote, establish or strengthen economic integration at the regional and subregional levels;

(*d*) To increase considerably their imports from other developing countries;

(*e*) To ensure that no developing country accords to imports from developed countries more favourable treatment than that accorded to imports from developing countries. Taking into account the existing international agreements, current limitations and possibilities and also their future evolution, preferential treatment should be given to the procurement of import requirements from other developing countries. Wherever possible, preferential treatment should be given to imports from developing countries and the exports of those countries;

(*f*) To promote close cooperation in the fields of finance, credit relations and monetary issues, including the development of credit relations on a preferential basis and on favourable terms;

(*g*) To strengthen efforts which are already being made by developing countries to utilise available financial resources for financing development in the developing countries through investment, financing of export-oriented and emergency projects and other long-term assistance;

(*h*) To promote and establish effective instruments of cooperation in the fields of industry, science and technology, transport, shipping and mass communication media.

2. Developed countries should support initiatives in the regional, subregional and interregional cooperation of developing countries through the extension of financial and technical assistance by more effective and concrete actions, particularly in the field of commercial policy.

VIII. ASSISTANT IN THE EXERCISE OF PERMANENT SOVEREIGNTY OF
STATES OVER NATURAL RESOURCES

All efforts should be made:

(*a*) To defeat attempts to prevent the free and effective exercise of the rights of every State to full and permanent sovereignty over its natural resources.

(*b*) To ensure that competent agencies of the United Nations system meet requests for assistance from developing countries in connexion with the operation of nationalised means of production.

IX. STRENGTHENING THE ROLE OF THE UNITED NATIONS SYSTEM IN
THE FIELD OF INTERNATIONAL ECONOMIC COOPERATION

1. In furtherance of the objectives of the International Development Strategy for the Second United Nations Development Decade and in accordance with the aims and objectives of the Declaration on the Establishment of a New International Economic Order, all Member States pledge to make full use of the United Nations system in the implementation of the present Programme of Action, jointly adopted by them, in working for the establishment of a new international economic order and thereby strengthening the role of the United Nations in the field of world-wide cooperation for economic and social development.

2. The General Assembly of the United Nations shall conduct an over-all review of the implementation of the Programme of Action as a priority item. All the activities of the United Nations system to be undertaken under the Programme of Action as well as those already planned, such as the World Population Conference, 1974, the World Food Conference, the Second General Conference of the United Nations Industrial Development Organisation and the mid-term review and appraisal of the International Development Strategy for the Second United Nations Development Decade should be so directed as to enable the special session of the General Assembly on development called for under Assembly resolution 3172 (XXVIII) of 17 December 1973, to make its full contribution to the establishment of the new international economic order. All Member States are urged, jointly and individually, to direct their efforts and policies towards the success of that special session.

3. The Economic and Social Council shall define the policy framework and coordinate the activities of all organisations, institutions and subsidiary bodies within the United Nations system which shall be entrusted with the task of implementing the present Programme of

Action. In order to enable the Economic and Social Council to carry out its tasks effectively:

(*a*) All organisations, institutions and subsidiary bodies concerned within the United Nations system shall submit to the Economic and Social Council progress reports on the implementation of the Programme of Action within their respective fields of competence as often as necessary, but not less than once a year;

(*b*) The Economic and Social Council shall examine the progress reports as a matter of urgency, to which end it may be convened, as necessary, in special session or, if need be, may function continuously. It shall draw the attention of the General Assembly to the problems and difficulties arising in connexion with the implementation of the Programme of Action.

4. All organisations, institutions, subsidiary bodies and conferences of the United Nations system are entrusted with the implementation of the Programme of Action. The activities of the United Nations Conference on Trade and Development, as set forth in General Assembly resolution 1995 (XIX) of 30 December 1964, should be strengthened for the purpose of following in collaboration with other competent organisations the development of international trade in raw materials throughout the world.

5. Urgent and effective measures should be taken to review the lending policies of international financial institutions, taking into account the special situation of each developing country, to suit urgent needs, to improve the practices of these institutions in regard to, *inter alia*, development financing and international monetary problems, and to ensure more effective participation by developing countries—whether recipients or contributors—in the decision-making process through appropriate revision of the pattern of voting rights.

6. The developed countries and others in a position to do so should contribute substantially to the various organisations, programmes and funds established within the United Nations system for the purpose of accelerating economic and social development in developing countries.

7. The present Programme of Action complements and strengthens the goals and objectives embodied in the International Development Strategy for the Second United Nations Development Decade as well as the new measures formulated by the General Assembly at its twenty-eighth session to offset the shortfalls in achieving those goals and objectives.

8. The implementation of the Programme of Action should be taken into account at the time of the mid-term review and appraisal of the

International Development Strategy for the Second United Nations Development Decade. New commitments, changes, additions and adaptations in the Strategy should be made, as appropriate, taking into account the Declaration on the Establishment of a New International Economic Order and the present Programme of Action.

## X. Special Programme

The General Assembly adopts the following Special Programme, including particularly emergency measures to mitigate the difficulties of the developing countries most seriously affected by economic crisis, bearing in mind the particular problem of the least developed and land-locked countries:

*The General Assembly.*

*Taking into account the following considerations:*

(*a*) The sharp increase in the prices of their essential imports such as food, fertilizers, energy products, capital goods, equipment and services, including transportation and transit costs, has gravely exacerbated the increasingly adverse terms of trade of a number of developing countries, added to the burden of their foreign debt and, cumulatively, created a situation which, if left untended, will make it impossible for them to finance their essential imports and development and result in a further deterioration in the levels and conditions of life in these countries. The present crisis is the outcome of all the problems that have accumulated over the years: in the field of trade, in monetary reform, the world-wide inflationary situation, inadequacy and delay in provision of financial assistance and many other similar problems in the economic and developmental fields. In facing the crisis, this complex situation must be borne in mind so as to ensure that the Special Programme adopted by the international community provides emergency relief and timely assistance to the most seriously affected countries. Simultaneously steps are being taken to resolve these outstanding problems through a fundamental restructuring of the world economic system, in order to allow these countries while solving the present difficulties to reach an acceptable level of development;

(*b*) The special measures adopted to assist the most seriously affected countries must encompass not only the relief which they require on an emergency basis to maintain their import requirements, but also beyond that, steps to consciously promote the capacity of these countries to produce and earn more. Unless such a comprehensive approach is adopted, there is every likelihood that the difficulties of the most seriously affected countries may be perpetuated. Nevertheless, the first and most pressing task of the international community is to enable those countries to meet the shortfall in their balance of payments positions. But this must be simultaneously supplemented by additional development assistance to maintain and thereafter accelerate their rate of economic development;

(*c*) The countries which have been most seriously affected are precisely those which are at the greatest disadvantage in the world economy: the least developed, the land-locked and other low-income developing countries as well as other developing countries whose economies have been seriously dislocated as a result of the present economic crisis, natural calamities and foreign aggression and occupation. An indication of the countries thus affected, the level of the impact on their economies and the kind of relief and assistance they require can be assessed on the basis, *inter alia*, of the following criteria:

(i) Low *per capita* income as a reflection of relative poverty, low productivity, low level of technology and development;
(ii) Sharp increase in their import cost of essentials relative to export earnings;
(iii) High ratio of debt servicing to export earnings;
(iv) Insufficiency in export earnings, comparative inelasticity of export incomes and unavailability of exportable surplus;
(v) Low level of foreign exchange reserves or their inadequacy for requirements;
(vi) Adverse impact of higher transportation and transit costs;
(vii) Relative importance of foreign trade in the development process.

(*d*) The assessment of the extent and nature of the impact on the economies of the most seriously affected countries must be made flexible, keeping in mind the present uncertainty in the world economy, the adjustment policies that may be adopted by the developed countries and the flow of capital and investment. Estimates of the payments situation and needs of these countries can be assessed and projected reliably only on the basis of their average performance over a number of years. Long-term projections, at this time, cannot but be uncertain.

(*e*) It is important that, in the special measures to mitigate the difficulties of the most seriously affected countries, all the developed countries as well as the developing countries should contribute according to their level of development and the capacity and strength of their economies. It is notable that some developing countries, despite their own difficulties and development needs, have shown a willingness to play a concrete and helpful role in ameliorating the difficulties faced by the poorer developing countries. The various initiatives and measures taken recently by certain developing countries with adequate resources on a bilateral and multilateral basis to contribute to alleviating the difficulties of other developing countries are a reflection of their commitment to the principle of effective economic cooperation among developing countries.

(*f*) The response of the developed countries which have by far the greater capacity to assist the affected countries in overcoming their present difficulties must be commensurate with their responsibilities. Their assistance should be in addition to the presently available levels of aid. They should fulfil and if possible exceed the targets of the International Development Strategy for the Second United Nations Development Decade on financial assistance to the developing countries, especially that relating to official development assistance. They should also give serious consideration to the cancellation of the external debts of the most seriously affected countries. This would provide the simplest and quickest relief to the affected countries. Favourable consideration should also be given to debt moratorium and rescheduling. The current situation should not lead the industrialised countries to adopt what will ultimately prove to be a self-defeating policy aggravating the present crisis.

*Recalling* the constructive proposals made by His Imperial Majesty the Shahanshah of Iran[4] and His Excellency Mr. Houari Boumediène, President of the People's Democratic Republic of Algeria,[5]

1. *Decides* to launch a Special Programme to provide emergency relief and development assistance to the developing countries most seriously affected, as a matter of urgency, and for the period of time necessary, at least until the end of the Second United Nations Development Decade, to help them overcome their present difficulties and to achieve self-sustaining economic development;

2. *Decides* as a first step in the Special Programme to request the Secretary-General to launch an emergency operation to provide timely relief to the most seriously affected developing countries, as defined in subparagraph (*c*) above, with the aim of maintaining unimpaired

essential imports for the duration of the coming twelve months and to invite the industrialised countries and other potential contributors to announce their contributions for emergency assistance or intimate their intention to do so, by 15 June 1974 to be provided through bilateral or multilateral channels taking into account the commitments and measures of assistance announced or already taken by some countries, and further requests the Secretary-General to report the progress of the emergency operation to the General Assembly at its twenty-ninth session, through the Economic and Social Council at its fifty-seventh session;

3. *Calls upon* the industrialised countries and other potential contributors to extend to the most seriously affected countries immediate relief and assistance which must be of an order of magnitude that is commensurate with the needs of these countries. Such assistance should be in addition to the existing level of aid and provided at a very early date to the maximum possible extent on a grant basis and, where not possible, on soft terms. The disbursement and relevant operational procedures and terms must reflect this exceptional situation. The assistance could be provided either through bilateral or multilateral channels, including such new institutions and facilities that have been or are to be set up. The special measures may include the following:

(*a*) Special arrangements on particularly favourable terms and conditions including possible subsidies for and assured supplies of essential commodities and goods;

(*b*) Deferred payments for all or part of imports of essential commodities and goods;

(*c*) Commodity assistance, including food aid, on a grant basis or deferred payments in local currencies, bearing in mind that this should not adversely affect the exports of developing countries;

(*d*) Long term suppliers' credits on easy terms;

(*e*) Long-term financial assistance on concessionary terms;

(*f*) Drawings from special International Monetary Fund facilities on concessional terms;

(*g*) Establishment of a link between the creation of special drawing rights and development assistance, taking into account the additional financial requirements of the most seriously affected countries;

(*h*) Subsidies, provided bilaterally or multilaterally, for interest on funds available on commercial terms borrowed by the most seriously affected countries;

(*i*) Debt renegotiation on a case-by-case basis with a view to concluding agreements on debt cancellation, moratorium or rescheduling;

(*j*) Provision on more favourable terms of capital goods and technical assistance to accelerate the industrialisation of the affected countries;

(*k*) Investment in industrial and development projects on favourable terms;

(*l*) Subsidising the additional transit and transport costs, especially of the land-locked countries;

4. *Appeals* to the developed countries to consider favourably the cancellation, moratorium or rescheduling of the debts of the most seriously affected developing countries, on their request, as an important contribution to mitigating the grave and urgent difficulties of these countries;

5. *Decides* to establish a Special Fund under the auspices of the United Nations, through voluntary contributions from industrialised countries and other potential contributors, as a part of the Special Programme, to provide emergency relief and development assistance, which will commence its operations at the latest by 1 January 1975;

6. *Establishes* an *Ad Hoc* Committee on the Special Programme, composed of thirty-six Member States appointed by the President of the General Assembly, after appropriate consultations, bearing in mind the purposes of the Special Fund and its terms of reference;

(*a*) To make recommendations, *inter alia*, on the scope, machinery and modes of operation of the Special Fund, taking into account the need for:

(i) Equitable representation on its governing body;
(ii) Equitable distribution of its resources;
(iii) Full utilisation of the services and facilities of existing international organisation;
(iv) The possibility of merging the United Nations Capital Development Fund with the operations of the Special Fund;
(v) A central monitoring body to oversee the various measures being taken both bilaterally and multilaterally;

and to this end, bearing in mind the different ideas and proposals submitted at the sixth special session, including those put forward by Iran[6] and those made at the 2208th plenary meeting, and the comments thereon, and the possibility of utilising the Special Fund to provide an alternative channel for normal development assistance after the emergency period;

(*b*) To monitor, pending commencement of the operations of the

Special Fund, the various measures being taken both bilaterally and multilaterally to assist the most seriously affected countries:

(*c*) To prepare, on the basis of information provided by the countries concerned and by appropriate agencies of the United Nations system, a broad assessment of:

(i) The magnitude of the difficulties facing the most seriously affected countries;

(ii) The kind and quantities of the commodities and goods essentially required by them;

(iii) Their need for financial assistance;

(iv) Their technical assistance requirements, including especially access to technology;

7. *Requests* the Secretary-General of the United Nations, the Secretary-General of the United Nations Conference on Trade and Development, the President of the International Bank for Reconstruction and Development, the Managing Director of the International Monetary Fund, the Administrator of the United Nations Development Programme and the heads of the other competent international organisations to assist the *Ad Hoc* Committee on the Special Programme in performing the functions assigned to it under paragraph 6 above, and to help, as appropriate, in the operations of the Special Fund;

8. *Requests* the International Monetary Fund to expedite decisions on:

(*a*) The establishment of an extended special facility with a view to enabling the most seriously affected developing countries to participate in it on favourable terms;

(*b*) The creation of special drawing rights and the early establishment of the link between their allocation and development financing;

(*c*) The establishment and operation of the proposed new special facility to extend credits and subsidise interest charges on commercial funds borrowed by Member States, bearing in mind the interests of the developing countries and especially the additional financial requirements of the most seriously affected countries;

9. *Requests* the World Bank Group and the International Monetary Fund to place their managerial, financial and technical services at the disposal of Governments contributing to emergency financial relief so as to enable them to assist without delay in channelling funds to the recipients, making such institutional and procedural changes as may be required;

10. *Invites* the United Nations Development Programme to take the

necessary steps, particularly at the country level, to respond on an emergency basis to requests for additional assistance which it may be called upon to render within the framework of the Special Programme;

11. *Requests* the *Ad Hoc* Committee on the Special Programme to submit its report and recommendations to the Economic and Social Council at its fifty-seventh session and invites the Council, on the basis of its consideration of that report, to submit suitable recommendations to the General Assembly at its twenty-ninth session;

12. *Decides* to consider as a matter of high priority at its twenty-ninth session, within the framework of a new international economic order, the question of special measures for the most seriously affected countries.

*2229th plenary meeting*
*1 May 1974*

\*

\*		\*

The President of the General Assembly subsequently informed the Secretary-General[7] that in pursuance of section X paragraph 6 of the above resolution, he had appointed the members of the Ad Hoc Committee on the Special Programme.

As a result, the Ad Hoc Committee will be composed of the following Member States: ALGERIA, ARGENTINA, AUSTRALIA, BRAZIL, CHAD, COSTA RICA, CZECHOSLOVAKIA, FRANCE, GERMANY, (FEDERAL REPUBLIC OF), GUYANA, INDIA, IRAN, JAPAN, KUWAIT, MADAGASCAR, NEPAL, NETHERLANDS, NIGERIA, NORWAY, PAKISTAN, PARAGUAY, PHILIPPINES, SOMALIA, SRI LANKA, SUDAN, SWAZILAND, SYRIAN ARAB REPUBLIC, TURKEY, UNION OF SOVIET SOCIALIST REPUBLICS, UNITED KINGDOM OF GREAT BRITAIN AND NORTHERN IRELAND, UNITED STATES OF AMERICA, UPPER VOLTA, URUGUAY, VENEZUELA, YUGOSLAVIA *and* ZAIRE.

NOTES

[1] Resolution 2626 (XXV).
[2] Resolution 3201 (S-VI).
[3] Resolution 2626 (XXV).
[4] A/9548, annex.
[5] *Official Records of the General Assembly, Sixth Special Session, Plenary Meetings*, 2208 meeting, paras 3-152.
[6] A/AC 166/L 15; See also A/9548, annex.
[7] A/9558 and Add 1.

# Notes

1. If the output from the import substitution industry is an input for the export sector, the competitive position of firms producing for foreign markets can be eroded. Furthermore, by restricting demand through high tariffs and other restraints, the domestic currency's exchange rate is artificially inflated, making it more difficult to export traditional products. High levels of protection have also produced distortions in domestic prices which have led to a bias against agricultural production. Finally, important learning and productivity effects, as well as other competitive benefits from trade, are often sacrificed.

2. Outward-looking trade policies receive support from empirical analyses which show ties between export expansion and growth. For example, Michaely (1977) correlated the rate of change in exports as a percentage of national product against the change in per capita product for 41 countries over 1950–73 and found a significant positive relation between the variables. Cohen (1968) employed a multiple regression to assess the relative impact of export earnings and foreign aid on LDCs' gross national product. In each of the two time periods tested, the export variable's coefficient was significant and considerably larger than that for the foreign aid term. Similar techniques were used and results achieved by Emery (1967). Kravis (1970) also demonstrated that external markets for developing countries, *unconstrained by artificial trade barriers*, are potentially more favourable than nineteenth-century markets were for the periphery countries, and that LDC export expansion is correlated with growth.

3. One participant argued that because free trade between developed market economy countries and LDCs represented 'unequal exchange' the latter had suffered more from liberalism than from protectionism. In his view, a strategy of industrialisation based on exports to developed countries would not be in the interests of LDCs since it would conflict with collective self-reliance, and since a large share of the benefits would go to transnational corporations. Another participant also argued that the problem of market access for LDC exports was a false one on the grounds that this trade was of interest to only a small number of countries, and that it involved selling their products at a give-away price (unequal exchange), and that much of the trade was controlled by transnationals.

4. As noted, an empirical investigation by Arthur Lewis (1978) has a major bearing on this point. Lewis clearly demonstrated that the trade expansion which occurred over 1960–73 was unprecedented in the historical record, and that LDCs should not count on such growth rates in formulating their

trade and development strategies. However, the fact that LDCs failed to achieve practically every important development target of importance during this period casts doubt on the proposition that growth can be transmitted from developed to developing countries without basic changes in the transmittal mechanism (i. e., the basic institutional framework within which the LDCs and DMECs operate).

5. While one must be sympathetic to the objectives of the basic needs strategy, there is a potential problem associated with time frames. Through its contribution of higher foreign exchange earnings and important learning effects, the outward-oriented strategy may allow attainment of higher living standards in the future than would be achieved if one adopts a basic needs approach. However, this proposition has been countered by proponents of basic needs who argue that the problem of human poverty and suffering is so severe as to require direct and immediate attention. Also, it is held that the resulting improvements in *human capital* may be equally as important as the productivity effects associated with an outward-looking approach.

CHAPTER 2

1. Kleiman (1976) notes that

> some of the effects of protracted colonial rule may be permanent. Linguistic and cultural assimilation, caused originally by enforced trading with nationals of the colonial power, may in time lead to the concentration of this trade on a voluntary basis. More generally, the creation of some of the circumstances fostering trade with the metropolitan country should be viewed as sunk costs, irrelevant to present decisions: the existing pattern of trade may be optimal, even if the developments which brought it about were not. Furthermore, even if the present pattern is suboptimal, the cost of transition to a better one may outweigh any ensuing impact.

2. By comparing the metropolitan state's share in the trade of former colonial associates with similar data for a control group of developing countries, Kleiman (1976) develops an index of 'enforced bilateralism' which shows the extent to which trade relations of the colonies have been distorted in favour of the developed nation. The results suggest that former colonial associates' exports to, and imports from, the United Kingdom were three times the normal level for LDCs, while similar ratios for the French associates were about eight times the developing country average.

3. Examples of studies which have tied concentration to higher prices and profits are Bain (1951), Bell and Murphy (1969), Mann (1966) and Yeats (1974). The concentration ratios employed in these investigations are statistical measures which show the percentage of sales controlled by a given number of the largest firms in a market. For a discussion of the use and problems with measures of market concentration see Adelman (1951).

4. Factors limiting competition are often referred to as 'barriers to entry'. Barriers to entry are characteristics of an industry which determine the

difficulty potential entrants experience in penetrating a market. Bain argued that entry barriers determine the 'condition of entry', or the extent to which established firms can raise prices above competitive levels without new entry. He concluded that the major entry barriers are product differentiation, largely through advertising, absolute cost advantages, and scale economies.

5. Using Kleiman's bilateral trade enforcement ratios as a guide, the Italian, Belgian, and Portuguese colonies appear to have been far more trade-dependent on the metropolitan state, while the United Kingdom's associates seem to have had a greater degree of self-determination.

6. Prior to 1966, French manufactures were imported by many associated African states at tariffs considerably below those applied to goods originating in other industrial nations. However, based on conditions set forth in the Treaty of Rome, preferential access to these markets (reverse preferences) were extended to all EEC members in 1966. Imports from the United Kingdom also received preferential treatment in such diverse markets as India, Malaysia, and Jamaica, thereby creating conditions where import competition was lessened.

7. Analysis based on unit values must be treated with caution since product differentials, quality, or styling variations may be reflected as price differences. However, for homogeneous products like iron and steel the influence of these factors should be minor. In fact, several economists have used iron and steel unit values to assess the accuracy of wholesale price quotations employed by the US Bureau of Labour Statistics.

8. Over 1963–9, France's share of OECD iron and steel exports to Chad fell from 53 to 35 per cent, in Dahomey from 62 to 39 per cent, and in Senegal from 63 to 41 per cent. Separate tests reveal a significant correlation between changes in French market shares and the pattern of relative import prices. Those countries which heightened competitive pressures seem to have benefited through lower import prices.

9. Supplementary information shows the associates pay in excess for other French imports. In a previously published study, UNCTAD (1968) estimated these countries paid the following margins over world prices due to the monopoly position held by French firms: cotton textiles—23 per cent, sugar—63 to 105 per cent, motor vehicles—30 per cent, tools and hardware—38 per cent, machinery—25 per cent, electrical apparatus—8 per cent, and petroleum products—12 per cent.

10. Between 1960–2, Kleiman estimated that 42 per cent of the exports of the United Kingdom's African colonial associates went to the home market (as opposed to 1·7 per cent to France), while the French colonies sent 53 per cent of their total exports to France, and only 1·6 per cent to the United Kingdom. The figures are even more skewed on the import side: French colonies received 61 per cent of their imports from France, and only 2·8 per cent from the United Kingdom.

11. In a related study dealing with unit values of US machinery exports, Hufbauer and O'Neill (1972) find evidence of a strong direct relation between size and relative prices. For example, they suggest 'A noteworthy feature of the regression analysis is the strong and highly significant effect of the quantity variable. Whether the elasticity of 0·23 reflects price discrimi-

nation based on lower sales and service costs for large buyers, or discrimination based on orthodox monopoly considerations, we cannot say. In any event, the quantity effect means that a small importing country pays a much higher price for its machinery.'

12. Individual developing countries generally find it too costly to maintain an efficient diversified market intelligence service for gathering information on terms offered by alternative sources of supply. To a limited extent, some LDC diplomatic missions perform such functions, but there appears insufficient coordination and specialisation. In cases, some developing countries rely on information supplied by market intelligence sources headquartered in the developed countries. In this situation, the United Nations suggests that a joint LDC intelligence service, located in major export centres, offers an excellent opportunity for fruitful collaboration.

13. The UNCTAD (December 1974) banana study provides particularly useful information concerning the market power of transnational corporations with which the LDCs must deal. For example, this investigation shows that the three largest banana-importing firms control 100 per cent of the market in Canada, 90 per cent in the United States and Switzerland, 78 per cent in Belgium and Italy, and 70 per cent in the Federal Republic of Germany.

CHAPTER 3

1. Viatsos (1978) provides a comprehensive survey of the potential problems and benefits associated with LDC economic cooperation and integration.

2. Several factors suggest more attention should be devoted to inter-regional preferences. Experience with customs unions among neighbouring countries, or on a regional basis, have been disappointing due to a lack of beneficial trading opportunities or the problem of distributing gains. Inter-regional preferences could bring together more diverse economies, producing a wider volume of goods, and thus should offer more beneficial trading possibilities.

3. Trade creation and diversion may be explained as follows. In a three country world, *A* and *B* form a customs union to the exclusion of *C*. In other words, *A* and *B* abolish trade restrictions among themselves, while imports from *C* are subject to a common external tariff. For products in which *A* and *B* are competitive, the elimination of tariffs causes the replacement of some high cost production by imports from the partner country. This *trade creation* effect is considered favourable to general welfare since it rationalises production within the union. Secondly, *A* and *B* may also begin to import from each other products that previously came from *C*. Thus, tariff discrimination induces trade away from *C*. This *trade diversion* effect is generally held to be unfavourable since it results in a less efficient world production pattern.

4. Several of these standards have potentially important implications for LDC trade and other forms of integration. Given that benefits are related to the size of the union, the maximum advantage lies in a *global* system of trade preferences. Also, available data show that considerable variation exists in individual LDC tariffs on common items, and that these tariffs may reach

several hundred per cent. These two factors also suggest the maximum advantage will occur from establishing the widest integration scheme possible.

5. Bela Balassa cites cases where a doubling of output resulted in a 20 to 30 per cent decline in costs, and also refers to a study showing that about 50 per cent of the interstate differences in labour productivity in Brazil are explained by the size of the manufacturing establishment, with the remainder being due to differences in capital per worker and plant scale. However, a more pessimistic view of the potential for achieving scale economies through economic integration is taken by Morton and Tulloch (1977, pp. 310–13).

6. Transport innovations may have made developed countries more efficient in shipping and widened the freight cost differential between industrial countries and LDCs. Since competitive pressures in developed countries are stronger, Little, Scitovsky and Scott (1970) suggest that

... containers and other forms of innovation in transport will be introduced there first and will not spread to developing countries' trade for a long time. These innovations might be accompanied by a fundamental change in the whole system of rate fixing since it would seem rational to base the charge on the container rather than on its contents. The result might be a big reduction in freight on exports of manufactures between developed countries, putting exports from developing countries at a severe disadvantage where the freight element is important.

To the extent that these innovations are used on major North – South routes, it would provide a bias against some intra-trade since other developing countries' goods might be rendered non-competitive by these reduced freight costs.

7. Yeats (November 1978) shows that there may be sizeable inaccuracies in some countries' import–export statistics due to problems associated with proper recording and treatment of transhipments. There is some reason to believe that transhipments may be influencing the trade statistics reported by Kuwait, although there is no way to distinguish this exchange from normal trade.

8. The tariff differential for developing country $i$ over developed country $j$ in the $k$th LDC market $(T_{ik})$ can be derived from,

$$T_{ik} = t(f_{ik} - f_{dk}) \qquad (3\text{–}3)$$

where $t$ is the tariff rate applied by developing country $k$, $f_{ik}$ is the *ad valorem* freight rate for shipments from $i$ to $k$, while $f_{dk}$ is the *ad valorem* freight rate for exports from the developed country.

9. Equation (3–3) shows why this must be the case. Essentially, the two-tier system results in setting the term $f_{ik}$ equal to zero. Given non-zero transport costs for exports from developed to developing countries, this is sufficient to cause $T_{ik}$ to be negative, i.e. to always generate preferences in favour of the LDCs.

10. If a tariff $t$ is applied to a free-on-board valuation base, the duty collected is $p_b t$ where $p_b$ is the f.o.b. import price. Under a c.i.f. procedure the duty collected is $(p_b + r)t$ where $r$ represents unit transport and insurance costs.

Algebraic manipulation shows the percentage point increase in import duties ($P_d$) associated with a shift from a f.o.b. to a c.i.f. base can be approximated from,

$$P_d = \frac{p_h + ftp_b - p_b t}{p_b} = ft \tag{3-4}$$

where $f$ represents *ad valorem* transport and insurance costs. In Table 3.7 the term $P_d$ is referred to as the f.o.b. margin and shows the difference between the duty collected under an f.o.b. and c.i.f. system expressed as a percentage of the free-on-board price of the good. In the table; the 'c.i.f. tariff' has been computed from,

$$t_{\text{cif}} = \frac{(p_b + r)}{p_b} \tag{3-5}$$

11. Objections to the two-tier valuation system on the basis that it encourages trade between 'distant' developing countries at the expense of 'nearer' ones, and therefore involves a misallocation of resources are invalid. What the system does is remove the interaction of tariffs and transport costs which *discriminate* against distant countries. Trade is still influenced by relative freight costs, but without the further confounding effect of the c.i.f. tariffs. Some misallocations may occur as trade is diverted from developed to developing countries, but the arguments advanced under the *collective-self-reliance* strategy outline a number of benefits which should offset these negative results.

CHAPTER 4

1. Kreinin and Finger (1976) estimate that, during 1956–73, buffer stocks of 120,000 tons and 4 million tons would have been needed to limit annual price fluctuations for tin and copper to 15 per cent around their trend. Stocks of these magnitudes for the two commodities would have involved a cost of more than $7 billion.

2. Laursen (1978) recognises the importance of this point in noting that

> the history of commodity agreements is not very encouraging. The practical difficulty is mainly to predict the correct long-run price above which the buffer stock should sell, and below which it should buy. If this price is predicted incorrectly, the scheme will either accumulate commodities, and therefore use up its funds, or it will deplete its stock. In addition, the buffer stock may actually stimulate destabilising speculation if it is too small.

3. Avramovic supports this allegation by noting that the lower relative prices realised by the Ghana marketing agency between 1966 and 1969 could be explained by the timing of a considerable portion of sales to meet urgent foreign exchange needs rather than an attempt to take advantage of price fluctuations on world markets. More generally, he notes that the lack of

*choice* as to when to sell has been the unacceptable feature of traditional trade, and an effective way of improving producer staying power is to advance credit for a portion of their marketable surplus. With cash available for payment of taxes and debts, primary product producers will have the option of holding stocks until the off-season to realise better prices.

4. Crop shortfalls by the Soviet Union are another cause of commodity price instability. On occasions, these deficits have led the USSR to enter world markets, particularly for grains, with purchases of a magnitude sufficient to produce rapid and sizeable run-ups in commodity prices. Research by UNCTAD also shows that changes in commodity prices and revenues are closely tied to the industrial nation's business cycle. The fact that instability in LDC export markets often has its root causes in actions by industrial or socialist countries makes a compelling case for the international community's adoption and support of measures such as the common fund to stabilise commodity prices.

5. Alfred Maizels (1976) notes, 'the inclusion of all processed commodities in the GSP schemes of developed countries, if possible at zero rates of duty, would assist in stimulating the growth of processing industries in the developing countries, particularly in those which do not possess a diversified manufacturing sector'. This suggestion deserves attention since utilisation of the GSP approach for processed commodities could be a way of liberalising trade and still controlling potential disruptive effects on domestic industries.

6. Since the demand for tropical beverages such as coffee and tea is price inelastic, abolition of these internal taxes would not increase exports by more than marginal amounts. Several economists have suggested alternative policies which are worthy of consideration. One proposal is to retain, or even increase, these taxes and to transfer back to the producing countries some agreed portion of the tax yield. Another alternative is for the LDCs to impose a uniform export tax which would operate as the importing countries reduce their duties to negate any price effects. Either of these alternatives seems likely to afford greater benefits to the LDCs than the simple abolition of the revenue duties.

CHAPTER 5

1. Diaz-Alejandro ties many present TNC problems to their forerunners in noting that

> while Northern observers prefer looking at the future belittling the past, history lies heavily on Southern perceptions of the present. The political and economic abuses of colonialism, the close and open cooperation between foreign governments and companies, are viewed not as phenomena which ended in 1945 or 1955, but which evolved into subtler manipulations which are with us today. ITT type scandals, which in the North are viewed as aberrations, are viewed by the South as merely the tip of the iceberg.
>
> Carlos Diaz-Alejandro, *Transnational Corporations and Developing Countries*, UNCTAD working paper.

2. Differences in the extent of transnational operations seem to be the major reason why the US and Japanese economies are so much more open to LDC exports than are other industrial nations. For example, the United States and Japan import close to 20 per cent of all manufactures from developing countries, while the corresponding ratio for most European countries is less than half this figure. Donges and Riedel (1977) suggest 'the primary reason for these differences can be traced to the countries' direct participation (through TNCs) in manufacturing for export in developing countries and the existence of appropriate marketing outlets for LDC manufactures'. Thus, TNCs seem to have been a major factor leading to developing country export expansion.

3. Franko stresses the problems in trying to assess the actual influence of TNCs in international trade given the very inadequate empirical information on this subject. Specifically, he states that

> the role of the non-US enterprises in the international trade of host countries has in the past been even more obscure than their role in foreign manufacturing. Despite the fact that large parent firms based in Switzerland, France, Belgium, Holland and Italy own over 1,000 foreign manufacturing subsidiaries, few if any official statistics covering these countries' foreign investments and foreign subsidiary sales – much less foreign affiliates exports – are available. Although foreign investment value statistics are available for UK, Japanese, German and Swedish enterprises, no surveys of their role in international trade appear to have been undertaken.

4. A key point that has not been dealt with adequately in these studies concerns the influence of the technology adopted by the transnationals on production processes employed by domestic firms. It may be that the capital-intensive technologies used by TNCs force local firms to utilise similar methods to be competitive. This interrelation, if it exists, would make comparisons between foreign and domestic production techniques of little practical utility.

5. Empirical studies by the ILO provide a basis for quantitatively assessing the employment creation through these linkage effects, at least within very broad limits. Through analysis of over 20 developing country input–output tables, the ILO derived general factors for employment creation based on industry value added. As a rule, it appears that the *maximum* secondary effects may be equal to the direct employment effects. Thus, if TNC activity creates 5,000 jobs the linkage effects may produce the same number of positions in supplier industries. However, on average, the secondary effects appear to be about half the size of the direct employment creation.

6. This section draws from Franko (1975).

7. World Bank statistics cover only public and privately guaranteed debt. The Bank staff have estimated that private, non-public guaranteed debt might add another 20 per cent to these figures.

CHAPTER 6

1. To a large degree, differences in LDC market shares in the developed market economy and centrally planned countries are due to fuels. While DMECs import about three quarters of their fuel requirements from developing countries, the corresponding proportion for the CPCs is only about 25 per cent. However, even excluding fuels the *level* of centrally planned imports from developing countries is well below that of the developed market economy countries.

2. Much the same picture emerges concerning the relatively poor performance of the socialist countries even if petroleum shipments are excluded from the totals. For example, in a comparative study of imports of 21 key commodity processing chains, Yeats (1979, pp. 48–63) found that the USSR imported only about $7 per capita of the components in 1974 as opposed to $49 for France and the United Kingdom, $53 for Japan, and $59 for the Federal Republic of Germany. This investigation also found that the USSR's imports were highly weighted towards unprocessed goods while the Western countries had a greater percentage of manufactures in the total.

3. It must be acknowledged that various factors contribute to the relatively poor trade performance of the socialist countries. A primary reason is the lack of traditional ties between the socialist and most developing countries. Lack of traditional contacts also explains why appropriate transport and financial institutions have not evolved to service East–South trade. Finally, there is no doubt that foreign policy of the DMECs has often been a factor working against broadened commercial contacts between developing and socialist countries.

4. Statistical comparisons support this contention. For example, the year to year changes in CPC imports from developing countries averaged 19 per cent as opposed to 12 per cent for the developed market economy countries. Also, when an exponential trend function was fitted to each group's imports, the standard error for the CPCs, expressed as a percentage of the trend, was almost 40 per cent higher than that for the DMECs.

CHAPTER 7

1. Leontief suggested that these perverse findings were due to higher labour productivity in the United States than in its trading partners. In support of this proposition, he demonstrated that US exports employed relatively more labour than did import competing goods. Irving Kravis also has shown that leading US export industries generally paid higher wages than import competing industries. Both Leontief's and Kravis' findings suggest a third factor, namely human capital, was important in explaining US trade patterns.

2. The selection of items was supplemented by detailed analyses of manufactures imported by developed from less developed countries to see if additional products needed to be taken into account. On this basis, several items such as batteries, lamps, and miscellaneous manufactures were added to the NBER list since relative value added in other countries appeared well

below the United States average. However, a major conclusion of this portion of the analysis was that products manufactured by labour-intensive processes in the United States were also manufactured by relatively labour-intensive processes in other countries. Lary used these findings to justify extensive use of United States production statistics as a guide to factor proportions.

3. This performance is all the more impressive when one realises that some of the labour-intensive goods (particularly textiles) are subject to nontariff barriers which have a differential regressive impact on LDCs. Specifically, many industrial nations have negotiated 'voluntary' export restraints under which developing countries curtail exports or face other, more severe, limits on market access. Since these restraints appear to be placed disproportionately on labour-intensive products, the potential spread between the LDCs' market performance in these and other exports should have been greater than indicated in Table 7.1.

4. A factor influencing the decline in developing countries' market shares for labour-intensive foods is the effect of the EEC's Common Agricultural Policy (CAP), and the fact that many industrial countries heavily subsidise agricultural exports. Under CAP, agricultural imports from non-EEC sources are subject to a variable levy which significantly raises landed costs. Sampson and Yeats (1977) provide estimates of *ad valorem* equivalents for these charges which suggest they have a major impact in diverting imports from LDCs and other agricultural producers to intra-trade among Community members.

5. The European countries' customs unions (EFTA and the EEC) have an influence on this relation. Specifically, protocols between EFTA and the EEC permit duty free trade in manufactures so a common external tariff applies to the United States, Japan, several other developed nations, and the LDCs. Thus, the tariff provisions of these common market members provide a bias against imports from non-European countries.

6. An extension of this analysis to individual industrial countries suggests that total imports of manufactures would increase by over 200 per cent if France brought its developing country market share up to the US average, the increase for the Federal Republic of Germany would be 108 per cent, and that for the United Kingdom would be 97 per cent. However, this line of analysis must be approached with caution since the market shares are undoubtedly influenced by proximity to other trading partners, language, cultural ties, complementary financial structures and a host of other independent variables.

7. Using indices of value added per employee, as well as LDC shares in international trade over 1965–76, several adjustments were made in product classifications. If the components were becoming less capital-intensive, coupled with an increase of at least 5 points in the LDCs' market share, this 'performance' criterion was used to switch some Group III products into Group II.

8. Two qualifications should be noted. Firstly, several types of complex manufacturing processes are candidates for off-shore assembly processing in developing countries. To the extent that some Group III products are suitable for OAP activity, this procedure may allow LDCs to move into

these product lines sooner than expected. Secondly, some three-digit products such as tools (SITC 695) have components which are produced by labour-intensive techniques. Given this diversity, LDCs may make inroads into some lower level markets, but are not expected to do well for the three-digit product in general.

9. Although they employ a different methodological approach, Watkins and Karlik (1978) come to very similar conclusions about the future composition of developing country exports. This analysis also suggests that the LDCs are likely to become competitive in a broad range of fabricated metals.

# References

Morris Adelman, 'The Measurement of Industrial Concentration', *Review of Economics and Statistics*, 33 (May 1951), 269–96.

Dragaslov Avramovic, 'Common Fund, Why and What Kind', *Journal of World Trade Law*, 12 (October 1978), 370–403.

Joe Bain, 'Relation of Profit to Industry Concentration', *Quarterly Journal of Economics*, 65 (August 1951), 297–304.

Frederick Bell and Neil Murphy, 'Impact of Market Structure on the Price of a Commercial Banking Service', *Review of Economics and Statistics*, 51 (May 1969), 210–13.

Benjamin Cohen, 'Relative Effects of Foreign Capital and Larger Exports on Economic Development', *Review of Economics and Statistics*, 50 (May 1968), 281–4.

J. Coppock, *International Economic Instability* (New York: McGraw-Hill, 1962).

John Cuddy, 'The Common Fund and Earnings Stabilization', *Journal of World Trade Law*, 12 (March: April, 1978), 107–20.

J. Donges and J. Riedel, 'The Expansion of Manufacturing Exports in Developing Countries: An Empirical Assessment of Supply and Demand Issues', *Weltwirtschaftliches Archiv*, Band 113, Heft 1 (1977), 58–87.

J. Dreze, 'Quelques Réflexions Sereines sur l'adaption de l'industrie Belge au Marché Commun', *Comptes Rendus des Travaux de la Société Royale d'economie Politique de Belgique* (Bruxelles: Royal Economic Society, 1960).

Corwin Edwards, 'Barriers to ·International Competition: Interfirm Competitive Behavior', in R. Hawkins and I. Walter (eds.), *The United States and International Markets* (Lexington: D. C. Heath, 1972).

Robert Emery, 'The Relation of Exports and Economic Growth', *Kyklos*, 20 Fasc. 2 (1967), 470–86.

J. M. Finger and A. J. Yeats, 'Effective Protection by Transport Costs and Tariffs: A Comparison of Magnitudes', *Quarterly Journal of Economics*, 90 (February 1976), 598–611.

David Forsyth, 'Restrictions on Multinationals in the Developing World', *Multinational Business*, 4 (Fall 1977), 1–7.

L. G. Franko, *Multinational Enterprise, the International Division of Labour in Manufactures, and Developing Countries* (Geneva: Centre d'Etudes Industrielles, 1975).

John Galbraith, 'The Defense of the Multinational Corporation', *Harvard Business Review* (March–April 1978), 83–90.

C. Glezakos, 'Export Instability and Economic Growth: A Statistical Verification', *Economic Development and Cultural Change*, 21 ( July 1973), 42–57.

Derek Healey, *Integration Schemes Among Developing Countries: A Survey* (Adelaide: Centre for Asian Studies, 1977).

Trevor Heaver, 'A Theory of Shipping Conference Pricing and Policies', *Maritime Studies and Management*, 1 ( July 1973), 17–30.

G. Helleiner, *World Market Imperfections and Developing Countries* (Washington: Overseas Development Council, 1978).

E. A. Hewett, *Foreign Trade Prices in the Council for Mutual Economic Assistance* (London: Cambridge University Press, 1974).

G. C. Hufbauer, *Synthetic Materials in the Theory of International Trade* (New York: John Wiley, 1966).

G. C. Hufbauer and J. P. O'Neill, 'Unit Values of U. S. Machinery Exports', *Journal of International Economics*, 2 (August 1972), 265–76.

Tayseer Jabar, 'The Relevance of Traditional Integration Theory to Less Developed Countries', *Journal of Common Market Studies*, 9 (March 1971), 254–67.

Donald Keesing, 'Outward Looking Policies and Economic Development', *Economic Journal*, 77 ( June 1967), 303–20.

Ephraim Kleiman, 'Trade and the Decline of Colonialism', *Economic Journal*, 86 (September 1976), 459–80.

A. G. M. Koch, *Current Pricing Behavior in Liner Shipping* (Bergen: Institute for Shipping Research, 1968).

Irving Kravis, 'Trade as a Handmaiden of Growth: Similarities Between the Nineteenth and Twentieth Centuries', *Economic Journal*, 80 (December 1970), 850–72.

M. E. Kreinin, *International Economics: A Policy Approach* (New York: Harcourt, 1975).

M. E. Kreinin and J. M. Finger, 'A Critical Survey of the New International Economic Order', *Journal of World Trade Law*, 10 (December 1976), 493–512.

Sanjaya Lall, 'Transfer Pricing by Multinational Manufacturing Firms',

*Oxford Bulletin of Economics and Statistics*, 35 (August 1973), 173–93.

Hal Lary, *Imports of Manufactures from Less Developed Countries* (New York: National Bureau of Economic Research, 1968).

Karsten Laursen, 'The Integrated Programme for Commodities', *World Development*, 6 (April 1978), 423–36.

J. C. Leith, 'Export Concentration and Stability: The Case of Ghana', *Economic Bulletin of Ghana*, 1 (1971), 45–55.

Arthur Lewis, 'The Rate of Growth of World Trade, 1830–1973', paper presented at the symposium *The Past and Prospects of the Economic World Order*, Stockholm, 1978.

S. B. Linder, *An Essay on Trade and Transformation* (New York: Wiley, 1961).

Ian Little, Tibor Scitovsky, and Maurice Scott, *Industry and Trade in Some Developing Countries* (London: Oxford University Press, 1970).

A. I. MacBean, *Export Instability and Economic Development* (Cambridge: Harvard University Press, 1966).

J. Macieja, 'Lowering Material and Energy Inputs for the Polish Economy in the 1980s' (in Polish), *Gospodarka Planowa* (September 1978), 428–44.

S. Magee, 'Information and the Multinational Corporation: An Appropriability Theory of Direct Foreign Investment', in Jagdish Bhagwati (ed.), *The New International Economic Order: The North–South Debate* (Cambridge: MIT Press, 1977).

Alfred Maizels, 'A New International Strategy for Primary Commodities', in G. K. Helleiner (ed.), *A World Divided* (Cambridge: Cambridge University Press, 1976).

Alfred Maizels, *The Industrialization of Developing Countries*, mimeo (Geneva: UNCTAD, 1979).

H. M. Mann, 'Seller Concentration, Barriers to Entry, and Rates of Return in Thirty Industries', *Review of Economics and Statistics*, 48 (August 1966), 296–307.

B. F. Massel, 'Export Instability and Economic Structure', *American Economic Review*, 60 (September 1970), 618–30.

J. Mead, *The Theory of Customs Unions* (Amsterdam: North Holland, 1955).

Michael Michaely, 'Exports and Growth: An Empirical Investigation', *Journal of Development Economics*, 4 (March 1977), 49–53.

Michael Michaely, 'Income Levels and the Structure of Trade', paper presented to the symposium *The Past and Prospects of the Economic World Order*, Stockholm, 1978.

Kathryn Morton and Peter Tulloch, *Trade and Developing Countries* (London: Croom Helm, 1977).

M. V. Posner, 'International Trade and Technical Change', *Oxford Economic Papers*, 13 (November 1961), 312–29.

Wilfred Prewo, 'The Structure of Transport Costs on Latin American Exports', *Weltwirtschaftliches Archiv*, 114 (April 1978), 305–27.

Frederic Pryor, 'Trade Barriers of Capitalist and Communist Nations Against Foodstuffs Exported by Tropical Underdeveloped Nations', *Review of Economics and Statistics*, 29 (August 1966), 177–93.

Gary Sampson and Alexander Yeats, 'Do Import Levies Matter? The Case of Sweden', *Journal of Political Economy*, 84 (August 1976), 881–91.

Gary Sampson and Alexander Yeats, 'An Evaluation of the Common Agricultural Policy as a Barrier Facing Agricultural Exports to the European Economic Community', *American Journal of Agricultural Economics*, 59 (February 1977), 99–106.

R. Snape and G. Sampson, 'Effects of the EEC's Variable Levies', *Journal of Political Economy*, 88 (October 1980), in press.

Jan Tinbergen (Coordinator), *Reshaping the International Order: A Report to the Club of Rome* (London: Hutchinson, 1977).

J. Tumlir and S. Robinson, *What is Feasible in Legal Regulation of Restrictive Business Practices in International Trade* (Geneva: GATT, 1975).

United Nations Commission for Asia and the Far East, *Intraregional Trade Projections: Effective Protection and Income Distribution*, 2 (Bangkok: United Nations, 1972).

UNCTAD, 'The Economic Consequences of Reverse Preferences', *Research Memo. No. 28* (Geneva: United Nations, 1968).

UNCTAD, *Level and Structure of Freight Rates, Conference Practices and Adequacy of Shipping Services* (New York: United Nations, 1969).

UNCTAD, *The Marketing and Distribution Systems for Bananas* (Geneva: United Nations, December 1974).

UNCTAD, *Import Cooperation Among Developing Countries* (Nairobi: United Nations, March 1975).

UNCTAD, *An Integrated Programme for Commodities* (Geneva: United Nations, October 1975).

UNCTAD, *Role of Transnational Corporations in the Trade of Manufactures of Developing Countries* (Nairobi: United Nations, 30 December 1975).

UNCTAD, *Economic Cooperation Among Developing Countries* (Nairobi: United Nations, March 1976).

UNCTAD, *Commodities: Main Issues* (Nairobi: United Nations, April 1976).

UNCTAD, *New Directions and New Structures for Trade and Development* (Nairobi: United Nations, May 1976).

UNCTAD, *Payments Facilities for Expanding East–South Trade* (Geneva: United Nations, 16 December 1977).

UNCTAD, *The Main Issues for UNCTAD in the 1980s* (Geneva: United Nations, July 1978).

UNCTAD, *The Control of Transfer Pricing in Greece* (Geneva: United Nations, August 1978).

UNCTAD, *Dominant Positions of Market Power of Transnational Corporations* (New York: United Nations, November 1978).

UNCTAD, *The Processing Before Export of Primary Commodities*, mimeo (Geneva: United Nations, April 1979).

UNCTAD, *Evaluation of the World Trade and Economic Situation and Consideration of Issues, Policies and Appropriate Measures to Facilitate Structural Changes in the International Economy*, TD/224 (Manila: United Nations, May 1979).

US Department of Commerce, *Annual Survey of Manufactures, 1976* (Washington: Government Printing Office, June 1978).

US Government, *The Role of Equity Capital in East–West Economic Cooperation* (Geneva: Economic Commission for Europe, January 1979).

C. Viatsos, 'Crises in Regional Economic Cooperation Among Developing Countries: A Survey', *World Development*, 6 (June 1978), 719–70.

J. Viner, *The Customs Union Issue* (New York: Carnegie Endowment for International Peace, 1950).

Stephen Watkins and John Karlik, *Anticipating Disruptive Imports*, prepared for the Joint Economic Committee of the US Congress (Washington: US Government Printing Office, 14 September 1978).

Lary Wipf, 'Tariffs, Nontariff Distortions and Effective Protection in US Agriculture', *American Journal of Agricultural Economics*, 53 (August 1971), 423–30.

Alexander Yeats, 'Further Evidence on the Structure–Performance Relation in Banking', *Journal of Economics and Business*, 26 (February 1974), 95–100.

Alexander Yeats, 'A Comparative Analysis of Tariffs and Transportation Costs on India's Exports', *Journal of Development Studies*, 14 (October 1977), 97–107.

Alexander Yeats, 'Do International Transport Costs Increase with Fabrication? Some Empirical Evidence', *Oxford Economic Papers*, 29 (November 1977), 97–107.

Alexander Yeats, 'Monopoly Power, Barriers to Competition, and the Pattern of Price Differentials in International Trade', *Journal of Development Economics*, 5 (June 1978), 167–80.

Alexander Yeats, 'On the Accuracy of Partner Country Trade Statistics', *Oxford Bulletin of Economics and Statistics*, 40 (November 1978), 54–60.

Alexander Yeats, 'Recent Changes in Developing Country Exports', *Weltwirtschaftliches Archiv*, Band 115, Heft 1 (1979), 149–65.

Alexander Yeats, *Trade Barriers Facing Developing Countries* (London: Macmillan 1979).

# Index